Endorsements
Brush My...

*The honesty of this book gives it en............wer – a power to move the reader
to appreciate grief but also to reflect on how to live with its reality as well as
help others. Amidst all the pain, Emma-Jane's voice shines clearly and honestly
throughout as she takes the reader through her family's story.*

*Will I have to brush my teeth in Heaven? is a book which does not dwell on
simple pieties, but the deep wrestling that Emma-Jane expresses so openly to her
readers will spur a deeper reflection on loss, hope and faith these are issues that
hold significance for all of us.*

GORDON CORERA, Journalist and Author

*It is hard to read this book without a steady flow of tears. Yet the raw and uncen-
sored thoughts of the author are precisely what give us permission to ask deep
questions which affect us all – of identity, purpose, forgiveness, injustice and
hope beyond death. Emma-Jane bypasses cliches and sound bites and instead
offers powerful reflections on these borne out of her own unwanted journey.*

*It is said that the house of suffering always yields more wisdom than the
house of pleasure. This book brilliantly challenges and educates us not only on
how to navigate unexpected and unwanted situations in our own lives but also
how to best help others who themselves are suffering.*

JAMES DE COSTOBADIE, Vicar Latimer
Church, Christchurch New Zealand.

Losing a child is one of the most tragic events that a family could possibly experience, but to lose two children.... unimaginable. This book takes you on a journey of grief, heartache and uncertainty but most importantly a journey of love, faith, and hope. Love comes before grief...and love will be here after; we grieve because we love.

Emma-Jane's raw and beautiful honesty about navigating the difficult journey of losing not one, but two of her children provides a unique insight into a subject that is not talked about openly in our society. Her words and resilience will provide hope and understanding to many bereaved parents who will sadly also walk this path. You will need tissues at hand, as Emma-Jane shows you that you can survive this unspeakable loss.

It is a privilege to be invited to share a glimpse into the lives of Samuel and Ben, two much loved boys who will never be forgotten and who continue to shape the lives of their beautiful family.

KERRY GORDON, CEO Precious Wings

Children aren't meant to die before their parents. The pain of losing one child is difficult enough for most of us to imagine; the pain of losing two is nothing short of unfathomable.

In this searingly honest but always hopeful story, Emma-Jane McNicol shows us all a path for not just surviving but thriving in the face of some of the most difficult moments in our lives.

Ultimately, this book is a testament to Emma-Jane's faith and love for her family. As readers we feel lucky to have been introduced to Samuel and Ben - two boys that in their short lives taught us all so much.

LAUREN QUAINTANCE, Journalist

This is a beautiful book. It is often painful and upsetting to read; Emma-Jane tells her story of unbearable loss with searing honesty and profound insight. And yet through it all she demonstrates how faith in Christ can hold us, even when we feel we are losing the ability or strength to hold on to Him. None of us welcomes pain, grief or loss into our lives. But when it comes (as it invariably does), it changes us, and resets our compass to nurture and cherish what really matters in this life. My compass has been reset by this family's story of sorrow, joy, resilience and ultimate hope, and I believe it will do the same for you.

STUART TOWNEND, Songwriter

Will I have to brush my teeth in Heaven?

HOLDING ON TO HOPE IN THE DEATH OF A CHILD

EMMA-JANE MᶜNICOL

Ark House Press
arkhousepress.com

Cataloguing in Publication Data:
Title: Will I Have To Brush My Teeth In Heaven?
ISBN: 978-0-6456366-8-0 (pbk)
Subjects: REL012010 [RELIGION / Christian Living / Death, Grief, Bereavement]; REL012170 [RELIGION / Christian Living / Personal Memoirs]; REL050000 [RELIGION / Christian Ministry / Counseling & Recovery]

Design by initiateagency.com

CONTENTS

DEDICATION

When doctors need to tell you bad news about the health of your child, they often start breaking the news softly by letting you know that you have a very special child.

When I think about my children, I think that I have not one, not two, but three very special children. I dedicate this book to each one of them.

To Tom, Ben and Samuel, each of you is special to me and God created each of you in his image. You are special to him and he loves you. You have each taught me so much, and you are each forever in my heart. Thanks for letting me be your mum. Sorry you had no choice.

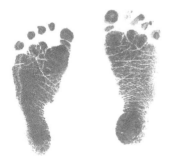

CHAPTER 1

The Birthday Cake

Today is Samuel's first birthday.

His older brothers Tom, aged eight, and Ben, aged five, walk to school in Eastbourne, England with Debbie our friend. Their discussion is about Samuel and what he might be doing for his birthday. Their conversation soon turns to what Samuel looked like as a baby and they start to discuss birth weight. Samuel was born weighing nine pounds and eight ounces.

Ben asks Tom, 'What was I, when I was born?'

Tom responds, 'You were eleven pounds and six ounces.'

'Wow,' says Ben, 'I must have been a very expensive baby.'

Debbie and Tom laugh.

Tonight, the boys share Samuel's birthday cake. It is chocolate, with thick chocolate icing, and Maltesers placed perfect distances apart around the circular frame of the cake. The cake was made for us by my friend

Robyn as a loving gift. When she hugged me and handed it to me she said, 'No mum should ever have to make this cake themselves.'

Though the cake looks perfect, there is an imperfection about it.

This cake has no candle.

I am Tom, Ben and Samuel's Mum. I share this cake with Tom, Ben, and my husband Roddy tonight, but Samuel, the birthday boy, won't be able to join us. He will spend his first birthday elsewhere, in a place far beyond my reach. Though my arms reach out to him, I cannot hold him. I cannot sing to him on his birthday. I cannot celebrate with him. Though I long to do these things, my desire can never break reality.

Will Samuel have cake on his birthday? Will there be any special celebrations? In the place where he is, will he look like a human being in the body of a one year old? Will he still be a baby, or will he be an adult? Or something in between? This is what we will discuss openly as a family around the dinner table tonight. It will not feel odd. It will not feel awkward. It will be our regular conversation. Such discussions are our new normal.

Ben eats the chocolate cake with urgency, in the hope that he may get another piece. His love of all things chocolate is evident in his huge smile and the brown speckle-coating on his face. He is well. Ben is happy. He will be with us all for many, many more celebrations, I think. You can't but smile when you look at Ben. He has a contagious smile that draws you in.

Cake eaten, it must be time to play some football. 'Tom, Tom, let's go and play,' says Ben. I look at my watch. It should be time for bed, but it is Samuel's birthday so, as a treat, they can play outside together a little longer.

When they come in from play, the boys head to bed. As is the tradition in our home each night before they go to sleep, we chat together and we say prayers to God, short messages to him discussing our day, our hopes and fears, sharing conversation with a God we believe is listening. Tonight, the boys thank him for this nice day, and for their brother Samuel who is 'the bestest brother ever'.

They hug and kiss Roddy and me, and once we have gone back downstairs, they talk together and pile up pillows on their bed to bounce on and fall off, all designed to make the other brother laugh. Roddy and I hear the laughter, together with the bangs of bodies landing on the floor, and we are thankful that despite our own grief and darkness it has been a happy day for Tom and Ben. We got through this day, and they actually enjoyed it.

The next celebration in our family will be Ben's birthday in September. He will be six.

CHAPTER 2

Island Days

When I was six, I lived in Fiji.

I had been born in another island country in the south western Pacific Ocean: New Zealand. My parents and two of my grandparents were also New Zealand-born.

New Zealand is often portrayed in novels as the place to escape to – a land of dreams and possibilities. But for those of us privileged enough to be born there it is no dream, but the only reality we know – until we travel.

And we Kiwis are known for travel. That is why when I was six I lived in Fiji. Dad had been transferred with his banking job to the capital city, Suva.

From being your average Kiwi kids attending the local state school back in New Zealand, we now lived a privileged life in a company-owned house with a couple of acres of land and a swimming pool, and staff to help us maintain it. Those carefree times made it childhood on overdrive for me and my older sister Joanna. We had no TV, so Joanna and I spent a lot of time outdoors.

One day, Dad helped us make a tepee out of the banana palm leaves in our expansive garden. We decided to spend the night there like true adventurers with quite a distance between us and the main house. We set up camp with Dougal our dog lying at the front of the tent on guard-dog duty for the night.

It was pitch dark. Sleep eluded us as we kept hearing weird and different sounds around us and wondered what they may be.

At one o'clock in the morning, Mum and Dad woke to the sound of children's knuckles banging on their window. We had given up on being adventurers and wanted to be let into the house, desperate for our own comfortable beds and proper shelter away from the wild Fijian bush. We city-born kids were clearly not always up for all the adventure Fiji had to offer.

My best Fijian friend was Kalesi. She looked after our house and in return she was paid and had use of a house just down the driveway on our property. In the daylight hours when I was not at school, I could usually be found not far from Kalesi's side. Kalesi used to cuddle me a lot and she smelt good and safe and secure. She exuded warmth and love. She was always friendly and my enduring memories of her are ones of laughter and joy. Kalesi and I were best of mates.

I was always the entertainer and could be found doing random dancing in her bure (house), often on top of her heavy wooden table so as to impress, as there was usually an audience of her local friends clapping and spurring me on for more. I was often with them and all their happiness encouraging my performance until dinner time.

At dinner time, I rushed home; although I loved the Fijian people I did not like their food. Kalesi's husband, Thai, used to say to me that if ever

I was naughty he would punish me by taking me out to a restaurant and ordering me the local delicacy, fish heads and dalo (a root vegetable). That was incentive enough to behave. Fortunately for me, he never did carry out this punishment.

One day, I returned from town grumpy. I was hot, bothered and frustrated, and needed someone within range to deposit my anger. Kalesi was in the firing line and I spoke abruptly to her; it is true that we often hurt the ones we love the most. My rude treatment of Kalesi prompted Mum to punish me by sending me to my room to think about how my actions had caused another's hurt. Clearly, Mum was biding her time to work out what further punishment I would receive.

Even though I was only six years old, how I felt during that time alone in my room is still a clear and vivid memory. I was confused and frustrated, but as I calmed down and reflected on what I had said I became aware that I had been horrible to my closest friend. I felt bad about that.

Guilt welled up inside. I wanted to be better. Yet there was this thing inside of me that took pleasure in being bad.

It dawned on me there in my room that I could not just decide to be good in my own strength, I had to have external help. I had heard from adults in my life – my parents, my grandma and my teachers at church – that in our own strength as humans we could not be good – we needed God to help us. I had been told this was the reason he had sent his son Jesus to die for us, to take our punishment for the sin we had caused. If we accepted Jesus into our hearts, then he would come in and take over the driving position and redirect our lives, with him in control and not us.

On that day in my room in Fiji at age six, I knelt down in my room and talked to this person Jesus I had been told about. I asked him to come into my life and take control. I had decided I could no longer do it alone.

No doubt I would have still gone on to receive my earthly punishment from Mum as she was no pushover. But I knew from that day on that Jesus had forgiven me and I was his. I had a peace. A little light had flicked on inside me and started to burn in my very core.

***

Over the Christmas holidays, we went home to New Zealand to celebrate my grandparents' fiftieth wedding anniversary with my mum's extended family.

Grandpa had lived a fairly humble life as a postal worker. His family had emigrated to New Zealand from England when he was a young boy, no doubt in search of a better life for their children away from the clay pits that my great-grandfather had worked in. Grandpa was only twelve years old when his father died. His mother did not linger for long in the grief of her husband's passing. She turned to her young son Arthur and told him, 'Now that you are the only man in the house, you have to work to provide for the other members of the household.' My grandfather did not rebel; he took his responsibilities seriously and worked hard for his mother and sisters. He was a good and kind man who lived a life of service.

While we were visiting during the holidays, Grandpa took me to the play area not far from his house. As I went to play in a wooden maze in the play area, I gave Grandpa my necklace to put in his pocket to keep it safe. When we got home, we found that Grandpa's pocket had a hole in it. The necklace chain was missing but the shaped, solid pendant was still there. I kept that pendant, and it reminds me of him.

Six weeks later, Grandpa died. Dad was in New Zealand on a business trip, and phoned mum to tell her the news that her father had died. It was the first time I had seen my Mum cry. It must have been hard for Mum, not being there for her Dad when he died and not being able to attend the funeral or to comfort her mother and siblings and gain comfort from them. My Mum has always been very family-centred. I heard Mum's tears and saw that she was sad, yet I can't recall offering any deep comfort. It was my first experience of the death of a family member.

Dad completed his posting in Fiji and we returned to Wellington, New Zealand to see out the rest of Dad's career, and for Joanna and me to complete our education. In returning home to Wellington, I missed the freedoms of my life in Fiji. Life in Wellington seemed far more hectic and structured. We lived very close to the centre of town, and Dad seemed to be absent from the home for long days as his executive role placed demands on his time. Yet I always knew that my parents were closest of friends, and if he could have shaken off the worries of work he would have been around a whole lot more. Sundays were big days of social activity, both at church and always with the hospitality my parents extended. There was a constant stream of people through our house. If those walls could talk they would have many a tale to share.

Mum and Dad were an encouragement to Joanna and me at school, but they were never the type of parents who micromanaged our lives. They told us the boundaries and we tended to fit within them. Schooldays weren't the rebellious years; we saved that for later.

Mum and Dad had each grown up with parents who, whilst very different in terms of personality, were maybe similar in that they had fairly closed views on what a person could and couldn't do, and these rules were to be followed. Mum and Dad had learnt a lot from having a more expansive view of the world. They had lived in London for two years and later in Fiji. They seemed to appreciate that there was not just one way of living. It may have been a subconscious decision, but I think they gave Joanna and me a lot more freedom of expression than they had been allowed in their youth.

They placed trust in us and gave us room to discover who we were, within the safety of knowing what they believed. I think their relaxed attitude helped to shape us towards greater independence. We knew we were loved, but were never smothered.

I was a carefree child. There wasn't much in my life to be worried or troubled by. My best friend was most certainly my Gran – Mum's mum. Gran was as every gran should be: kind, loving and a lot of fun. She came food shopping with us on a weekly basis. Her needs were less than ours, so she would finish her shop first, then wait for us on a bench outside the shopping mall. Inevitably, every time we went to pick her up, she would have some stranger sitting with her in deep conversation. She was a people-puller. A magnet for interaction. She was not designed to be widowed and at home alone.

Gran and I connected. I had a life full of friends my own age but, despite those contacts, most days I would give Gran a phone call and chat with her about my day. I always knew that she cared, and she would listen no matter how long I went on for – and believe me, I can talk.

Her influence on my life was great. During our conversations she often told me about her faith in God and the reasons why she believed. She was authentic and was no fake. She was a real and present witness to me. I knew that she told God everything – she was a real woman of prayer. Sometimes I would share a room with her if she was staying the night at our house. If she couldn't sleep, I would wake up to hear her praying aloud, telling God all her thoughts and concerns. I am certain that her grandchildren have all benefited from those prayers she prayed for them, deep into the future.

When school days were over, I decided to take a gap year in the United Kingdom before starting university. Just before I left to travel, I went to visit my Gran for what we all knew would be the last time. She was in a hospice receiving end-of-life care for bone cancer.

Gran sat in her armchair, and at her request I read to her from the Bible. She chose the twenty-third psalm, a powerful poem reflecting on the fact that we do not need to be alone in death, as Jesus walks with us like a Shepherd with his sheep.

When I finished reading the psalm, I looked up. Gran put her hand out to hold onto mine. She said, 'This is not goodbye. We will meet again on the other side.'

Up until that moment, Gran had not talked to me about my leaving for overseas, and certainly not about her own dying. As her fragile hands pressed mine, I knew she understood, but that she was prepared for her next stage. She was calm and at peace, in readiness for what was to come. Her desire to encourage me was because she wanted each of her loved ones to hold onto faith and to follow where she was going.

I travelled to the United Kingdom and was determined to send Gran a postcard so she could get it before she died. I wanted to deny the inevitable passage of time. I sent it at the earliest possible opportunity, but she never read it. She died before my postcard reached New Zealand. My best friend had gone on her own journey from this life, and no matter how close I had been to her, I could not journey to be with her right now.

I cried a lot at the passing of Gran. I was in England, far away from the rest of my family and still trying to break in with the contacts I had made at my new workplace. I did not experience the corporate outpouring of grief as I was away from the familiar. I did not unload on my workmates, but instead chose in my time off to take walks out in the countryside to be alone and to think of Gran and to mourn her in solitude. I did my grieving alone.

CHAPTER 3

Head Over Heels

University saw me back in Wellington doing a double degree: Law and a Bachelor of Arts majoring in English, Theatre and Film. I was studying in my hometown but without my family around. Mum and Dad had taken early retirement and headed down to live in the country town of Akaroa on the South Island.

When I completed my course, I was able to practise as both a Barrister and Solicitor in New Zealand – but I wanted to head back to the United Kingdom for some work experience and further travel.

Without much forward planning, I landed on my sister Joanna, who was working as a Nurse in London. After not many weeks, I had little money and, in the end, no money. I was feeling low about the situation I had found myself in, but Joanna encouraged me, saying that one day my luck would change and I would get a job.

She was right. Just when I was thinking I should have accepted offers for jobs back in New Zealand, I got my career break as a Solicitor in the legal department of the European Investment Bank UBS Warburg. A six-month contract turned into a permanent position, and I would remain with the organisation for nine years.

I found a flat in southwest London, and became great friends with one of my flatmates, Sarah. Over time, Sarah and I spent more and more of our spare time together.

We both signed up to a skiing trip to France. I had tried to ski in New Zealand, but each time had been hampered by bad weather conditions and one time even a volcanic eruption. I was still a novice in the sport, as was Sarah. We thought we could learn together and have a fun holiday.

Before the trip, we attended a meal at the house of the trip organiser. Among the group was a general practitioner from Scotland named Roddy McNicol, who stood out in my memory of that night. We had a private chat, both perched on the stairs outside the main room as there were too many people in the room. Maybe we were both similar in not wanting to take the best seat in the house and that was why we found ourselves outside in the cold, sitting on the stairs. Or an alternative view is that maybe this was no chance meeting; this was planned well in advance for us.

On the ski trip, Roddy was one of the practical jokers of the group. He was constantly laughing and having fun, with a real beam on his face and a definite sparkle in his eyes. His jokes and his all-encompassing smile always made me laugh.

By the final day of skiing, I had finally developed the level of ability required to ski down the slopes with the rest of the gang. I went down a slope, heart pounding, and tried to pace myself by taking small breaks off-piste.

During one such break, Roddy skied over to join me and said, 'Don't worry, take your time. We have all the time in the world.'

A sigh of relief escaped my body as I felt a calmness – previously unknown to me when attempting to ski – seep through me.

After the ski trip, many of us stuck together as a group of friends. One time, Roddy and I were alone, and he asked me whether I would like to go out with him. I was pleasantly surprised as I had started to think I had misread some of the signs of his earlier attention, and that he was not interested beyond a strong friendship. He said, 'I didn't want to rush you. I wasn't sure how you would feel about going out with someone from another country.'

To be honest, it had hardly crossed my mind. I was not thinking of future plans, and after all he was Scottish, so weren't we all from different countries? That was what London was all about for many of my acquaintances. Country of origin did not define our friendships.

In January 2000, Roddy and I had our first trip out to New Zealand together. It was on this trip that Roddy took the opportunity to ask me and then my Dad if he could marry me. Mum and Dad were living in Akaroa at the time and one day Roddy suggested a trip into town. The purpose of the trip was that he needed to get something before he could ask me something, apparently. So, we headed into town to look at jewellers' shops and try on rings. We chose one and the shop assistant suggested putting it on my finger, but Roddy whipped it away from her as he had a better plan. On our drive back to Akaroa he pulled off to the side and suggested we take a short walk to a lookout in the hills overlooking the beautiful Akaroa Harbour. There he proposed.

When you look at a world globe and locate Scotland and New Zealand, you soon realise that we were from the exact opposite ends of the earth. The amazing thing we discovered was that my great-great-grandfather, who was Scottish, had journeyed from Roddy's home town of Mearns (now Newton

Mearns) to find a new life for his family in New Zealand. Three generations later, I was effectively marrying the 'boy next door'.

Roddy and I came from similar family backgrounds, but despite the similarities I think it was still very much a cross-cultural marriage.

I was naively relaxed about making the 'biggest decision of my life'. It's a big one, who you will marry. Yet our future together did not faze me. There was something about Roddy's personality and demeanour that just calmed me. I often wonder why I did not spend any more time analysing my answer to his marriage proposition. I just knew that my answer was 'yes'. I was fairly head over heels in love with him.

I will never know what life would have been for me or for him had we not married each other, but I can say that through all we have faced, his calm and measured temperament has helped me to remain the same, even during turbulent times.

***

At eight o'clock on a Friday night two months before our wedding, I was heading home from work. I got off the Tube (London underground railway) at Tooting Broadway and headed for the main high street, Trinity Road, and my shared flat in Wandsworth Common. As I emerged onto the pavement, I heard a loud noise and saw the faces of the people in front of me change to panic.

The next I knew I was being attended to by an ambulance crew. I would later learn that a drunk driver had taken a wrong turn at the lights. Instead of driving straight up the road he had driven at an angle across the pavement, taking me with him as his car rammed me into a jewellery shop window. Fortunately, the shop had its metal shutters drawn down for the night, which prevented me from flying through the glass frontage. I'm told the driver was so drunk he got out of his car and wandered over to the kebab shop next to the jewellers and tried to order a kebab.

Despite my injuries, I had some level of consciousness. I was able to tell the ambulance crew Roddy's mobile number, and he came racing across London from his flat. It was a chilling time for him as he imagined all manner of long-term injuries and even potential loss of my life.

I was taken by ambulance to St George's Hospital emergency department, then transferred to the coronary care unit because of a worrying drop in my heart rate. I felt so sorry for the man who had driven into me. I thought how bad he would feel once he sobered up and realised what damage he had caused and how close he came to killing or seriously harming me. He was lucky I was a physically strong person – an event like that may have ended the life of a less physically able person. Yet later, when he appeared in court, he was verbally unrepentant and in fact defiant, despite the evidence in the case against him.

The streets had been extremely busy that night. It was a summer's Friday evening in the curry capital of London. Many people were out and about, heading to and from the restaurants. Why was it me that was hit and not someone else? Why had I got that train and come out of the Tube at the precise moment the driver was taking a wrong turn? Is it all just random selection? Is it a result of a chaotic world? Or is there a plan in all of this confusion?

Weeks later, recovering under the watchful and attentive eye of Roddy, sitting in the lounge of his flat surrounded by all the flowers that had been kindly sent to me by friends and family, I felt sober. I said to Roddy, 'It so easily could have been flowers sent for my funeral.'

This time, I had been spared. I came away from the accident with permanent physical scars but nothing that would stop me from carrying on with life as I had known it before the accident. Yet it could have easily gone a different way. In the time it took to recover from my injuries I was prompted to think about the fragility of life. We can make all these plans, and yet no one really knows what is around the corner for each of us. How can we predict? Why do we plan? What is this life all about?

For now, I had life. With a renewed joy in the life that we had each been given, Roddy and I were married in October 2000 in Christchurch, New Zealand at St John's Church, Latimer Square, a beautiful, historic grey stone church just behind the famous Christchurch Cathedral.

There was a lot of joy on that day. We celebrated that the wedding itself was able to happen as my life had been under threat.

There was also a sadness that we each felt. Roddy's mum, Flora, was not with us. She had died when Roddy was only twenty-one, after battling cancer for seven years. She had made it to the first son's wedding but not to any of the other three. When Roddy talked to me about his Mum, tears would come to his eyes. I was given a glimpse of some of the pain he experienced as a young man, without his Mum to confide in or guide him. I couldn't imagine what it would be like to suffer such grief and loss. I listened to him, but I had no words to offer, other than I was sorry and I wished it had not happened.

Other members of Roddy's family and some of his friends were able to be with us that day. In his speech, Roddy's dad Daniel talked of how happy Roddy was as a child. He said when Roddy and I were both in the house together there was a lot of laughter. Daniel envisaged that our house would be filled with laughter.

That was everyone's prediction on that day. The future for us looked rosy.

CHAPTER 4

Our Three Boys

Tom

I t was on my twenty-eighth birthday that Roddy first suggested we should think about starting a family. I admit it came as a bolt out of the blue for me. We had been married a couple of years but had never really discussed having children. None of our immediate London friends who were our age had children. We would be the first, it seemed.

I also wondered whether we should start a family yet, as we did not own any property and had never really discussed where we would live geographically long term.

Roddy said, 'If we are fortunate enough to have a child, then a child is very adaptable. They can travel in a backpack until they start school at five.'

Actually, this point made sense to me. We could delay the 'where shall we live' question for a few more years. We both wanted children someday.

Maybe it was better to start a family now, while we were still young. Later in our life we might discover it was not possible to conceive, or we would have an increased risk of having a child with a disability.

Early into my first pregnancy, I had some blood spotting. We didn't know if this was a sign of miscarriage. I had an appointment at the hospital to check. The sonographer showed me a light flickering on the screen and said, 'That is baby's heartbeat, everything is alright.'

I was so happy. Up until then I had not believed the pregnancy was real. It was early days, only six weeks in. Seeing that flickering heartbeat, I felt a lurch in my own heart. I started to feel very excited that the baby was real. I was this baby's mum. The maternal instinct kicked in.

I suffered from severe morning sickness that did not go away until just after delivery. I was not able to keep much food down.

I still worked fulltime at UBS, which meant long hours. Tube travel was the worst thing for the sickness. It was so hot down on those trains. I would easily feel sick and faint. It was the days before pregnant mums on the London Tube wore 'baby on board' badges to alert people to offer them a seat. I never liked asking for a seat, so I just stood and clutched my trusty sick bags and tried to endure the journeys. *Think of something pleasant and this will all just go away.* Yeah, right.

We developed a new routine for getting me to work. Running into London with my clothes in my backpack was not going to work through pregnancy. We lived in Fulham, South London. Roddy worked in Primrose Hill, North London and I worked in the City, East London. Roddy would drive me to the Marble Arch Tube stop, midway between, so I would have a shorter journey on the Tube.

We made a joke of my numerous sick episodes. Blue plaques were appearing around London to commemorate famous people who had once resided there. Roddy suggested we erect our own plaques to mark every famous spot in London where I had been sick – unfortunately it was that common. My worst episode occurred one day when I just made it up out of the tunnels of the Tube to the street above, to be sick in the gutter outside. A mother walking by with her daughter said, 'Disgusting, at this hour!' She clearly thought I was drunk. I was too ill to tell her it was not what she thought.

Morning sickness seemed to be my only real concern. All reports were that the baby was developing well, so it was just a test of my endurance, and a race to the finish line. Nine months seemed forever and we were tired of waiting.

When the contractions first started at home, Roddy and I still couldn't believe it was all happening. Between the contractions we laughed and joked about becoming parents, like a pair of giggling teenagers. We were both so excited to meet our new baby.

Thomas Daniel McNicol was born at 2.39 am at Chelsea and Westminster Hospital after only a three-hour labour. Our midwife advised us that if we were to have any more children we should move closer to the hospital, as next time may be even quicker.

We were all amazed the baby chose to come exactly eleven years to the day after my Gran died. My sister Joanna would later have her first child born on the same date that my grandfather – Gran's husband – had died. Family connections, and new generations linked with the old. I like that. It makes this sometimes-chaotic life seem more ordered and planned than otherwise appears at first glance.

Roddy and the Scottish midwife became very jokey as they were discussing names for our baby boy. At one stage, I thought it was the midwife who would be choosing. Maybe I was still high on gas and air, but I felt disconnected from their euphoric conversation. I felt like I was in another world, trying to reach theirs, as I told them that I liked the name Thomas.

So much joy on that day. That is how a baby should enter the world.

Tom was a mini Roddy. When Roddy first took the baby to his surgery to see the staff, they were all calling Tom 'little Roddy'. One night in my breastfeeding-blurred daze I woke in the middle of the night to see Roddy's adult face beside me in bed. I thought it was Tom, but blown up with some kind of infection. I screamed so loudly in Roddy's ear. This caused Tom to wake up and demand yet another feed. That night, I saw what people were all talking about. They looked like two peas in a pod.

***

I returned to work when Tom was five months old. I was not allowed a longer leave of absence. I had to re-stake my claim on my job. The man who had covered my maternity leave took great delight in telling my colleagues that all I would now talk about was teething and nappies. I smiled, and just waited for the day the handover was complete, then sighed with relief at having my own job back.

Work was work and home life was home life. This was the corporate world, and my maternity leave had not taken from me my ability to do the task at hand.

Roddy arranged for Tom to go to childminders near his general medical practice in Primrose Hill. Sandy and Chrissy were two Sri Lankan ladies with permanent smiles tattooed on their faces. If it had been me working as a childminder, I think I would have developed an unhealthy dependency on painkillers. I enjoy time with my own children, but willing submission to other small people for prolonged periods of time is exhausting. The constant demands of babies and toddlers would drive me insane. Hats off to those who choose this career and thrive.

Sandy and Chrissy had the special level of patience and love required for running a childcare business. Being based in central London meant that many of the children in their care were from different nationalities. When we picked Tom up, we could often smell tempting curries coming from the kitchen. A glance round the room made you wonder whether you had mistakenly entered some apprenticeship for the United Nations. It was a warm and nurturing environment, and the ladies laughed at everything their mini tribe attempted. They adored their extended family.

A couple of years later, Roddy and I started to think about having a second child. We wondered how Tom would find it when he was no longer the centre of attention and instead had to share our love with a baby brother or sister. I wanted Tom and the baby to be best of friends and form a special bond, but I knew this was no given. It would have to be worked at.

Ben

Baby number two was due in September 2005. Again, I suffered from a long period of morning sickness. I wanted to spend time with Tom before my attentions were taken by the new baby McNicol, so I chose to go on maternity leave in early July 2005.

The day before I was due to go on maternity leave, I was just about to leave our flat when I decided to hang out the last bit of washing, even though I was already later than usual. After a few minutes' delay, I waddled – baby was expected to be big – off to the Tube.

As I was approaching the steps down to the waiting train at Gloucester Road Tube station, I thought about putting on a sprint. One glance at my overextended belly made me think better of it.

I let that train go and I caught the next Circle line train, heading for work in the city. Near Tower Hill station our train came to a halt. We were told to disembark. There had been a power failure somewhere on the line and the trains were not running. How annoying, I thought.

Heading up from the Tube station to the outdoors, I had no idea where exactly I was. I spotted a UBS umbrella somewhere in the mass of people. I decided to follow it, as it was the company I worked for. I just hoped that the holder of the umbrella still worked for UBS and had not changed jobs, leading me elsewhere.

Following that umbrella got me to my destination. En route, we passed Aldgate Tube stop. A fire engine turned up, but people were still going in and out of the station so I was not too bothered. I got to work, made a complaint to my secretary about the trouble of Tube travel in London and dashed, or rather waddled, into a meeting.

How glad I am that I did not run and catch that earlier train. It was Thursday the seventh of July, 2005.

When I came out of my meeting an hour later, I was given messages to call Mum, Joanna and Roddy. *There must be something wrong with Dad.* He had been perfectly well the last time I had spoken to him, but why else would they all be on the phone to me in work hours? With this concern in my mind, I rang Roddy – only to hear that they had all been worried about my safety.

That morning, bombs had exploded on the London Underground. One exploded at Aldgate, one stop further on from Tower Hill where at the time of the explosion I had been told to get off. Had I got that earlier train, I do not know what would have happened to me that day.

Being so close to danger, and only one day out from the maternity leave which would take me out of Tube travel for a while, I again thought of the close shave I'd had with death. Many didn't survive the London bombings that day, and their families have been devastated through the loss. Many that survived have been injured to a point that their lives have been significantly altered.

Why did I survive and they did not? I didn't just think about myself. I thought about the baby I was carrying. There was a small whisper of reassurance that this baby was going to live. Survival was part of the plan.

The next day, I still went to work, but this time I travelled by bus. I was heading along a surprisingly quiet Oxford Street in central London on a very empty bus when I got a phone call from my boss. He was kindly suggesting I didn't have to go in to work that day – I could do my final handover on a later day.

I told him I was fine to continue, but mentioned the eeriness of the bus journey. It was eight in the morning and the London streets were almost as empty as the bus. People were in hiding.

It was a sad and worrying time for Londoners. I realised that my children were to grow up in a world that appeared less secure than the relative safety I had been privileged to experience in New Zealand. What a different world I was bringing this baby into! What changes would he or she see in their lifetime, I wondered.

***

Thank goodness we had taken the midwife's advice and now lived in a flat around the corner from the hospital. Our second baby was born within thirty minutes of me feeling contractions.

Benjamin John Galt McNicol entered the world at 0.50 am. He was healthy and huge, weighing in at eleven pounds and six ounces. The midwives were all joking about his size. One asked whether we had already enrolled him in school as he might be needing to go very soon.

I got the joke, but I was still thinking, *But he is my little baby! Please don't make him grow up too fast.* Roddy and I thought baby Benjamin looked gorgeous, and we were thrilled to have him as part of our lives.

Roddy returned home to our flat later that morning to tell Mum and Dad the news. They had flown over from New Zealand to help us out at this time, and had been babysitting Tom while we were at the hospital.

Roddy said to them, 'Poor Tom,' thinking that Tom's world would be shaken by the arrival of this new baby. It was soon to be proved that it was not poor Tom, but lucky, proud and happy Tom. He loved his baby brother from the very first.

One day, Mum was looking after both boys while I was across the road at a friend's. She was in another room and initially thought all was well as it was quiet. Then she started to wonder what quietness meant, and should she be concerned? *Best to check*, she thought.

She put her head around the door and saw Tom sitting down next to Ben, who was lying on a rug on the floor. Tom was simply looking at Ben, interested in him, not harming him at all. He adored his brother, and in time his brother would reciprocate that adoration.

In those early days, I decided that whilst baby Ben needed me for food and personal care, it was Tom who would need me most at the emotional level. I gave Ben cuddles and comfort when feeding him, but my main attention was focused on Tom and helping him to readjust. Who knows, maybe they would have sorted out a good relationship as siblings no matter what I focused my attention on, and my input may have been unnecessary. It may be an inherent thing – we either like our sibling from a young age or we don't. Whatever the reason, my desires for the boys were answered and they quickly became the best of friends.

The boys depended on each other a lot. They each had an inner confidence, but this was developed and strengthened by the knowledge that wherever they went, they had a best friend who would not let them down.

Their different personalities complemented each other. Tom was the conscientious big brother, always checking that Ben was okay and not getting into danger. This was not in a tattletale way. It was when there was genuine need for the alarm to be raised.

Two times, Tom alerted me to dangers facing Ben. When Ben was only one year old, I had answered the phone whilst in the midst of toilet cleaning. Tom shouted, 'Ben is about to drink the poison.' Sure enough, Ben was found with the toilet duck in hand, ready to take a swig. Tom again raised the alert when Ben was about to drink the perfume from an air-freshener plug we had installed when we had a sickness bug.

In the playground at school, Tom would always first check that Ben had someone to play with before he went off with his own friends. This may account for why Ben often ended up playing with the boys in Tom's class more than those in his own. On the days I was working in London, the boys went to breakfast club together before school. The teacher in charge told me how lovely it was to see Tom helping Ben pour the cereal or butter his toast. She said it was unique, and not what all siblings did for each other. I was amazed as, at home, Tom claimed he could not spread his own toast, but clearly if it meant doing it for Ben then he would do it.

Ben was a laid-back second child. He breezed along, loving life and in turn being very easy to love. He was so happy, bouncy and cuddly he easily fitted in to our family unit. He gave us all a lot of laughs. Ben's jokes were simply the worst in terms of content, but his excellent delivery and infectious smile caused us to laugh anyway.

Ben liked to perform, and he was good at it. His performance ability was evident to me at his Nativity play in his reception year (prep, or the first year in school). His performance as one of the three wise men really stood out. Many people came up to me afterwards and commented that Ben was destined for the stage. His reception yearbook shows a photo of Ben dressed up in oversized glasses and a lady's dress, and of course a great big smile. His teacher commented in the book that this was Ben's favourite photo of the whole year. He loved role-play and drama and was a natural.

The boys' shared passion was football – Manchester United, to be precise. Tom's friends were all collecting Match Attax football trading cards, and the names and placements of the teams were very important. Tom checked the English Premier League on the computer, and at that time Manchester United was the top team. So, Tom decided it would be a good team to follow. Ben agreed – whatever his big brother said was usually followed. Their joint allegiance for everything Man U started that day.

Even at their young age, they would both have done well in any pub in England discussing football with the locals. Their knowledge of the different clubs, the games and the placements, learnt in part by those Match Attax cards, was amazing.

They loved actually playing football as well. Ben's favourite position was goal keeper. He loved leaping in any direction and throwing himself into the mud – rugby was not far off. Tom liked striker or midfielder, so it was a winning training combination. They would play football for hours in our back garden. It would often end in rough and tumble with each deliberately tripping over the other, ending in raucous laughter.

Ben, independent from Tom, loved the television programme *Total Wipeout*, a British game show where contestants were challenged on an obstacle course over water. The most iconic piece of the action was when contestants had to jump over four large, slippery, red balls – aptly named 'the big balls' in our household. On rainy days, when the boys were not making a tent with the cushions of our old couches, they made a *Total*

Wipeout obstacle course. This was Ben's great joy. He would pretend he was taking part in this game as he leapt about the house, full of the action of it all. During *Total Wipeout*, the contestants usually called out something silly at the top of the slide, to spur them on as they were about to take the first leap onto the course. Ben had this part already planned. At the top of the slide he was going to call out, 'I am doing it for my family.' He would then launch himself into the air and slide along the carpet. He was annoyed that he had to wait until his eighteenth birthday to be eligible to enter the competition. He was keen to sign up now.

But Ben had to wait.

Samuel

Many of Ben's friends started talking about babies. At school, they studied the care of babies. A lot of his wee pals were gaining baby brothers or sisters in their households, and I think it was all aimed at helping them to adjust. Ben started asking us if we would have another baby. Tied up in the novelty of it all, he told me all the things he would do if he had a baby brother or sister. He would give him or her a dummy and generally help care for the baby.

Ben's questioning came at the same time that Roddy and I were thinking of having another child. Although the boys were so close, I thought they would be able to learn to share that love with someone else in the family.

We were now living in Eastbourne on the South Coast of England. I was working as a Solicitor for a Swedish bank, and had a long commute to work in the City of London – a four and a half hour round trip three days a week, not counting the times the trains were delayed. Roddy was concerned that sickness and travel, as we had seen in my previous pregnancies, did not mix. I knew this was just what I had to put up with. It was not, in my opinion, a reason for not having a third child. I was approaching my thirty-fifth birthday so the earlier we had this child, the better. A now-or-never mentality hit me.

***

With my third pregnancy I had the usual morning sickness, having to make well-timed excuses during a fun family holiday with Roddy's siblings and their families in the Cotswolds. I felt like the party pooper at times, but I felt so rotten I just had to escape. Sickness was to be expected – all just part of an ordinary pregnancy for me. I was determined to keep this announcement under wraps, as surely the joy for all of us could wait until after the first scan?

Baby's first scan was at twelve weeks, a medical check that was part of the ordinary process run by our local hospital. This scan was primarily meant to check baby's growth and development to see that it fitted with the dates we had provided.

In previous scans with the two boys, I had felt so excited. To me, these scans felt like Christmas come early. It was the first look at my precious baby. Up until that point in a pregnancy I had only experienced sickness, but none of the joy of being pregnant. In these scans I started to see my baby forming, and realised that if I just held on and put up with this sickness it would all be worth it in the end. The scan was a glimpse of the good times to come, evidence that a real life was present and it wasn't just a figment of my imagination.

I wanted to feel like that this time as well. I lay down on the hospital bed, expecting that my niggling concern about this pregnancy and my age would be unfounded.

In this routine check, the hospital takes a measurement from the baby's neck to see that it is 'normal'. This is called a nuchal fold scan. The sonographer scanned our baby. She presented us with the results. From her measurements, our baby had a one in sixty-four chance of having Down's Syndrome.

Somehow, when statistics like that are presented, I find that we often jump to think we are that one in sixty-four. I was no different. This felt like confirmation of my earlier premonition. We were offered an amniocentesis test which would confirm whether our baby had Down's Syndrome. We were also told that unless we did this test then, we would not be able to find out any further down the track what baby's condition was until delivery. No subsequent scans could reveal any more about Down's Syndrome.

We knew there was a risk of miscarriage with an amniocentesis test, so we chose not to have this test. We knew that even if the baby had Down's Syndrome we would not be terminating the pregnancy, so there was no point in putting baby's life at risk by doing the test. We left the hospital that day expecting a test of our patience ahead, as we imagined a twenty-eight week waiting period to find out the result.

I was so upset. In the hospital car park before Roddy left me to return to work, he held me. He tried to encourage me to be strong and to think positively. I think he was also trying to convince himself not to go down a path before the facts were known.

He said, 'On the statistic we were given, there are sixty-three other people who will be born without Down's Syndrome. We may just as easily have that other child, and not the one who has Down's Syndrome.'

He was right. However, it was natural to consider that I might be the one.

The hospital was also concerned. They put me in touch with a specialist nurse who dealt with special care babies. She phoned later that day to discuss what the statistics meant, and what life with a child with Down's Syndrome could mean. I was told a lot that I had previously been ignorant of. I had not fully realised that many with Down's Syndrome also suffered from a variety of physical complications, primarily heart abnormalities. It dawned on me that baby's life, if he or she had Down's Syndrome, would be more than just a learning disability. It was highly likely they may need operations and ongoing medication. If baby did have Down's Syndrome what would life really be like?

Prior to our first scan, not many people apart from Roddy and I knew of this pregnancy. When these complications were raised, we could have elected to terminate without too much fuss. We may have in time gone on to have another pregnancy and given birth to a healthy baby.

Yet this baby, whatever his or her complications were to be, was in our view a gift from God. He or she was loved by God even in their current state. As the baby was growing in my womb, God knew our baby and God loved our baby. We had to trust that God would only allow our baby to have as much as we could all handle and we could care for.

Our faith and belief that God is in charge, which we each already had rooted and established in our hearts, was to be tested in the months, years and decades ahead.

***

I collected Ben from Nursery and went to see my friend Charlotte to tell her about the scan. It is with her permission that I say Charlotte and I hold different world views. For Charlotte, life is the world around us – what we see as real and solid, and nothing more. My world view is that there is a God. That God has all this world in his hands, and he controls it, and we are accountable to him for what we do in it.

Despite our different world views, Charlotte and I were the closest of friends. We cried together that day, the first of many tearful times together. I commend and acknowledge her continuing friendship with me through the hard times. Some friends desert you when faced with the sniff of trouble. She has never done that. She has had the wisdom to listen to my world view and accept it as the view I hold, and to support me and my family at every step, despite her own personal opinion on our decisions. Having friends who hold different world views but who respect you and love you for who you are is priceless.

It is also important at times of uncertainty and fear to have friends who do share your world view, so you can be as open as possible, gather strength, and gain support. My friend Pippa, who was later to become this baby's godmother, was my next port of call. I rang Pips because she was a good friend, and also because in her career she worked with many people with special needs. We had a long chat about what life would be like for us if baby were to have Down's Syndrome. We of course realised that any disability would be on a spectrum. There was no way of telling where our baby would fall on that spectrum. Even if we did the amniocentesis test and confirmed that the baby had Down's Syndrome, we would not know what level of learning or physical problems he or she would have.

When at twelve weeks into your pregnancy doubt is cast on the health of your baby, the joy of expectant motherhood is somewhat diminished. No matter how hard I tried to think we may not be the one in sixty-four, I also thought there was every possibility we could be. Why should we be immune from trouble? My mum always told me not to cross my bridges too soon, but I was already well and truly across this bridge and planning the next logical moves from there.

Roddy and I had said prayers for the health of this baby when it was forming and developing. At no point do I think the outcome of this baby's development was due to lack of prayer on anyone's part. I was rapidly (because I had crossed those bridges) having to accept that maybe Down's Syndrome was God's will for our child's life. It was an adjustment.

We did not tell our whole community of family and friends about our concerns. It didn't seem appropriate at this early and uncertain stage. Roddy and I just had to live with the concern, and hope and pray we could cope on the day, and in the future, with whatever condition our baby presented.

***

Despite our concerns, it was great that we had reached the stage where we could now tell the boys we were going to have a new baby in our family. On hearing the news, Ben beamed. He ran over to me, pulled up my top and rubbed my tummy lovingly. He said, 'Ahh, baby is so smooth!' He was quick to start planning what he and baby would be doing and instructed us on how we were to look after baby. The boys' enthusiasm was wonderful to see, but as Roddy and I looked at each other through the smiles, we each had a quickening heartbeat. What would life really be like for this baby? What would come of all these hopes and dreams the boys had for their baby sibling?

With the knowledge that we would know no more about the baby's health at subsequent scans, we chose to take Tom and Ben along to the hospital for the second scan at twenty-one weeks. I thought we should at least give Tom and Ben some of the fun bits of having a baby, as there could be harder times ahead.

I lay on the bed hearing about the various parts of the baby's body that the sonographer was seeing on the scan.

Then she paused and said, 'Mrs McNicol, I would like to be able to tell you that I can see everything clearly, but I am sorry to say that I cannot see the four distinct chambers of baby's heart. We are going to have to refer you through to a senior consultant at Hastings Hospital to check this further.'

From my minimal internet investigations on Down's Syndrome, I realised that one of the most common physical problems was heart abnormalities. I thought the sonographer's words confirmed that our baby had Down's Syndrome.

It was a quiet, wet and difficult hour's car journey that afternoon from Eastbourne further up the coast to Hastings Hospital. The consultant had agreed to stay late to deal with our scan. We got to Hastings for six o'clock, and we left with further information on our baby's health. First, the good news: baby was a boy. We elected to find out the sex, though we hadn't before in other pregnancies. I thought it would be nice to know, as again I had a premonition that at the time of delivery a name for baby may not be our top priority. It seemed wise to use our energies toward things we knew for certain we had to deal with, as opposed to constantly dealing with unknowns.

The bad news was that the consultant confirmed there was a problem with one of the walls forming in the chambers of baby's heart. She was also concerned about one area of the brain formation which showed to her some abnormality, but she was not certain about this. She referred us to a further consultant at St Thomas' Hospital in London. We were given an appointment for four pm the next day.

During the train journey up to London, I did the only thing I know to do in times of difficulty: I pleaded with God. I asked him directly, 'Please may it only be baby's heart. Please, no more.' I was quite polite, I thought.

Yet as we were checked over by the consultant at St Thomas', everything that the Hastings Consultant had said was confirmed, and one additional complication was detected. It appeared that the baby had no, or very little, stomach bubble. This was an indicator to the consultant that there could be some complication with the baby's oesophagus, meaning that the baby may be unable to swallow into his stomach. All the hospital could offer would be to have further weekly scans and hope that over time a clearer picture of a growing stomach bubble would develop.

We were drip-fed bad news at each new medical appointment.

The consultant asked us to consider having an amniocentesis test. This test would help to establish what they were dealing with. Having all of the information they could gain prior to his delivery would give the medics a better chance of caring for him, and giving him all the correct assistance that would be needed to give him the best chance at life. The test would tell us whether the baby had any known chromosomal condition. We consented to this procedure as it was now considered best for his overall long-term care. I was certain that the test would prove Down's Syndrome.

Roddy and I returned by train to Eastbourne that night, both shell-shocked. Roddy had intended going on from London to Birmingham for a work conference on diabetes he had booked in some time ago. Instead, he decided to come home with me that night and leave early the next morning to make the conference.

We were both numb. The world around us seemed oblivious to the serious issues playing out in our heads. People were laughing and joking on the train, but we felt changed already. We felt the tremendous weight of a future life with a child who had disabilities. We never spoke about it directly, as we had no certainty yet. I suppose it was still only a possibility, but it was looking more and more certain that our child would have special needs. I think we both thought we would have to make the right decisions for this child at key stages in his life.

The task ahead seemed daunting. Too daunting to even verbalise. Despite the fact we had no diagnosis, we could no longer expect that it would be good. The road ahead for our child looked rough, and we felt responsible for it.

On Friday, Roddy had to go to Birmingham and I had to take care of the boys. Once we knew the results of the amniocentesis test, we would have to make decisions for our baby boy. We were frightened about what they might be, or what the results would mean for us all as a family. This was the hardest part of parenting I'd had to face so far, and our wee boy had not yet even been born. As loving parents, we all want to make the right decisions for our children, and yet there was so much uncertainty still in our situation. We had no clear direction.

What we did know was that this baby had some abnormalities. We expected the tests to reveal one of the chromosomal conditions, as surely that was in line with the complex problems of his makeup. I looked up on the internet the other two conditions he was being tested for: DiGeorge and Edwards' Syndrome. The information that I read was hard for me to take in.

I have always found uncertainty hard. If you know the results, you are probably going to be given a lead by the medics as to what to do. Certainties can direct your thinking more. You can feel like you can 'deal' with it and find a path that will put you back in control. With uncertainty, however, you find yourself going down all the possible roads and imagining the worst. I don't think this is being negative. I think it is being realistic and preparing yourself for what might happen. I was crossing countless bridges in my head. Every bridge seemed to lead to a fog at the other side.

That weekend in my tasks with the boys, I was given an extra measure of patience and strength. Despite my tears each night when they were in bed, I did feel the presence of a greater Being, close and loving me, despite my sadness and utter confusion.

During the weekend I turned to God. I had found throughout life that when you are alone and have just your thoughts to call on, there is a natural drawing to talk in your head with someone else. I talked in my head with who I believed to be God. I knew nowhere else to go.

I found great comfort in reading in the Bible about Hannah, in the opening chapters of the book of Samuel. Hannah had not been able to have any children, but after petitioning God she was given a child named Samuel. She dedicated Samuel back to God, returning him to the temple at the tender age of two years, so he could serve in the temple for the rest of his life.

In response to what I read, I prayed that God would help us to know his will for this baby's life. As I rested my hand on my stomach, I felt the baby move inside. I started to favour the name 'Samuel' for this child, as it had been Hannah's choice for her child. The boy Samuel in the Bible was born through seemingly impossible circumstances, and he was born to be dedicated to God for His service. Kneeling at our bed that night, I too dedicated my baby's life to God's service. I asked that God would use us and Samuel in whatever way he willed. In my heart and in my sadness, I handed my baby back to God. Dealing with Samuel in my own strength alone already seemed an impossible task. I needed extra help.

For Roddy, away from us at a medical conference, it was a hard and difficult weekend. He returned to us near the end of the weekend and his face was blank. His spirit appeared empty – he was fully drained. It felt that part of him was in a faraway place that we could not reach. He was even despondent with Tom and Ben when they tried to cajole him.

My friend Magda saw me later in the week and asked if Roddy was okay. He had been on the same bus as her, returning from London, and she had been about to say hello but the look on his face dissuaded her. She said he looked in deep thought. If Roddy had been a drug-taking man, you would have known he was on a trip. A wild one at that.

I will not be telling Roddy's story here as that is for him to share, as and when he wants to. It is sufficient to say that it was a very low point for Roddy. I chose not to prod and ask. I just let him see this period through.

I spent my energies pleading with God for Roddy and his faith to hold, despite the uncertainty. I also asked those who were close to us to pray for him. One friend came to pray with us that Sunday afternoon. As she prayed, I saw tears cascade down Roddy's cheek. He was hurting and confused. She prayed not that we would make the right decision but that we would be saved from making the wrong one. This was wise and it proved to be insightful.

CHAPTER 5

Waiting for Samuel

A few days later, Roddy phoned me with surprising news from the consultant. The amniocentesis test had proved negative to Down's Syndrome, Edward's Syndrome and DiGeorge. They were going to do some further checks, but so far all of the major chromosomal disorders had been ruled out by the results.

It was good news indeed. I started to think maybe our baby just had physical problems and not a known chromosomal disorder. We had good news, but still no certainty as to what was affecting our boy.

I was now under the watchful eye of the consultants at St Thomas' Hospital, London, with weekly appointments to check on his development. Our biggest hope was that at one of these appointments the consultant would give us the good news that the baby's stomach bubble was getting larger, confirming that there was no problem with his oesophagus.

We never had that joy. Each week, I pleaded with God for the miracle. Each week, I had to accept the disappointment that baby was unable to swallow the amniotic fluid around him. This resulted in polyhydramnios – an accumulation of excess amniotic fluid. I was getting physically very large.

I was thankful for the physical size of Ben as a baby. My body had been able to hold on to a baby as big as Ben, so I thought it would also be strong enough to hold this baby and all the excess fluid.

The consultant, however, was concerned with the build-up of fluid. She did not want my waters to break prematurely and baby to be born too soon. She wanted to perform a drainage procedure and warned it could trigger early contractions and the baby being born early. In her opinion, the benefit of draining the fluid to potentially prevent early delivery out-weighed the risk of this triggering an early labour.

***

I attended these hospital appointments in London after work, which was also in London. At week twenty-nine of baby's life, I turned up in work clothes for the scan and heard the news that the fluid level was so high the consultant could not risk another week. I was advised to have the drainage immediately. This meant I had to stay in hospital so that, if necessary, he could be delivered there. If everything settled down after the procedure and the expected contractions were stalled, then he could be given a further length of time to grow before delivery. I was not given the option to pop out and get anything for myself. This was what he needed, and this was where I would stay for the next couple of days.

Consent I did. I was going into the unknown. I did not know what to expect. There had been mention at earlier scans about this procedure, but I thought I'd have more warning when it actually came.

I lay on the bed and watched my baby on the screen beside me as the consultant carefully managed the procedure. She continually scanned him throughout the procedure so she could see what his movements were. She wanted to protect him.

She used a very fine needle to enter the lining of the womb, and drew out the amniotic fluid. It was such a delicate procedure as one slip of the needle could cause harm to the baby by touching him or his home. I watched as he kicked and moved his arms up dangerously close to the needle. I prayed without ceasing that the procedure would be successful, and that God would allow baby to stay safely there until his due date came.

There was a noise of pouring water in the background as the medics drew off over three and a half litres of fluid. Every now and then her assistant had to change jugs. The fluid kept coming. In different circumstances this might have seemed comical; the procedure was so delicate, but the swapping of plastic jugs seemed so basic.

The procedure was completed. I was told to rest and they transferred me to the delivery ward. There was a high risk that contractions would start at any time. My body would think the loss of fluid was my waters breaking and it could trigger the start of the birthing process.

Sure enough, about one hour after the start of the drainage procedure, contractions began. At the pulse of each contraction, I pleaded with God to keep baby in place and not to let him be delivered prematurely. I knew that only if baby came at his proper due time would he have his best chance of survival. I wanted to be able to at least give him that. There was nothing else I could do. I was entirely helpless, at the mercy of nature.

Bizarre things can happen in a London hospital. Space is often a vital commodity. Sometime in the middle of that first night, a midwife entered my room to draw the curtain around my bed. Another expectant mother was wheeled in to deliver her child on the other side of the curtain.

I waited and looked out the window at the changing colours of the lights on the London Eye until she completed delivery of her apparently healthy child and was taken off to the postnatal ward. I have no idea if she knew I was present the whole time. I was gently trying to whisper to my baby to tell him not to get any ideas from what he was hearing; I did not want him arriving tonight.

The contractions stopped a few hours in. They did not return until the day our consultant thought it was a good time for delivery. The procedure had been successful. Tiny miracles do happen.

On a physical note, I also felt considerably lighter, almost as if the pregnancy was not there. It made me realise just how much I had been stretched in order to accommodate all the excess fluid. It was a wise decision by our consultant to do the drainage. I felt assured we were getting top care for this child.

It gave me courage, to know that he may make full term. Interestingly, at this stage I did not struggle with why he had been given these challenges. I just pressed on with desiring his continued protection. I was ready for battle but had no idea what the battlefield would look like.

***

As I left hospital a few days later to return to Eastbourne, I had a real hope that our boy would survive. I was not ignorant of the fact that his physical condition had not changed. I believed what the consultant said.

I knew the earthly reality we were facing. However, I also believed in the unexpected – the delights that can sometimes happen.

I was on a rollercoaster and just had to strap in and hope for the best. I prayed God had some miracle in mind to bring together baby's oesophagus and allow baby to live and be a part of the ongoing life of our family. When life got tough, messy and complicated, I resorted to the only resource I had called on since being six years old in my bedroom in Fiji. I knew no other way.

***

All too soon, my fluid levels were on the rise again. At each hospital appointment, my consultant tried to convince me to give up work and check in to the prenatal ward to be kept under twenty-four hour watch by the medics.

The medics' concern was that my waters would break due to all the excess, and unless I was in the hospital, baby may be under considerable pressure and may not be delivered alive. If they could control and monitor the delivery closely, they believed he would have a much better chance of survival. They did not want me to be at work. They did not want me to be in Eastbourne, which was at least a two-hour ambulance trip to St Thomas' Hospital. They wanted me under their eye and control.

I was caught by the need to also look after Tom and Ben. I was concerned it would be so tough on them if I was away from home for many weeks prior to the delivery as well as once baby was born.

I decided on a compromise. I would start my maternity leave, but I would allow myself one week at home with the family before I checked into the ward. I clocked out of work for the next stage.

***

It was odd, arranging things at home. Then packing for what would be a long and uncertain time away from home. I visited a chemist shop to get all my baby essentials and the maternity products that, despite how my baby developed, I would still need. An eager employee came rushing up to me, wanting to sign me up for their baby club. I tried to smile and just walk on, but she was persistent and kept going on about how excited I must be about having a new baby.

I was not letting myself get excited. I had not planned a nursery. I had only succumbed once, in a moment of weakness, to buying one pair of baby socks – surely, he would need socks?

I was trying to remain measured and calm. Any other alternative just felt like building up for a great big disappointment. I am a Solicitor; aren't we meant to be logical and measured? Haven't I trained for years to be able to argue both sides and live life through reasoning and sound judgment? I was having to draw on these professional skills in my personal life. *Don't get excited so you won't get disappointed. Tell yourself that often enough, and maybe one day you will believe it.*

It was clear, despite the apparent lack of chromosomal issues, that our baby boy had a great number of physical problems. We were so uncertain how things would pan out.

I did not sign up to the club and the lady was probably left wondering why. I am normally a warm, emotive person, but during this period of my life I had a method of detachment from my surroundings that seemed to work well. If you numb yourself strongly enough to pain, then maybe you won't actually feel it?

The one thing I could not numb myself to was the boys' love. It was wonderful having time with Tom and Ben. That was the only joy. The only time when I didn't have to clam up. Their life, love and enthusiasm made it hard to be cold and measured.

The sting in it was that they were both so excited about having a new baby in the house. Even though they knew there would be complications, they did not understand to what level.

The boys knew their baby brother had a heart defect, so they often talked in their nightly prayers that his heart would be mended. Then they often added on the end, 'and we pray that we don't have heart attacks.' Roddy and I had to assure them that even though baby's heart was sick it was not contagious, and they would not suffer a heart attack because of it. The boys prayed consistently and with faith each night that God would heal baby and that he would be kept safe. We, as their parents and the parents of the new baby, were greatly encouraged by the constant petition that these young boys made. They trusted with such a hope that there was a God who would answer their prayers in the way they wanted. Childlike trust and childlike faith on display, but boy did it hurt to watch whilst having all the adults-only knowledge rooted in my confused and numbed heart.

In my own personal inner life, I had a dilemma. I knew the facts as presented to us by the medical experts and I accepted them as true. I also believed that there was a God who could perform miracles.

I didn't know which strand of prayer God was wanting me to bring to him. Did he want me to be in prayer and fasting for a miracle to occur? Or did he want me to be building up my own strength in order to face the future with a disabled child – was this God's will? I felt torn between asking for a miracle and accepting the will of God.

In the end, whilst my prayers acknowledged my understanding of God's total ability to perform a miracle, I also acknowledged that we wanted to be praying for the will of God to be revealed in this baby's life.

I had snippets of hope along the way, as friends would tell me of their belief that all would be alright in the end. That this was just a time of testing for us, but if we trusted God he would resolve all earthly issues for this baby. Some who were close to me even said they thought he could be the 'miracle baby'. These thoughts and dreams dared me to have hope and to carry on.

With this hope in mind, I left Eastbourne and my family behind. I caught the train to London, taking the two-hour trip alone. This next stage would involve a lot of alone time, calling on those inner resources we all apparently have but rarely get a chance to connect to. I voluntarily checked myself into the antenatal ward at St Thomas' Hospital. I was to remain under hospital care for one month prior to delivery.

**

Hospital life was an odd existence for me. I am a doer and not a sitter. Extended periods of waiting were challenging. I had to hope that time would pass quickly and safely for baby. I wanted no regrets. Another challenge – sitting, waiting, ready for the battle.

The antenatal ward of St Thomas' Hospital London is best described as a holding bay. It reminds me of a detention centre. Expectant mums were there for a variety of reasons, but in the end the common denominator was that we were all waiting. Waiting and being watched. Staff were looking for any change in our condition so that the medics could be on hand to assist immediately.

This hospital ward reminded me of the television programme I used to watch as a child called *Mind Your Language*. It was about an English language class for new immigrants to the United Kingdom. I imagine in the modern world of political correctness it would not be screened – it was a comedy based on ethnic differences, and was not always complimentary and understanding of other cultures. But as I sat at St Thomas' Hospital – an English hospital in the heart of London – there were approximately twenty-five patients on the ward at any one time. It was rare to meet a fellow patient who could speak English, let alone who was English. I too was a migrant – a native New Zealander adding to the mix of inmates. The diversity in culture represented on that ward allowed many interesting friendships to form.

Two ladies would sit and watch television together each afternoon. One was a dominant African lady and the other a very quiet lady of Nepalese origin. The African lady would often add in her views of what they were watching, and her companion would nod in an understanding manner. In this way they passed their waiting hours.

One day when the African lady had left the ward, I was able to speak with the Nepalese lady alone on our shared ward. As I asked about her pregnancy she shared her story. I was surprised and saddened. She suffered from a condition called lupus, and it was expected that all of her vital organs would one day fail. She lived a life of constant medical supervision and medication. She had become pregnant but it was unplanned. She had been told that at her stage of lupus she was not expected to be able to carry a baby full term. She was currently at twenty-two weeks, but she believed the medics who said that either she or the baby would die should the pregnancy progress too much further. The baby was drawing too much from her already-weakened vital organs. Despite being so close to being able to give birth to a premature baby – who may possibly survive given modern medicine and intervention capabilities – she knew that in the next two weeks things would come to a head. The expected result was that she would deliver her baby but the baby would not survive. She was very matter of fact in the way she described her story.

I was so saddened by her story, and thought about this unborn life. I was wanting a miracle, but she was so accepting that this would not happen. She had no reason to hope, and I felt a deep pain for her and the baby. It must have been so hard for her to be there on that ward where others were all talking of their hopes and dreams for their babies, and she knew that her baby would not survive. How did she find strength?

One night, only a few days after my conversation with her, this dear lady was taken from our ward. The time had come to deliver her baby. I had woken from sleep with all the commotion. Even though I knew it was too early for the baby to survive, I longed for a miracle. Yet I never saw her again – not back on the ward and not later in neonatal intensive care – so I assume her baby did not survive. I prayed that she had survived and could cope with all she had to face in the future. Beautiful people who touch our lives.

***

Many patients were on the ward because they had a condition that could jeopardise their baby's safe delivery. This might be because of blood pressure issues or difficulty with carrying multiple babies. Many assumed I was in the ward because I was expecting twins, as I was so large. They would tell me this when we chatted over mealtimes together. They often said I must be excited to be expecting twins. I just let them talk.

The reason I was there was so different from the others I met. I had always kept good health throughout pregnancy. I was there not for my health but because my baby was not well. I didn't often engage with others as I felt very odd and different.

I desperately wanted to connect with someone who might understand what we were going through. Someone I could share ideas and coping strategies with.

In all my meetings in the hospital I only sensed a greater isolation, as our boy's position was not common.

One day, I was asked if I minded a group of medical students coming with the consultant on his morning round. I did not mind as I am willing to assist with medical training.

A large group came to my bedside. They were crowded into my bay, two deep. The consultant asked the medical students questions about my condition. He was wanting them to work out why I was there. They read my monitor readings which all appeared perfectly good and healthy, and looked perplexed.

'Who would like to examine the baby?' the consultant said. One brave girl stepped forward.

I was prodded and poked as students felt my womb and tried to feel my baby. They could not. This surprised them. It is usual at this advanced stage of pregnancy for the baby's features to be almost visible through the skin, but of course, because I had all the excess fluid, my baby was not so easy to feel.

One student suggested, 'Maybe the baby is in breach position. It felt odd up top.' But this was not correct.

In the end, the consultant had to tell them I was there because of the polyhydramnios.

From the expressions on their faces I could tell I was an interesting case and not ordinary. I felt like an unusual exhibit at some zoo.

I tried to remain brave, but inside, sadness and hurt were welling up. My mind was protesting: *I don't want to be an interesting case! I crave to hear the words 'normal', stable', 'good'.* Anything like this would have been so reassuring. In my time in hospital I never heard those words directed at me.

***

I was being constantly checked for blood pressure and other observations, which were all going well – so in my mind it was totally unnecessary. Numerous times I wanted to scream at the staff, 'Hands off, I'm fine,' but I knew I had to grit my teeth and bear it. It was not their fault I was an odd incumbent of their ward. As tiredness set in, it was yet another test of my patience.

I felt so trapped on that ward, just filling in time. Until my waters broke there was really no need for me to be there. The medics just didn't have any alternative place to put me. The ward was under immense pressure for bed space, so I decided to be proactive and ask if there was anywhere nearby I could go so I was not taking up an expensive hospital space. My persistent asking eventually won through. I was moved to a patient hotel just across the path from the entrance to the hospital. It was such a relief to be there and out of the bubble, and to get a decent night's sleep.

The patient hotel was designed for patients who had to travel a distance to get to the hospital, so overnight accommodation was a help. Many were oncology patients or disabled patients. The stories I heard during shared meals were many and varied. I was reminded again of the bravery of many in this fallen world. Some people's lives and stories are so full of hurt. One thing I had was a lot of time. I would re-think their stories later and feel burdened for them.

It was not common for a pregnant person to be at the patient hotel, so talk of my excitement at the birth of the baby was a topic of conversation. I felt like an anomaly again. Many times during these discussions, I didn't know how to respond. I knew many of the people there had life-limiting illnesses, so who was I to complain? Why not let them believe in my excitement?

I felt very lonely. In my room alone I often talked with my baby as if we were in a team together. I promised him that I would do anything and everything to help him, and that together we would prove the medics wrong. It was a form of coping strategy, I suppose.

It was also a time where I felt totally bonded and connected with this young boy. While he was inside me, I knew he was safe. I also knew that God knew all about him and His hand was forming him. I took all my concerns to God on a regular basis as he was available day and night. There is no rest time for God. I asked for his hand to form this baby as he had planned. I pleaded with God for a miracle on each of the medical points.

***

Medically, what we knew about our baby at this juncture was that he had a confirmed heart defect, known as AVSD. The four chambers of the heart were not properly formed, which means that 'blue' deoxygenated blood mixes with 'red' oxygenated blood. If this was left untreated, he would become seriously sick. He would require heart surgery to repair the chambers. I was given lots of information to read about heart babies.

But he was not just a heart baby. We had additional complications, the biggest being the unformed stomach bubble which strongly suggested a gap in baby's oesophagus. The scans could not tell us whether the gap in the oesophagus was large or small. Our best hope was for a small gap. This meant he could be operated on very early in his life to join up the gap. However, if the gap was large, then he would have to stay in hospital for as long as it took for him to grow, and in turn for the oesophagus to grow to a point that they could operate and connect it. This could mean he would be in hospital for up to one year, just waiting to grow in order for them to operate. Not surprisingly, we were all wanting a small gap.

The brain abnormalities of our baby were always loosely referred to as suspected but not confirmed. The medics believed he had brain abnormalities, but they could not give a detailed report on this until he was born and given more detailed scans. Then, with the brain having been fully developed, they could explain what parts were of concern. What the early in utero scans could not decipher was whether he had formed strong lungs or not, as these are not revealed until baby is born.

We brought our petitions to God and left them at his feet. Apart from looking after my own physical health and staying close to the hospital, there was absolutely nothing that Roddy or I could do to alter what would be revealed when baby was born. It continued to be a testing time in our lives.

***

During this time away from Eastbourne, I missed home life so much. I felt cheated of a proper maternity leave. In particular, I missed the boys and their reassuring words and cuddles. I felt so pulled. I knew I had to sacrifice this time from them in order to give our baby the best chance of survival, but it was still incredibly hard not to be there for my children on a daily basis.

I looked forward to their visits to me on the weekends, but I also found these times confusing. I wanted so much for their excitement about their baby brother to be mine. I kept a journal at this time, and I want to share what I wrote about one of the weekend visits from Roddy and the boys:

> When wee Ben saw me on Saturday he got down on his knees and hugged baby and again declared that baby was his best friend and he loved baby so much. He asked when would baby be coming out of mummy's tummy? It was so hard. I had to fight the tears that were welling up inside me as I do not want the boys to think that I am too sad. They need to feel confidence that everything is OK otherwise they will find it hard to leave me.

I found it hard to be relaxed with them. Prior to this baby's complications I don't think I had been an overly protective mum, but this seemed to change. I felt so protective of the boys.

One Saturday, we took the boys to the play area behind the hospital. I noted in my journal how I felt disconnected to the fun they were having. I had an urge not to let them go on any of the play equipment just in case anything bad happened to them. I wanted to wrap them in cotton wool to keep them safe.

I knew this was not how I would normally react with them. I was living in a complex hospital environment where everyone was keeping still in order just to grow their babies, and here were these wild people throwing themselves around with careless abandon. I found it unsettling. I wanted to hold on to them and sit them in a corner, reading, having no potential for harm. It was irrational but very real.

***

I have been blessed with great family and friends. They did not disappoint at this time. My parents arrived from New Zealand to help Roddy with the boys at home, and of course eventually to meet their new grandson. They brought with them a book of encouragement made for us by a group of women in their church. I had attended this women's group back in 2005 when we spent some months living in New Zealand whilst I was on maternity leave with Ben, so I knew many of the people who had made the book. I was so touched that they had taken the time and effort to make such a beautiful and personal gift for me. Each contributor had been asked to think of a verse from the Bible or a poem that had been of encouragement to them when they faced a hard time. They individually displayed this for me in the book. I received it as a true gift of love.

My sister, Jo, kept regular contact. As always, the geographical distance between us was difficult for us both. Joanna would often tell me how I had been specifically chosen out of all the people in the world to be this baby's mother. Her words of encouragement helped me to feel loved and special. The concept of being special delighted me, and I tried to focus on that, not on the concept of being weird.

Melissa, my friend from my gap year in the United Kingdom, was now living back in Australia, but she still took time to send a lovely hamper of fruit and treats to the ward, and made regular phone calls to keep in touch.

My friend Charlotte made a special effort to regularly come up to London on her day off to pop in to see me for an hour, just so I didn't feel cut-off. Shortly before our baby was due, Charlotte presented me with a lovely quilt that she had made specifically for him. She is a busy lady and it made me cry, which made her feel she had failed to encourage me – but of course she had not failed. Her kindness and love were so evident. When friends go the extra mile to make us realise we are loved and special to them, it can be emotional.

Janet, Emma and Sarah wrote letters to me in hospital – yes, good old-fashioned letters with a stamp. They wanted me to feel connected with the Eastbourne community.

Work colleagues from my days at UBS took time to visit me, and gave me magazines and crossword puzzles to help distract me and fill in time. There were many more who did things to help, looking after the boys by having play dates or offering to make meals for the family.

I mention a variety of these kind acts and gestures because they inspire me to do likewise. If there is someone in need in my community, practical gestures can show my love no matter what the distance is. I can be as creative or as practical as I like – all are welcome at such times. I will take time to think how I can help and act.

I am forever thankful to my family and friends for the continuing love and goodwill they have shown to me and my family. Whilst my hospital existence was isolating, my support network was not. I knew that if they could do anything to change our situation they would, but it was beyond their reach. So their response was to display their love to me and the family at this time in other practical ways.

My greatest support through all of this was God. The gentle voice of love and courage that he daily whispered in my ear. It was an intense period of testing and trusting.

***

Then came a day when the waiting was over. On Monday the twenty-second of March 2010, I left the patient hotel to walk the short distance across to St Thomas' Hospital. I was booked in to be induced at eleven that morning. Roddy arrived, and together we went to meet the midwives.

Baby was exactly thirty-nine weeks. His delivery was ordinary, with one exception. As we were approaching the final stages of pushing, suddenly there were lots of people in the room. In previous deliveries it had only been me, Roddy and the midwife. Now we had a room full of medics, and beeping machines being prepared for action.

In the midst of my pain delivering this baby I also felt a lot of pressure to perform on time, and not to waste the multiple doctors' valuable time. I felt like shouting at them to go away. I didn't want to have to work to their timetable.

Confusion reigned. I had a physical desire to push, but a fear of what would be revealed when he was born. All of these people were in the room setting up various apparatus to help him when he was born, but I wanted to protect him.

There was beeping and noise, lots of noise. Noise in my head and pain in my body. The whole purpose of waiting close to the hospital had been so that he could be delivered in this safe and controlled manner, yet I wanted to halt the ultimate outcome, to breathe him in and not let him out.

At five thirty-five that evening, our baby boy arrived into the world. I never got the first cuddle I had been promised. He was quickly taken by the medical team and whisked away to intensive care.

CHAPTER 6

Life with Samuel

I did not get to see our baby again until eleven-thirty that night. There had been a complication with the placenta and its removal. It just would not budge. The doctors were starting to talk about taking me to theatre to have the placenta surgically removed. Just as I was about to be whipped off to theatre, it came.

As I lay on the hospital bed and watched the nurse methodically and slowly stitching me up after the delivery, I started to think about our boy. He had breathed – this was great news as it meant his lungs were working. Yet what I had not heard from him was any cry. Our baby had entered the world in silence.

While the nurse stitched on, we had a visit from one of the consultants from Neonatal Intensive Care, commonly referred to as NICU, who had checked our baby over once he was on the ward. It was still early hours, but what the doctors could tell so far was that all that had been predicted at the antenatal stage was confirmed, and they had found one additional issue. Our baby had a cleft palate inside his mouth. This meant he would have difficulty feeding, and he would require an operation when he was a few months old to repair the palate.

The consultant said that from the outside our baby appeared totally normal, and had weighed in at a healthy nine pounds and eight ounces. The doctors also confirmed that he was breathing on his own with no assistance.

I cannot recall the time that Roddy and I agreed on our baby's name. How sad. Everything else got in the way and took precedence. It was so different to when we named Tom and Ben – the joy and laughter of those moments seemed like a distant memory. At some point we agreed on the name Samuel Roderick McNicol for our third and much-loved son.

That night on my first visit to Samuel, I looked at him and was surprised. I had expected he would look different from our other healthy children. Yet he did not. As a newborn baby, Samuel looked just like his brothers had. He had a head of brown, almost auburn hair and rolls of chubby baby flesh. He looked gorgeous to me.

In time Roddy, Mum, Dad and I would all comment on how Samuel looked so like Ben had looked as a baby; you could tell they were brothers. Yet how different he was from Ben, our healthy, happy four-year-old. Samuel looked so normal yet had physical and, potentially, brain abnormalities.

Samuel looked out of place in NICU, an anomaly – a healthy-looking boy in a ward full of premature babies. The other five babies on Samuel's Bay in NICU were tiny little people kept in incubators to regulate their body temperature, as close as possible to still being inside their mother's womb. Samuel did not need an incubator. He lay in an open cot looking plump and out of place. He was the awkward one in the room – not too sure why he was there.

The only sign he had any need to be in NICU was the tube the medical staff had immediately fed through his nose so he would not swallow his saliva into the oesophagus that did not reach his stomach yet. He would need this tube up until the point that an operation could connect his two sections of oesophagus. Samuel also had a heart monitor attached with little stickers to his chest, the machine beside him beeping the regularity of each separate heartbeat.

***

I looked at Samuel for a long time. All this waiting, all this longing and here he finally was. A reality. A living, breathing reality, not just a black and white image on a scan. Samuel was my baby yet I felt frightened to touch him, even though I was encouraged by the staff to do so. I wanted to touch him and check that he was real, yet I had a strong desire not to give him any infection. I wanted to protect him.

As I sat and stared, I wondered about so many things, thoughts crumbling into fragments through my head. A scrambled post-delivery maternal brain trying to comprehend the levels of disability that apparently lay before me.

In the first moments, though, I was mostly wondering about him. I am a relational person (aren't we all in different ways?) but what I mean is that I find it easy to remember people's stories that they share – where they came from and who they are. I often forget names as names are less important to me. It is your story and what makes you the person you are that really interests me.

So I looked at Samuel wondering who he was and what made him tick. What would be his personal story? Did he have one already? If Samuel could express how he was feeling about being shot out of his cosy home inside my womb to land in a hospital ward connected to a machine with bright fluorescent lights glaring down on him and all these people constantly invading his personal space, what would he say? If he could express his first reaction to life here on earth. In silence, standing by his cot with Roddy that first night, I tried to take in all that was Samuel and all that made him special and unique.

My love for him consumed me. It was every bit as strong as the love I had for Tom and Ben, but for Samuel I felt a caution, as if I was scared to get too close because I may wake up one day and find it all to be a dream. This real live baby lying by me was mine, but I could not hold him or feed him. He was my untouchable. As he slept on, Roddy and I just stared as the machines beeped and lit up around us.

***

No plans had been made for our accommodation once Samuel was born. He was now the hospital's patient and I was no longer needed. All the focus had been on getting Samuel safely into the world. We had not thought about us, his parents, who were now a long commute from home.

I had not cleared my room at the patient hotel, so in the early hours of the morning Roddy went there and took that bed. I went back to the ward where I had just delivered, thinking I could sleep there for the rest of the night.

I walked back into the room that had been mine only hours before, but instead of finding my things as I had left them, I was greeted by a scene I will never forget. I opened the door and there were two proud parents sitting on the bed with their darling newborn baby swaddled in their arms. They were obviously caught in the moment of pure joy, holding their baby and admiring all of its tiny features. I blurted out some apology and went out to the ward corridor, alone and confused.

For the first time during that long day and night, I was close to tears. I had no idea where to go or where any of my belongings were. I stood abandoned in the corridor and was rescued by a passing nurse. She said they had moved me to a different room down the corridor. I went in to find my things dumped unceremoniously in a pile on the floor.

I was at last on my own, free to cry and pour out my sadness and jealousy at the scene I had just witnessed. How far removed it was from our reality.

***

Until they were able to get us room in the Ronald McDonald House, a facility for parents and siblings of children who are sick in hospital, I was kept in a small, separate room off the postnatal ward. I would hear the constant cries of newborns and know that none of their cries were my child's. I spent as much time away from there as possible, as of course I wanted to be where Samuel was.

I am thankful to one of the nurses on that postnatal ward. She was my gift at this time. I was in a very odd position, as the midwives had done their job of delivering the baby. I was seen to be healthy and well and recovering as normal, so I had been discharged, but still not officially. I was effectively unaccounted for. I had somehow slipped through the system, dropped off the radar. I was taking up a bed space but not under any medical team. I needed no further medical interaction for my own personal care. I had delivered a baby and been stitched up – job done – go home. The only problem was I could not take the baby. He was theirs for the unpredictable future.

What worried me the most was that no one had given me any assistance as to how to start pumping my milk without the option of having Samuel on my breast. I had mentioned my concern to one of the staff in passing, and they said I had to try to stimulate and manipulate the breast myself. To put it bluntly, I tried on my own but had achieved nothing and was still confused. I did not mention it to anyone. It seemed wrong to mention me when clearly all our attention was on Samuel.

In my room on my own on one of these early days, I really panicked. I knew the milk would dry up sooner or later, and that would be the precise time they would come and ask me to supply Samuel. He would be taken off hospital parental nutrition and need my supply. I thought, *Even though I am reluctant to ask for help I have to be brave and do it. This is not for me. It is for Samuel.*

I breathed in courage and opened my door and looked down the corridor for help. And then I saw Holly.

Holly, I assume, was a nurse on the ward. She came and helped me to work the breast and produce the thick first stage of baby's food. She showed me how to do this and how to store it, and most importantly she asked me about my baby. I was so touched that she acknowledged that I had a baby and she asked me to tell her all about him. She wanted to know what he looked like. It was so liberating to be finally able to talk about him as real. She was the first person to do so from the hospital staff on that ward. I was able to tell her about Samuel and then to cry as the floodgates opened. Then, amazingly, she asked if she could pray with me for him. She told me she was a Christian. I said I was, too, and I would very much appreciate her prayers.

Her pleas were answered. It was clear from the rows of milk bottles in the shared fridge with Samuel's name on them that I was able to produce a greater supply than the other mothers on the Special Care or Intensive Care Wards. It was one way I was able to feel I could help Samuel.

In time, I would donate excess milk to other babies who were on the ward and needed extra nutrition. Being able to produce milk helped me to feel needed. I have never been able to thank Holly – it is a big hospital – but I would like to. I have deliberately changed her name out of concern for possible repercussions for her. I suspect her actions may not be appreciated by all, and may not be following the rule book in its entirety.

But she helped and encouraged me at a very low point of my life. Thank you to all medical professionals who go the extra mile for their patients. At key times, your help and care are like a lifeline to the broken.

***

Mum and Dad brought Tom and Ben up from Eastbourne to see Samuel the day after he was born. The boys were so excited. What a joy for Roddy and me to be able to see them, and to witness afresh and anew their life and robustness. Their radiant smiles were such a contrast to the bleak hospital surroundings.

Before they could meet their brother, we had to first introduce them to the world of hospitals and in particular the rules of intensive care. They had to wash their hands thoroughly and then use hand sanitiser at the door before entry to his shared room. Only two people were allowed by his cot at any one time, and because of their age they had to be accompanied by an adult, so they had to see Samuel one at a time.

I thought Tom should go first as he was the oldest, but Tom said, 'No, Mummy, I think Ben should as he is very excited.' How kind! I knew Tom was just as keen to see his baby brother.

I held Ben's hand and took him along the corridor to see baby Samuel. Ben was skipping next to me as he could not contain his excitement at finally meeting his baby brother.

When Ben entered the ward I told him, 'This is Samuel.'

There was such a big smile on Ben's face. 'Can I touch him?' He was allowed to touch Samuel's cheek.

Ben asked me, 'Why does Samuel have such a big plaster? I think I will take it off, Mummy, and then he won't be poorly anymore.'

I smiled at Ben. If only it could be that simple. Wouldn't that be wonderful? To take off the big plaster and pick Samuel up and walk right out of that hospital and take him home. Samuel would not be poorly anymore.

Ben looked at all the other beds in the bay. 'Are these all Samuel's friends?' He wanted to know how many were girls and how many were boys. And he asked which one was Samuel's best friend. Ben thought Samuel was fortunate to have so many friends already. I think Ben saw the NICU ward as a type of boarding school where the babies get to hang out with each other. It was an interesting interpretation of Samuel's life so far.

It helped the boys that Samuel was very ordinary looking. After all the build-up in preparing them for the fact that baby would not be well and would require some extra time in hospital, they may have expected him to look different, but he didn't. They verbally acknowledged how lovely he appeared.

Mum tells me that Tom said to her at home that night, 'Granny, don't you think our baby is just so beautiful?' Mum said you could tell the pride and love he had for Samuel.

***

After the boys had each had some time with Samuel my Mum and Dad each had a visit. The timing of these first visits coincided with the routine visit from the eye specialist, who came to test all of the new babies' eyes to see whether they could detect any issues. There were six babies in Samuel's NICU room with one nurse per two babies. The eye specialist went around the bay, then stopped at Samuel's cot and tested his eyes. He failed the test.

Samuel had deformities in both eyes. The right was considered more serious than the left, but both had problems. Samuel was almost certainly blind.

If you are a parent, I don't know what it is you hope for or long for with your children, or what disappointments you have had to face. However, I do know that if on day two of their lives you are told they may never be able to see the world around them or see you, this news sends a dagger to your heart.

This was to be the story of Samuel's life. We were to be drip-fed bad news about his health on a regular basis. Daily daggers.

Once we heard about his eyesight, I asked Roddy whether he thought Samuel would be able to hear. So, the next time we saw the Ear Nose and Throat Consultant, Roddy innocently asked, 'Do you think his hearing will be affected?'

She said, 'Oh, no, he won't be able to hear.'

The way that she said it came out as if we were being rather foolish ever to expect that he might be able to. To put it bluntly, her lack of bed-side manner as regards an issue fairly fundamental to human existence was astounding. I hurry to add that her inability to handle the situation well was more the exception than the rule. In our dealings with the other medical staff, we were very fortunate that they were gifted with a great bedside manner.

Talk about a rollercoaster ride. We were now dealing with a child who had multiple disabilities. There were to be many further tests to establish just how bad his eyesight and hearing was, but it was clear enough to all that each of Samuel's main senses would be affected.

***

That second day of Samuel's life we also met up again with Mrs A. She was the lovely surgeon we met pre-delivery, who was on stand-by to operate on Samuel to join up his oesophagus as soon as medically possible. In her calm and measured manner, she advised us that from the results of the scan it appeared that Samuel's gap in the oesophagus was a middle-sized one, but because he was such a good-sized baby she thought they could operate on him immediately. It was her opinion that, at a stretch, she would be able to join up his oesophagus now, and he would not have to wait in hospital longer for it to grow.

What a relief! Prior to Samuel's birth, I had been praying they would be able to operate on his oesophagus earlier rather than later – but at that time we had thought it was his biggest issue.

Now we had been told he had all of these other complications, and it was hard to get our head around the imminent operation. Leaving no room for delay, the operation was scheduled for that night. It was only the second night of Samuel's life, and he was going under the knife.

Whenever I think of Mrs A., I think of quiet, unassuming and clearly very skilful. Her manner showed that she cared. This attitude gave us great confidence in her ability to do the task in a caring and professional manner. How different from others who feel that by loudness and assertion they can achieve greatness.

We were blessed to have her skilful, gentle hand operate on Samuel. Yet we knew it would not be easy.

We were confused. As Samuel's life progressed, we heard more and more complications about his body. Yet no one had as yet told us whether he had a known condition. It had been less than two days, but the heap of problems he had was growing rapidly. We were deeply concerned about his future.

We did not have time to linger on our concerns. For now, his operation was the focus. We signed the consent forms, and let the doctors prepare him for surgery.

Roddy and I were asked to leave his room, as were the parents of the other babies in his intensive care room. The insertion of Samuel's ventilator tube was deemed too distressing to be watched. They made us leave to protect us all from the trauma.

Roddy and I sat in the parents' room a few doors along the corridor, as Mrs A. explained further about the operation. Despite the closed door and the distance, I could hear rasps of a baby screaming along the corridor. I realised it was Samuel – it was such a piercing and distressing sound. I think of it now and realise that it was the first and only time I was ever to hear Samuel's voice.

A flustered NICU consultant came into our room. She said they were having tremendous difficulty putting the tube down Samuel's throat. She said, 'There is something funny about him down there.' Not exactly encouraging. They had given up trying to get the tube in on the ward. He was needed in theatre now, and the clock was ticking against us.

The plan was to take him down to theatre and hope that one of the ENT consultants would be able to sort something out with the tube. If not, the NICU consultant did not know what they would be able to do. They would have to reassess whether his breathing capability was healthy or not.

She advised us to go and see Samuel now to say goodbye to him before the operation.

All this was blurted out to us like a waterfall, a gushing of bad news. She was clearly flustered and had forgotten to check her medical journals on how to deliver bad news to parents. This was never something we blamed medics for. It was simply the fact of the urgency and immediacy of all Samuel's issues. In the heat of true emergencies there is little time for formality of communication.

It dawned on me that by consenting to this operation we may be saying our permanent goodbye to Samuel, before we had really had time to meet him and say hello.

***

We went to kiss Samuel goodbye. We took a couple of photos of him as we thought this might be it. We may never see him alive again.

A team of medics transferred Samuel into an incubator to take him down to theatre. Eventually, we were ready to walk the long route to the theatre. It was a procession: Samuel, the porter, a few medics and then Roddy and me walking behind.

Roddy and I held hands as we walked in silence, but with tears, for about twenty minutes through the many corridors of the hospital through to the children's theatres. We saw Samuel go into theatre, and we sat outside and waited.

Amazingly, the ENT consultant was able to place the breathing tube with no fuss. We were told to return to the ward and wait there for further news. The operation would take several hours.

Such confusion reigned in our minds that long, long night. Together we prayed for God's will to be done in Samuel's life. We knew no other petition to make and no other authority to call on. The balance of our child's life was well beyond our human comprehension and control.

Roddy and I waited together in the entrance foyer to the NICU ward. We were just waiting for the doors to open, to confirm to us the end of Samuel's operation and his return to the ward to recover.

Every time the doors opened, we looked up expectantly. There were a lot of false alarms. We were met with new babies being transferred in, or parents going in and out of the ward to be with their babies.

It was not until early the next morning that Samuel returned from theatre. We jumped up to greet him and the medical team accompanying him.

Our Samuel had survived the operation.

***

Samuel would be kept in an induced coma for about a week for his body to take the time to heal. Once this happened, he would be gradually brought round, out of the induced coma. It was hoped he could then be taken off the ventilator and get back to breathing for himself.

The ENT consultants were unsure why the NICU staff had trouble fixing the tube for Samuel, as it had been no problem for them to do so. This was encouraging.

Mrs A. came to report on how well the operation had gone, and how they had been able to stretch the oesophagus and join it up for Samuel. His body would just need rest in order for it all to heal.

CHAPTER 7

CHARGE Syndrome

T he next day we were able to get accommodation at the Ronald McDonald House approximately half an hour away from the hospital. There was a connecting shuttle bus service to St Thomas' Hospital from the house. I checked in to my new accommodation and Roddy returned to Eastbourne to work. He thought he should use his two weeks' paternity leave sparingly. While Samuel was being sedated there was nothing he could do, and his time with Samuel would be best used later when he came out of this post-operation state.

I went to visit Samuel, and sat at his bedside as he lay in an induced coma. I started to hear the medical staff use the word 'charge' whenever they discussed Samuel. Was Samuel a special charge? Did he have an extra surge of energy? Was he charged?

I asked what this was all about. They said they now had a strong suspicion that Samuel had a condition known as CHARGE Syndrome. They arranged for geneticists and our antenatal consultant to meet with me to discuss this the next night.

As Roddy was now back in Eastbourne, I attended this meeting alone. I sat with a group of medics around a circular table with a box of tissues placed deliberately within my reach. There were a lot of tissue boxes in my life at this time. The sole purpose of the meeting was to inform me of what was known about Samuel's condition, and to rapidly bring me up to speed with what the medics were thinking.

I had never previously heard of CHARGE Syndrome. I learnt a lot about it that night, and in the subsequent days, weeks and months.

I was told it is a rare genetic disorder that affects a random selection of society. Like many other disorders, it is a spectrum. The name 'CHARGE', first used in 1981, referred to a newly recognised cluster of features seen in a number of children.

Some individuals who had CHARGE Syndrome would only be affected by one or a few of the disabilities. Others, like Samuel, would have a range of the disabilities. The letters that made up the word CHARGE stood for each of the defects that had been grouped together to describe this overall condition.

- Coloboma – of the eye
- Heart – congenital heart defects
- Atresia – of the choanae, the apertures at the back of the nasal cavity
- Retardation – of growth and or development
- Genitalia – and/or urinary defects
- Ear – anomalies and/or deafness.

There were also several additional, minor characteristics of CHARGE Syndrome which we already knew Samuel had, as he had developed cleft palate and oesophageal atresia – where his oesophagus was not connected. There were many other areas of his body and brain that could be affected. We would only know as time went by and we saw Samuel grow and develop.

CHARGE Syndrome was also described to me as a condition where the middle section of parts of the human body were affected, or just not formed.

At this point of the meeting, our fetomaternal consultant, who had been responsible for my care since referral at the twenty-one weeks' scan, turned to me to apologise for not thinking about the possibility of CHARGE before Samuel was born.

I thanked her but had to be honest and assure her that it would not have made a difference. We would still have gone through with the pregnancy. In her defence, even when children with CHARGE Syndrome are born, the diagnosis is often difficult due to its rarity. She was not expected to know it was CHARGE given her readings of my scans. Roddy and I have never been in the business of blaming the medics.

***

With Samuel in an induced coma, I was able to go back to Eastbourne for a couple of nights at the weekend, and Roddy was able to go up to London to be with Samuel.

I took a photo of Samuel on my phone so I could look at it as I pumped milk at regular intervals through the day and night for him, back in Eastbourne. I put these bottles in the freezer, in the hope that they would be taken out, defrosted, and used for Samuel's feeds when he finally came home for me to care for him.

Being at home meant that when the boys were asleep I was also able to grab a chance to look at the internet, to find more information about CHARGE Syndrome. I had been warned by the medical team against doing too much research as it really is a spectrum, and each child born with CHARGE Syndrome may respond in different ways. There could be a lot of complications added to my situation by looking at the information on the internet and believing it might be true for Samuel, when it may not be. But it was a syndrome I had no knowledge of. I needed to begin somewhere if I was to be the carer of a child with it.

I decided to look at just the main websites of the CHARGE foundation. There were two things that struck me. Firstly, it seemed that few surviving people had all of the known features of CHARGE. It was more common to have a couple of the features of CHARGE. It was not common to have all of them. With the list of things we knew about Samuel, I already knew he was one of these very rare cases.

I found this hard to take in. The reality of it was distasteful. Why did our baby have to have it so bad? Samuel had all on the list, and more.

Knowing the amount of prayer that occurred during the time Samuel was in the womb, it was difficult to read that CHARGE Syndrome was a genetic condition caused by a mutation in a single gene – a regulatory gene that plays a role in turning other genes on and off.

It was just one gene. One gene out of the more than twenty thousand we all have. Just one went wrong, and it triggered other genes to turn on or not.

How could one part of Samuel's creation go wrong? Or had it? Had God somehow made a mistake and just forgotten to ensure that one of the genes in Samuel's body worked correctly, or was this all part of his master plan? I don't know the answer and maybe I never will.

Some bits I read on the website were encouraging: 'One of the hidden features of CHARGE Syndrome is the determination and strong character these children display.'[1] I also read how some of these children could become aggressive and strong-willed. I was not surprised. Wouldn't anyone feel frustrated, trapped in a body that could not perform like those of others? Weren't Samuel's disabilities enough reason for him to feel anger and confusion? I felt that way myself, and it was not my body going through these challenges.

My reading made me worried about what the future might hold for Samuel. I took time to think about how our family's lives would all be altered by having a child with severe disabilities who was so totally dependent on care. We would only know over time just how bad or good would be Samuel's response to the numerous operations he would face. It would be a challenging future with him in our lives, and there would be many ups and downs through the journey of his life.

Life with Samuel would be one of daily surrender to God for his help and strength in being able to cope with each new challenge. Previously, I had thought parenthood of able-bodied boys had been enough of a test for me. Samuel and his condition would be a continual test of that patience, stretched to the furthest degree. I had birthed a complete dependent.

That weekend on the internet I discovered that in the vast majority of CHARGE cases there is no known family history. Nothing to do with any gene that Roddy or I might carry created this condition in Samuel. It appeared to be a condition of spontaneous mutation. I think this is still the known position on CHARGE. Over the years, researchers may discover more about possible contributory factors, but for now we had to rest in the

---

[1]   https://www.chargesyndrome.org/about-charge/overview/ accessed 3 August 2020.

knowledge that there was very little known about why babies were born with this condition.

Also, I was aware it was a bit late to find out why this had happened. We had to accept that it was the reality of Samuel's life, and to find a way forward in navigating life with a severely disabled child.

***

A week after his operation, the NICU staff thought it was time to take Samuel off the ventilator and introduce him to breathing for himself again. This was planned as a gradual withdrawal from dependence to independence from the ventilator. We would see how he coped off the ventilator for an hour or so, and then let him show us when he was physically able to do all the breathing for himself again. It was envisaged that he would come off the ventilator and be able to breathe for himself as he had done prior to his operation. It would just take time for his body to readjust, and gain the energy to breathe.

With this end in sight, we were all geared up for the first attempt at extubation. I was encouraged to be a part of this process – to hold him, and to help him adjust to breathing again. As I held him, I could tell the staff were concerned. He did not seem to be doing well. He looked around for help, and his chest heaved and pulled.

He was kept off the ventilator for two hours, but all through this time I could tell it was taxing his tiny body. I felt no peace about him being able to breathe on his own in time. The doctors decided it had been too early, and they would put him back on a ventilator for a few more days to let him recover strength before his next attempt at extubation.

I left Samuel's bed while the medical team reinserted the ventilator. I'd had my hopes up that this day would be successful, and that we would be making some progress towards his full recovery after the operation.

It did not make sense. I could pick up that the hospital staff were unsure why this attempt had failed. I went into the parents' room on the ward and phoned Roddy to let him know how it had gone. Roddy had his own concerns that maybe Samuel's airways were affected. He had read in his own research that this can also be a part of the condition.

Yet I protested, 'He breathed for the first day on his own prior to the operation, so his breathing must be alright.' I started to wonder whether the operation had caused the problem, remembering the night when the NICU staff had tried to insert the tube, and their confusion about that process.

We had to just be patient and wait for the next attempt.

***

In the time between attempts at extubation, I had a regular pattern of life in hospital with Samuel. I would go each morning to the hospital and stay till evening with him.

We and the other parents in our room and on the ward were a support team. In time we learned the stories of each of those dear young lives. Many had been born premature. The youngest was a little baby whose parents had pleaded with the staff to keep her on support as she had been born just short of the 24 weeks. There were many parents who were strong advocates for their children.

There were also many parents who were weary. It is an emotional experience to have your child sick and in hospital, let alone having to deal with your own post-operative body, having just delivered a baby and having your hormones literally all over the place. We witnessed many desperate scenes. I often felt like I was in this bubble of hospital life. It is not called intensive care for nothing.

During my times on the NICU ward, I grew accustomed to the sounds and smells. The surgical fluids and the uniformed people. But most of all it was the incessant beep of the machines. Over and over again.

I struggled, listening to it banging inside my brain. Sometimes there were no other noises in the room. Despite human activity, the only constant sound was the persistent beeps of the bleating machines.

As a trapped listener, part of the noise frustrates you so much you wish you could tell it to shut up. But if it did shut up then Samuel would not be alive. So you don't want the beeps to stop.

But it is hard to breathe between the beeps. Hope hangs on each sound. Breath is held at each beep.

The alternative is silence.

Sometimes I took time to step away from Samuel's cot and gaze out the window, across to the Houses of Westminster. I considered what was going on there inside the very heart of British political life. The busy lives filled with apparent purpose. I would look out to Westminster Bridge and see the streams of tourists walking along, oblivious to the fact that through this window there were six wee babies, each born in different circumstances, but each fighting for their right to be a part of the hustle and bustle of that society outside.

***

On one of these days, I had an appointment with Samuel's cardiologist. Roddy and I had met him during our antenatal visits to St Thomas' Hospital for an initial discussion about what an operation for AVSD would require. Now that Samuel had been born, they had done various tests and echograms to produce a better image of the true state of Samuel's heart. The consultant wanted to discuss the results with me.

I entered the consulting room expecting to hear that it was imperative that Samuel have the operation within the next few months or he would die due to the condition of his heart.

I was surprised to hear the consultant's opinion that Samuel would live for years with the current state of his heart. It would just become weaker. If it wasn't operated on, it would not be until his early teens that his heart may fail and he would die. We were encouraged to consider consenting to an earlier heart operation rather than later, to prevent this deterioration.

I took the opportunity to ask the consultant whether he had other CHARGE Syndrome patients on his books.

He said, 'Yes, I receive a referral from a child with CHARGE about once every two years. I follow through with each one after the operation to see how their heart is coping and growing.'

I tentatively asked if he could tell me what these CHARGE Syndrome children were like. 'Can they communicate with you? Can they walk?'

I breathed in as he answered. 'Oh yes,' he said, 'they can be delightful. I had one little boy in only recently who I operated on as an infant. He is now four, and he is very talkative and lively.' He said he could not recall any issues with the boy's walking.

I thanked the consultant and left the room in high spirits.

I will never, ever forget my feelings of euphoria when I walked away from that cardiologist's room. It was the first time for some time that I was beginning to feel that Samuel may just pull through all of this and still be a very active part of our lives. I felt a sense of joy and purpose.

I told myself that although Samuel's life would initially be a series of painful and difficult operations, most of these operations would make a difference to his condition, and better his prospects for a brighter future. It dawned on me that the heart operation was now one of the least of his issues. Even if he did not have the operation, his heart would continue to operate. It would just gradually deteriorate – over years and not months. So it was a no-brainer to allow them to operate earlier rather than later, to give him the best quality of life possible.

I went for a late lunch and I couldn't stop smiling. I started to dream that Samuel may be like the little four-year-old the consultant had told me about. I started to have hope that he might just be able to come through all of this and have a place in our future. I was not foolish – I did fully admit that it was not going to be an easy life, but I thought each obstacle might be overcome.

I often think of this day when I look back and think about Samuel, when doubts creep in, telling me that I could not be trusted with the care and love of a disabled child – that once I was presented with Samuel's disabilities I ran away.

No, I say to myself, I did not react that way. I was fully, one hundred percent ready to embrace him and all his many disabilities and problems. I wanted to love and care for him forever.

I was given back some hope with the meeting that day. I treasure it, as I know that I was prepared to devote myself to care for Samuel in every way humanly possible.

If only I could be given that chance.

***

It was Easter weekend and Samuel was two weeks' old. Another ENT consultant wanted to meet with Roddy and me to discuss the way forward despite Samuel failing his first extubation.

Tom and Ben were in London with us for the holiday weekend and so they attended this meeting. They loved being with Samuel, and each weekend they were becoming a part of the furniture on the ward. The boys had their favourite nurses and they added cheer on the ward, as not many other babies had siblings present. The staff loved to interact and joke with them.

The boys really enjoyed going together to the large slide at the Evelina Children's Hospital, which was just next door to St Thomas' Hospital. It was a nice break from the rest of their new routine. They learned to assist in the breast pumping room, getting me my bottles for supply, putting dirty nappies in the bin, washing their hands with sanitiser, and being quiet when necessary. The boys just seemed to accept this new pattern of hospital life.

At this particular Easter meeting the boys' comments to the consultant were hilarious. They asked all sorts of personal questions about the ENT consultant's private life. He took it well and attempted to answer each question as diplomatically as possible.

He also tried to engage Tom and Ben, to help them understand Samuel's condition. He drew pictures to illustrate the procedures he was planning and was keen that we could all understand what the pictures represented. He was wanting, if we consented, to use a small camera to check Samuel's trachea (windpipe) to ensure this was not the reason for his failed extubations. We consented.

The results were excellent. Samuel's trachea was functioning as normal so this was not the cause of the failures. The ENT consultant had every hope that they had just attempted it too early and that next time Samuel would do better and be able to survive unassisted.

**

Samuel failed another attempt at extubation.

I was there, holding him, for one and a half hours as he struggled to breathe on his own. Eventually, the doctors decided to put him back on ventilation, as clearly he was not getting there on his own.

They were confused. Why was he continuing to fail? I left the room as they had the task of inserting a new tube into Samuel. I went out to the parents' room to phone Roddy and let him know of this second failure.

I had seen Samuel struggling and I was so confused. I kept a sporadic journal during our time with Samuel and I would like to share one excerpt from this time.

> 'When I see Samuel's pain and the ventilator tube being in, and the secretions being taken out regularly by the nurses, I cannot help but blame myself for putting him through all of this. As he looks up, I feel that his eyes are talking to me. I search for forgiveness from him, but it is not there. Yet so much is unknown of what he can see, hear or understand. Only time will tell.'

One of my struggles that became a recurring theme throughout Samuel's life was: what if he goes through all of these countless operations, the medics fix this and that, and he gets to a stage where he has some ability to be able to verbalise what he feels. Will he then say to me, 'Mum, why did you bother? Why did you put me through all of this?'

The most important question in my head was: what is best for Samuel? Would he want us to be pulling out all the stops to make his life better, when the best he could hope for was far from a full and active life as we envisaged it?

I really had an internal struggle about this. Whilst I believed that God was the giver and the taker of life, where did it start to be medicine that was giving Samuel life, and giving him a life that he himself was not happy with? As a mother, I would do anything and everything within my powers for Samuel, and work toward making his life the best that was possible given his many physical and no doubt mental limitations, but would he actually want me to do this for him? What was best for Samuel? That was my quest.

My quest did not have to continue for too long.

***

The ENT team decided to do one more procedure to check Samuel's breathing ability. This time, they wanted to put a small camera down his trachea and round the corner to see into his lungs. They took him through to the Evelina Children's Hospital to do this test.

I walked along with him and his medical team. Whilst the procedure was being done, I waited alone in the parents' room. After about half an hour, the consultant came back to chat with me about the results.

We sat together on a bench in some random corridor outside the parents' room, alone. The consultant in his white coat looked at me with an intensely earnest face and said, 'We have found what the problem is.'

Samuel had a condition known as bronchomalacia. His trachea and his lungs were perfectly formed. However, the bronchi which carry air into the lungs were not remaining open in Samuel's body. The bronchi in a healthy person are surrounded by strong cartilage, but when Samuel took a breath the bronchial tubes were floppy. They were collapsing, and not opening far enough to be able to let the air out of the lungs.

The consultant said, 'I am sorry, so terribly sorry, but I think that any form of operation on this would be futile, absolutely futile.'

It was a lot to take in. The word 'futile' meant the end of this journey.

No point. No alternative. Blank. Blank word. Blank heart. Blank hurt. Pain. Intense pain.

Slowly, as I sat silently there with the consultant, I did take it in.

The answer the consultant had given me made some sort of sense. Samuel had CHARGE Syndrome, which affects the formation of the middle of so many parts of the body, including the middle of Samuel's access to his lungs.

I looked at the consultant there beside me on that bench and thanked him for finally finding out for us what was wrong with Samuel's breathing. I did not question his interpretation. I realised it was not his fault that he was the bearer of bad news. He was only retelling the message from a higher authority: God.

The consultant's word 'futile' was God finally telling me what his will was for Samuel. God was taking him home. Medical intervention would be futile. There was nothing more we could do for Samuel here on earth.

I asked the consultant why Samuel had been able to breathe on his own at the start of his life. He said it was unexplainable. He did not know why that had happened. The consultant agreed it was miraculous. Given what he had seen with the camera, the earlier ease of Samuel's breathing seemed impossible.

I have often thought it was a miracle that Samuel could breathe on his own when he was first born. I think he was allowed to breathe at first so that we could be given those five weeks with him. Knowing what we know now, we realise he could have died at birth. I believe he was saved, not for him, but for us, his family, so that we could have him as a very real and precious part of our lives, be it ever so briefly.

The consultant asked me whether I wanted to see the video of Samuel's breathing. Despite the obvious pain it would cause me to watch, I did want to see this – and face it now rather than later. I have often wished Roddy had been beside me on that day to see the video with me. Had he known this would be the result, he would have been there. It was just that he thought we had forever with Samuel, and he was wanting to save his days so he could be with him once home.

Now I was being told that we would not have those forever days with Samuel.

I said yes, I would see the video. I walked back into that ward with the consultant, and we interrupted the other medics who had been chatting and looking at the video. They moved aside for me.

There was a silence, almost reverence, in the air as, before seeing the video, I took my time to be with Samuel.

I held Samuel's hand, and had a long look at Samuel lying there on his child-sized bed. He was kicking his feet and he seemed to be looking around. He had his arms stretched out wide as if he was any newborn, lying on his mat, having a playful kick. I took in that image of Samuel, and I can visualise it still in my head. There are no photos, but that image is engraved on my heart.

I asked to see the video and watched the screen. I saw an enlarged view of Samuel's perfect airway failing to open into his lungs as each breath was taken. Red. Passageways. Columns of human tissue, and then this small piece of flesh flapping before me, not strong enough to keep open. Failure and futility – modern medicine beaten by one small piece of weakened human tissue.

I could not believe that it had come to this. All the journey, from the first scan to this now before us, a tiny imperfection by measurement size but one of great magnitude in terms of our ability to survive as humans.

I watched the video for some time, just staring at it. It was like looking into an eternal space of red blood and cartilage, flesh. If only his bronchi had been formed normally then maybe we would have Samuel with us, but because it was imperfect we would have to let him go. These are still haunting images for me. That video is ingrained in my head for as long as I have memory. Yet I acknowledge, too, that there are so many parts of each of our bodies that we all take for granted. I did not even know until that day that I had bronchi. Yet mine had remained open without me ever thinking about it or acknowledging its apparently perfect creation.

***

The next day, Tom asked me, 'Will Samuel die?'

I knew I had to be honest so I said, 'Yes.'

Tom burst into tears, there in the hospital waiting room. I did not know what to do. I held him tight and confirmed our love for him, for Ben and for Samuel. Tom then asked whether other babies in the room with Samuel would die.

I said, 'No, we hope they won't.'

Tom said, 'That's not fair.' I had to agree, it wasn't fair.

I was concerned that Tom was feeling angry toward the other families who hopefully would not have to face the death of their child. I spoke to Mum about it and how best to handle Tom's feelings. She wisely suggested that now was the time to tell Tom that the little baby who had been opposite Samuel last week had died. I had not yet told the boys that fact.

I chose my moment when Tom and I were next alone together. I told him about the other baby's death, so that he would not think he was the only one to experience this unfairness of losing a brother. He looked up at me with a great big smile, suddenly glad, almost relieved. I wondered why.

He said to me, 'Mummy, that is great, as Samuel will have a friend.'

Here was me thinking Tom was concerned by the unfairness of us losing Samuel, but Tom was actually most concerned about Samuel being on his own in death and not having a friend to go through death with. That was Tom's version of unfair: facing death alone.

Tom and I ended up having a chat about what Heaven might be like. Tom said that Samuel would be lucky to meet Moses, Noah, the first Samuel who was in the Bible, and his mother Hannah. Tom said, 'Maybe they will look after him, Mummy.'

That night, Tom prayed, 'God, look after Samuel. Take good care of him. Please, please, make him comfortable with lots of people to play with.'

CHAPTER 8

Saying Goodbye to Samuel

would like to share with you an excerpt from the journal I kept during my pregnancy with Samuel, and his life. Much of his story has come from those jottings, but this entry seems worthy of direct quote.

'How do you wake on the morning you know that your baby is going to die? How do you make decisions about breakfast and what you are to wear? How do you chat with others at the breakfast table? What will be the topic of conversation? Most importantly, how do you ever become brave enough to enter the hospital and go to the sixth floor. I have to be brave for Samuel. Otherwise I would run a mile, but I have to be there for him.'

I had never previously seen a dead body. I was frightened at how I might react and whether I would have the courage to be with Samuel all the way. I did not know what to expect. I was scared, petrified.

I also knew that despite my own fear I had to be brave for Samuel. He needed his mother for the last time, and I did not want to fail him. My presence with him was all I could give.

***

It was Monday morning, three days after I viewed the video which sealed Samuel's fate. Roddy and I were due to meet the palliative care consultant in the morning, and we would then make a plan on what was best for Samuel. The professionals did not know how long it would take for Samuel to die. It may be that day, or it could take longer.

We were fortunate to have the support of two nurses who had taken a special interest in Samuel, and in us as a family. Sarah and Jill were both on duty that day, and they both wanted to take care of Samuel. They both individually expressed to us that they were 'pleased' we had made the decision not to prolong Samuel's life. They had each seen the pain he had experienced when the extubations failed, and personally they thought it was too much.

In the end it was Jill who was allowed to care for Samuel through this first palliative care shift. Jill was a great nurse and she was from Christchurch, New Zealand where my parents had their home, and so we had an instant connection. She was also your typical no-fuss Kiwi launching into our darkness with a huge dose of positivity. She was determined to make this a very special day for all the family. We are forever grateful to hospital staff such as Jill who go the extra mile to care for their patients and families. Jill later wrote to us the following words:

> 'Samuel touched my heart as soon as I laid eyes on him, with his cute wee face, super soft skin, and his strength. He is also a part of one of the most loving, wonderful families I have been lucky enough to meet. It was plain to see how much you adored him, and your main focus was always what was best for him, despite how hard it was for yourselves to make those selfless decisions.
>
> There are some babies that stick in your mind, and Samuel is one of mine. I still think of him often.'

Jill helped us to arrange taking footprints from Samuel's feet. She included Tom and Ben in this activity – they laughed, she made it fun. She also helped us dress Samuel for the first time. In NICU we hadn't been able to dress our baby in lovely clothes. He wore only a nappy, and depending on his body temperature then sometimes he had a blanket. Occasionally he was allowed socks, so my only baby purchase had come to some use.

It was a 'treat' to be able to dress him fully, and we all wanted a part in it. For the boys this was particularly special. For the first time, we were doing the things that Ben had planned for Samuel all those months prior with his nursery pals. We chose to dress him in a white babygrow that had plastic ducks as buttons down the front. Both Tom and Ben had worn this outfit as a baby.

Samuel looked so beautiful in his clothes. He looked like a real baby. Despite the tube, you could have convinced yourself he was 'normal'. We all just longed to pick him up and take him home as if this horrible reality was not happening.

Samuel was moved from the ward into a private room and we were then each given time with him. We each had a cuddle of him. During his cuddle, Ben broke down in tears and cried over Samuel, saying, 'My baby, my baby brother.' It had finally dawned on him that we would lose Samuel. He had been told Samuel would die, but each day of the weekend we went back to the hospital, and he was still there. Now Samuel was five weeks old and Ben was told this was to be his first and last cuddle. He sobbed. He had wanted this baby so much and had so many hopes and dreams for him. Samuel was indeed his baby brother and he wanted to protect him and save him from everything. Ben was only four years old, but his wee heart was deeply saddened.

Tom said to me that day, 'Mummy, why does Samuel have to die today? Why can't he live for another day?'

I had to say to Tom that if we let Samuel live another day then we would also want him to live the next day, and the next. 'There will never ever be a day that we want to say goodbye to him, but that wouldn't be fair to Samuel. While he's on earth he's in pain, and we don't want him to suffer anymore. This is why we have to be kind to Samuel and let him die.'

Tom tried to plead with me for just one more day. I found it hard as I knew that if I said, 'Yes, Tom, we will let him live one more day,' then his face would have lit up and he would have been happy – for that day.

I also knew that each day Samuel was in hospital it gave the medical team a reason to have to take bloods from him. This would cause him to suffer more. I felt that the best thing for Samuel was to let him go as soon as all the palliative medicine was ready. I had to be firm with Tom in order to best take care of Samuel.

These are some of the toughest moments in the journey – seeing others in your baby's family suffer. They loved Samuel so much they wanted to hold on to him. But you know the parental love you have to show is the one that will let him go. I knew for Samuel I had to be braver than I had ever been, to help him and the rest of my family through this time.

After our cuddles and family photos the drugs were ready, and we had to begin the process of letting Samuel die. I state this without any expression, because when you have to face these things in life there are logistics and practicalities that come into action alongside the reality of the event before you. Even to allow Samuel to die we had to wait for the pharmacist to draw up the appropriate pain medication. Time inevitably moves forward, and decisions made one day lead to consequences the next. Eventually, the medicines arrived, and the consequences had to be faced.

Tom and Ben went out of the room to be with Mum and Dad. The plan was that they would stay near the hospital, as no one knew how long Samuel would survive off the ventilator. It could be minutes, hours or days. Mum and Dad took the boys to the hospital gardens and waited.

As Samuel's tube was taken out, I noticed how lovingly the consultant removed the plaster that had been a permanent feature on his face, holding the tube in position. The big plaster Ben had wanted ripped off on Day One was now being taken away. The consultant tentatively pulled at it and wiped every few seconds to release the adhesive and relieve any soreness. I greatly appreciated the love that was shown and the delicacy and dignity given to Samuel by all the staff who took care of him on that day.

Once the plaster was removed and the tube taken out, the consultant whisked Samuel into my arms. I wonder whether he thought Samuel would only last for seconds. At the side of his mouth, Samuel was given some drugs to ease any pain he may experience. For the first time, I was able to hold baby Samuel free from that machine beeping and free from the encumbrance of the ventilator. Mother and baby having our first unimpeded cuddle.

Samuel 'looked' around. You could tell he was thinking: this is something different, it is a new experience. Roddy and I sat together on the couch, wanting to soak up every second with Samuel, to look intently at his hands, his feet, his face. I wanted to savour each moment. To breathe in the smell of him, to capture it permanently in my sense of smell and never let it go. I imagined being able to bottle his smell in some permanent manner, to hold onto it forever. I realised this was impossible, but I still kept breathing in the dream. Soaking up Samuel.

Roddy and I were left to be on our own with our baby as Jill, our nurse, waited just outside the door. There was no need for the intensity of care he had experienced the rest of his life. If he showed any signs of pain, we were to let her know and further drugs could be supplied.

He was so calm, so at peace. I was almost lulled into thinking everything was normal – I was just having a relaxing cuddle with my husband and baby. I tried so hard to give him comfort and to somehow pour my love into him through the action of gently rocking and reassuring him.

After about half an hour, I handed him to Roddy for a cuddle. He gently rocked Samuel while quietly singing to him a peaceful song of comfort. Later, Roddy passed Samuel back to me as he softly said, 'He is approaching his final breath.'

I could hear that his breaths were coming with greater pauses in between, and each time another breath came it was with a heave from Samuel's small chest. Then there was one loud heave, and we waited, and heard no more. I screamed a sound that must have been heard vibrating all around the hospital. It was a curdling sound of deep anguish as my baby, my precious boy, breathed no more.

***

Samuel died at four thirty-five pm on Monday the twenty-sixth of April 2010. He had survived one hour off his ventilator, and why he had been able to breathe for two days unassisted before his operation no one will ever be able to tell us. I believe it was a miracle, and it was allowed in order that we could have those five precious weeks with him. To hold him, to love him, and to care so much that eventually it was because we wanted him to suffer no more that we were able to give him back.

I will never stop loving and wanting Samuel. He has taken part of me with him to a place I have not yet been allowed entry.

CHAPTER 9

A Family Grief

There was a knock at the door and my poor Dad entered, asking for keys to the flat. Tom had fallen into the pond outside the hospital and was fully soaked. He needed a change of clothes. Jill took charge and sorted out Tom with theatre scrubs as an adequate temporary measure whilst his own clothes were put in the hospital tumble dryer.

The family all came back to cuddle Samuel, and to prepare him in his cot. The boys' first reaction on entering the room was:

'But Samuel is still here!'

'We thought he would disappear!'

Tom told me he never thought being dead would be like that. He thought dead people became invisible. We were able to explain to them that Samuel's body was still with us on earth, but that we believed his spirit had been taken to be with Jesus.

The boys were so happy to have his body. They each had a cuddle of him. Then they helped us and Jill to clean him and dress him. It was so natural.

The scene was all happening in front of me, but I do not know that I could fully take it in. I had kept courage as my daily weapon since the first scan until this point. I saw it as my purpose to be strong. I knew Samuel needed a double dose of my strength and courage. But he was gone and I was stunned – in aftershock at the calm that now seemed to invade the room.

Ben looked at Samuel lying in his cot and then up at me, and said, 'Mummy, is this what Michael Jackson looked like when he died?'

It was an odd question, but until then the only death Ben had been aware of was the hype on TV about Michael Jackson's recent passing, so I suppose he equated the two very different scenarios as one. Death is death. Do we all look the same as each other when we die?

In the days, months and years to come as parents, we would be asked many varied and interesting questions about death by our boys. They managed to amaze us each time with things we had not thought about or did not know the answer to.

We resolved to always try to answer any question that arose, with discernment so as not to overly concern them about unnecessary issues, but also with honesty. We knew no more about death than they did. Who were we to say what it was like to die? We had not experienced it ourselves. Who were we to say whether people in death remain the same age they were when they died, or whether they have a type of aging process in Heaven? How were we to know whether there are schools and sports stadiums in Heaven?

At the time, I was also conscious that the faith Roddy and I each had was a faith we as individual adults had chosen as our response to the life around us. It is a faith we have tried to share with our children. Whilst I wanted to reassure our boys of this faith in eternal life, I did not want to let them be ignorant of the fact that some people do not believe this and have other opinions. Whilst it is unwise, I believe, to bombard a grieving child with too many options and create confusion in a time when they need stability, I think it is important that they understand not all may choose a path of faith. I say this because one day they will grow up. They will enter the world without us by their side, and they will be challenged by the world around them and the beliefs others hold. They may then look back and question the conclusions about Samuel we gave them, and wonder whether they later believe it or not.

I did not want to use our faith as a simple plaster over their very real grief and confusion. They needed to nut out these issues for themselves and reach their own answers to life's dilemmas.

Tom and Ben would be free to question their own beliefs when that time may come, but I was also aware that if they were to question the faith we shared, they would have to begin their own journey of grieving all over again. Much of their childhood grief, whilst deeply felt, was also softened by their understanding of Samuel being in a place called Heaven where Jesus would keep him safe. If this hope were to be pulled from them in the future, would they still find strength?

There are various guides and rule books for how parents should deal with different life scenarios. I did not seek any of them for dealing with the boys' grief after the loss of Samuel. This was not because I had an attitude that I did not need help. It was simply because I was so involved in the practical effort of everyday coping with my own grieving heart and that of my family, the thought of taking time to read guide books to work out which was best was in the too-hard basket.

I followed my own logic. I was open and honest with the boys at each stage of their questioning. Roddy and I were also trying to navigate this strange pathway of grief and confusion for ourselves and each other. We tried to listen to each and every concern or question the boys had, in an open and free manner. In our household, no question was considered unaskable. I have to admit that many of the questions were unanswerable.

***

Leaving Samuel in the room he had died in, now safely wrapped in a shawl and lying in his cot, was one of the hardest moments of my life. I would never willingly have left him. I had been with him for almost a year. We had been a team, and I had been one of his strongest supporters.

I had no choice. I could have tried to set up camp in that room, but I knew that, inevitably, one day, I would be asked to leave the hospital. I had to somehow find the last of my strength for the day to leave my precious, much wanted and much-loved son. I did not know what I faced in the world now, without him in it.

As Roddy, Mum, Dad, Tom, Ben and I left the hospital that evening, we were waiting at a lift which had wards opening to both left and right. On one side was the neonatal special care and intensive care units where Samuel had lived for all of his short life. On the opposite side was the general neonatal ward.

I had not realised Tom had ever been aware of the other door. But as we left the sixth floor that day, Tom looked up to me and, pointing towards the door to the neonatal ward, said, 'Mummy, we would have liked to have gone through that door to visit Samuel, wouldn't we?'

I had to agree we would have. If only.

Outside the neonatal ward at that moment were two groups. One was a family party, ecstatic with blue balloons, clearly about to go in and welcome their new family member into their lives. The other group were two policemen making apparently urgent calls from outside the ward. It seemed there was a commotion inside the ward between one of the mums and her partner.

It struck me that in the time we had been with Samuel in the Neonatal Intensive Care Unit I had met many parents, and what stood out was their dedication to their child. If the children behind the NICU door were given a chance to go home it was obvious to me that many would be loved and cherished by the families they had been placed in. They were parents who were presently fighting for their child and not fighting each other.

Yet here was a scene where one child had been born to an obviously troubled start. What would he or she face in their life ahead, with parents already fighting in the hospital?

I do not question God's ability to keep the world under his control, but I do question many of the things that are allowed to happen in this world. Why can't all children be given an equal start? Each innocent child certainly deserves it.

Yet as I ponder these things, I am reminded that this world is imperfect. It is a world that is not how God planned it to be. I believe God has given humans the freedom to exist. If he did not allow us to make mistakes, would we really be creatures of our own free will? If he micromanaged perfect lives, would we be truly human?

I also thought, as I watched those policemen, of what it would be like if we entered that maternity room right now and were given the apparently healthy baby from a troubled background whose parents were fighting. Never presuming that they would have given the baby to us, but what if they had? If we brought him or her up in our home, would that child be able to replace Samuel? No, my mind protested loudly. Whilst there could be some good for us and possibly for the baby – controversial as to whether it would be better for the baby or not – having the other baby would never take from us the pain of losing Samuel.

A member of our family had died, and we would never be the same family again. No matter how many other children came into our lives, we could not step back to a time before Samuel existed and live as if he had not been. We had to learn to live without him here on earth, whilst internally our minds were protesting our new reality.

The old reality of a family of four had changed forever. We were five now. Samuel had etched his imprint on all our hearts. He was a permanent, if absent, member of our family.

The lift doors opened to take us down.

CHAPTER 10

Samuel's Homecoming

We returned to Eastbourne, but without our baby. He would be transported later by private ambulance.

I had had one short weekend at home, when Samuel was alive but in an induced coma after his operation, where Roddy had gone to be with Samuel and I had spent time with Tom and Ben and my parents. Apart from that flying visit, I had not been in our home or in Eastbourne for three months. It was not the homecoming that anyone had envisaged.

As uncertainties had been raised about Samuel's health from the start, I had not allowed myself to make too many preparations. I was not returning to have to deconstruct a nursery.

The socks I had allowed myself to buy for Samuel I keep in his box that the hospital passed to us when he died. It contains his name tags and his heart monitor leads. At times when I go through the things in that box, I am struck by how little we have to remind us of him. A couple of hospital knitted hats, a couple of name tags, one with his name and one just as Baby McNicol – his name before we named him.

***

The box contains a small specimen bottle with a few scraps of Samuel's hair. Instead of bringing me joy and connection to him, the sight of the hair takes me back to his cot.

I had been out of the ward to have my lunch. I returned to find that, without my permission, the nurse on duty had shaved half of his head in order to try to find a vein for a cannula to go in. She had inserted it into his head.

When I returned and saw his head shaved and the cannula sticking out, I was devastated. My reaction was that my boy had been violated, and I had been caught off duty at the time. 'Failed parent' feelings crept in. The nurse said to me, 'Just consider it as Samuel having a new and funky haircut.'

Later, after the video that seemed to seal Samuel's future, the consultant said the cannula on Samuel's head looked infected and I should tell the ward to remove it. When I told him the manner in which it had been inserted and without my permission, he was visibly shocked. Again, I realise it was not the nurse's fault. She said it had been hard to find a free vein, and this must have been the final option and not done lightly. However, I think it is important to know that I do not look on that bottle of hair with fond and happy memories. It draws pain and hurt. It is not a pleasant reminder of happier times.

As I look inside Samuel's hospital box, I long for that bottled smell I had imagined when being with him. But there is no bottle of Samuel-scented smell that remains.

***

In time, I had to go through all our baby clothes and accessories and take these to the charity shop. Whether they were bought by others specifically for Samuel or just hand-me-downs, it hurt the same. I was effectively saying that no baby of ours would ever wear these. I know I could have waited to do this task later, but when? When would it ever get easier? I could not envisage any time that it would, so I opted to deal with it earlier rather than later.

I chose a children's charity, Barnardo's, as it seemed appropriate. My sister Joanna was with me when I took the first delivery, and the lady in the charity shop exclaimed, 'What a lot of stuff! You must be downsizing. How quickly they grow out of all the baby stuff.'

I remained silent. When we got back to the car, Jo was in tears. The lady at Barnardo's had no idea – no one expects an infant death.

Even many of our friends who we had warned there might be complications found it hard to believe that Samuel's death had happened. It became evident that many had not really believed what we had said earlier. I think some had thought we were being over analytical and pessimistic, and that all would go well for us in the end. So for many of our contacts, the death of baby Samuel came as a shock.

***

When we went back to Eastbourne, I was still full of milk. I had to let my supply gradually reduce, which part of me resented. It was as if I was accepting the fact that Samuel had died. Lack of milk supply equated to lack of need for a mother.

With increasing anger at the futility of it all, I threw into the rubbish bin all the frozen milk I had pumped during the weekend I had been home. I was like a woman possessed. Outside, on our very public street, I used all my strength to aim those frozen bottles one by one into the big black bin. To me, each thump seemed to highlight the waste.

Clearly, my anger was also due to my heartbreak at the loss of Samuel. I was broken. There was so much nurturing I had wanted to give Samuel. There had been so many mums in the hospital unable to produce enough milk for their babies, and here was me with oversupply but no baby.

Bang, thump went the plastic bottles sharply into the bin, to defrost and be taken away as waste.

I felt empty. I kept putting a protective arm around my stomach, then realising that Samuel was not there. He no longer needed my protection. I had all the normal physical and emotional feelings of a mother who has only five weeks earlier delivered a baby – but I had no baby to hold and to care for. There was only air, useless air, all around me, without Samuel as a form within the air.

I felt useless. My experience has been that when you have a child it is like having an extension of yourself, yet one you cannot really control. A child has its own will, its own desires, but at least while it is very young, you are needed. You have this bonding time when you can nurture your child, so that when it grows it will be free, but it will know the love of a mother's arms.

Samuel was so young. I felt the need for him to be protected and loved by me still. Yet I could not give my love and protection to him. He was out of my reach. We had seen his body after he died, but it felt as if Samuel had disappeared from us; his spirit had gone. I wanted to call him back to tell him again that we loved him, and if I could that I would protect him.

Where was he? Out in the air? Up in the sky? I would look to the dark night sky and wonder. He was out there somewhere, but I could not go to him.

I felt his vulnerability and my inadequacy as a mother, deeply. There is no way of joining our dead child unless we too die, no matter what we personally believe happens once we die. We cannot deny that there is a finality about death that causes a separation. We can remember the child, but we do not know what their reality is now. It is not our reality. We are connected to the earth; they are elsewhere.

*****

We had only been home a few hours when Roddy said we should go and look at cemeteries. I suppose it was Roddy's need to do something practical, to fill our time, to have a purpose, to sort out the next stage. That was one of Roddy's coping mechanisms. I had no objection; I just followed.

Roddy was right that we needed to do this soon, but what a horrible job. Some of the cemeteries we saw were so grim. They were grey. Row upon row of grey stone and then broken stone and then discarded stone. My heart becoming blander and duller at each stop we made.

I experienced a real homecoming feeling when at the end of our cemetery tour we drove into Willingdon Cemetery. It did not take us long to agree that this was the place for Samuel.

Yet the act of choosing a cemetery was troubling for me. I thought, how can I say it is a nice place? Yes, it was at the base of the South Downs and had a beautiful setting, surrounded by open countryside with sheep and cattle on the nearby hills. But a burial is in the ground. You don't put a baby in the ground. Also, the cemetery was too far away. It was a ten-minute drive. He needed to be closer to us. A baby needs his family, and we needed him there with us.

That night, I dreamed that we buried Samuel in our own back garden. But in my dream I protested that he was not allowed to stay there. We had to dig him up and put him in the cot. I picked him up lovingly out of the cot. I held Samuel tightly, in my dream. I concluded that in my arms was the only truly proper place for him to be. I awoke clutching my empty arms.

***

We had a meeting with the funeral director in town. As I stepped out from the building onto the pavement, a mother with her newborn baby walked past me. As I watched her pram pass by, I was struck by the polar-opposite experiences we were having. It was wrong, so wrong. You bury old people. You arrange funerals for your grandparents, not your child. It was all so unbelievable.

No matter how much you think you are prepared for death, the stark reality of it, and the planning for the funeral and burial or cremation so soon after the traumatic event, when the reality of death has not yet sunk in, means you often operate in a dreamlike state. My experience was that at this time as a human being you are not really thinking clearly, yet you have to make so many important long-term decisions. You have to make plans.

Everyone wants to know what you want. You have no idea what you want or who you are or what you should be wanting to want. You are not you. You are in a different state entirely. But everyone wants to support you, yet you can't find you. You, is missing.

***

I suppose it would be an option just to shut the door and remove yourself from the world. But I never considered it a practical one, as maybe others wanted to grieve with me and my family. It would have been easier had we chosen a private ceremony –less to arrange. However, we had many people who wanted to come and show their support.

I also realised we would not be able to plan anything else for Samuel. There would be no first birthday, no first day at school, no graduation, no wedding day. How else were we going to celebrate and give tribute to his life but in a funeral?

***

Samuel was brought back to his home by hearse. I looked outside at the long, foreboding black car, parked, waiting for us to get in. I could see his little white coffin in it. I wanted to sneak out and grab it and bring him indoors and send that car away, never to return.

I have to accept that he never did truly come into our family home. Samuel was never part of our physical life beyond the hospital walls. He was never given the ability to come to his earthly home. One gene determined that.

Some people thought the fact that he was never physically at our home must have made it easier for me, as we had no memories of him in the house. I didn't turn a corner at home and see him there, as he never was there. Yet, surely, with a child who dies after you have known them for a while, it is those very memories that sustain you in your grief? Your knowledge of who they were and what they liked and how they fitted into your family.

With Samuel, we could only talk about what would have been. We did know, with his disabilities, that a lot of the ordinary things we think of for a child's life would not have been true for Samuel's. In many ways we grieved twice, firstly for the condition he was given and secondly for his death.

***

I think about the dreams and plans his big brothers had for Samuel, and I can understand the words my friend Charlotte sent to me shortly after Samuel died. She said, 'I still have sad moments thinking about the wonderful family life that Samuel has missed. I think of your trips and plans and remember how he would have fitted in and been so adored by you all. It seems crazy that such a lucky boy was so unlucky not to experience it all.'

Samuel's funeral was the first funeral Tom or Ben had ever been to. How wrong! They were meant to be involved in all the ordinary things of welcoming a new baby into their home, yet they were off to church, and on to the cemetery to see him buried.

It seemed right to us to include them in everything. At no point was anything hidden from them. Their brother had died, and this was now what happened to him. I thought they needed to see that. Children are smart enough to know when adults are hiding things.

These things about death and burials were not what I wanted my children to learn at a young age, but then I didn't want Samuel to die. What I did not want to happen had happened. I had to respond to the practicalities in a manner that met the unfortunate reality. Truth, we could handle. Lies or hidden areas would be hard to undo later when small children grew up and learned the truth.

I was warned by one of my work colleagues that he had been traumatised at a young age by being taken to a cremation. He advised me to protect the boys from that. We had chosen to bury Samuel, but I was aware that the act of burial itself may be difficult for the boys to understand. After all, I was struggling with it myself. Again, I thought it was right to include them and not make them feel that there were adult things happening that hid Samuel from them. As long as we were able to 'have Samuel with us', we would, and the boys would be a part of every stage. I had no idea whether this was the right approach, but it felt better than shrouding death and burial in mystery.

**

Ben opened the car door, jumped into the hearse and gave the coffin a big hug, saying, 'Ahhh Samuel! He is so gorgeous.'

We had managed to source forget-me-nots, which my sister Joanna and her family had kindly paid for, and which were beautifully displayed on top of a pure-white baby coffin. As I looked at that wee box, I envisaged Samuel's cold body inside. The funeral directors had offered for us to see Samuel's body at any time prior to the burial, but I had chosen not to see his body again. I wanted to remember him as I had last seen him, snuggled in his wicker basket, lovingly placed there by his brothers who had helped wash and clean and dress him after he died. I wondered whether I would ever regret not going to see his body again, but my mind tried to quash those wonderings.

Tom and Ben called the hearse a 'special car'. Later, when we were visiting Samuel's grave with Roddy's sister, one of the boys said to her, 'Fiona, have you ever been in a special car?' They were comparing funeral experiences. It all seemed crazy, but this was their new reality so they openly discussed it as normal.

To me, the loveliest moment in the special car was when Ben said, 'Mummy, we all have seatbelts, but where is the seatbelt for Samuel?' He was protecting his brother to the end. We were able to hug Ben and tell him that he was showing great concern for his wee brother, but as Samuel had died there was no longer any need to wear a seatbelt. We were to find that he would carry on protecting Samuel even after death by always referring to him, and talking about his baby brother openly and freely with anyone. To the full extent that any four-year-old can love someone, Ben did love Samuel.

***

I had never attended a British funeral, so I was unprepared for the ceremony of the occasion. The funeral directors were dressed in top hat and tails. The hearse was directed into the churchyard very slowly, with the funeral director walking at a slow pace in front of the hearse. I was not expecting the formality of it, yet I liked it. To me, it showed the reverence and respect for Samuel that he deserved. I felt it was a fitting tribute to his short life.

Inside the church, when the music started we proceeded down the aisle behind Roddy and Samuel. Roddy alone was carrying his son's coffin in his arms. I think it was a beautiful image of love and care for that wee boy right until the end, and it is a picture I hold dear in my heart – my husband holding his dead son with such care. I held Tom and Ben's hands, and Ben skipped down the aisle.

The funeral service was taken by our friend, Tony. He and his wife Anne had been very supportive to us as a family every step of the way with the pregnancy and short life of Samuel, so it seemed appropriate to ask him to take the service. We wanted to have someone who had actually met Samuel, and Tony had visited him only days before he died. At the service he spoke about how beautiful Samuel looked, how he had held his hand, and what a firm grip on his finger Samuel had had. Many in the congregation that day had not had the privilege of meeting Samuel. It was good to have someone affirm him as a real live being.

This is why I also wanted a photo of Samuel on the order of service. I wanted people to see our gorgeous boy and to acknowledge he was real. I thought it would help them connect with Samuel. Yet we did not have many photos of Samuel before he had the tube put in for his breathing. I had cried earlier that week at the chemist when I was trying to print photos of Samuel to see which one would look the best. I felt jealous of people who at least had a normal baby photo without hospital apparatus, as it seemed we had even been denied that.

I wanted to speak about Samuel at his funeral. I was his mum, I had carried him for nine months prior to his birth, and I had been with him most days since. I wanted to tell others some of the initial things I was thinking, about what Samuel's life could mean. I wanted people to see Samuel's life as not just some tragic event. Even at this early stage into my grief, I wanted to show that there was some purpose in his life and that he had made a lasting impact on our family.

In my eulogy I talked about each of my three boys, and how they had each taught me something during the time Samuel had been with us.

Starting with Samuel, I said that he had taught me to appreciate more the everyday things that we so often take for granted. Samuel never did leave hospital. He never had the privilege of breathing in fresh air. I don't know what he could see with his limited eyesight, but I knew he had not been introduced to a world beyond the hospital ward, so it was not likely that he had seen much. All the things we as able-bodied people can take for granted, he was not able to enjoy. For that I wanted to publicly thank him, for teaching me to be thankful for the privileges I had been given with my own life and health.

I spoke then of Ben and his intense and selfless love for his baby brother. He had even said that Samuel would be allowed to chew all the tyres off Ben's toy cars and he would not mind. This was a big call, as keeping cars in good working condition meant a lot to Tom and Ben. Ben was explaining that to be able to play with Samuel was more important than the actions that Samuel might take during that play, and that Ben would love him no matter what. Unconditional.

Then I spoke of what Tom said at home about Samuel's death. He said, 'Lucky Samuel, Mummy. Lucky Samuel, as he gets to see God and Jesus first, and God is making him a house.' His strong belief that Samuel was the fortunate one when all the world around us was thinking he was 'unlucky' was a reminder to us of the Christian hope that we hold. That God is indeed preparing a place for each one of us, and that after our time in this world – whether it be five weeks, five months or one hundred years – a time will come for each of us when we will die. Will God be welcoming us home as a known son or daughter?

***

I wondered how Heaven works when a child has not made a commitment to God themselves yet dies. The way I look at it, Samuel was born without fault. Did Samuel in some unconscious way sin in his lifetime? Was he truly innocent, or did he need to seek forgiveness?

Does the fact that a person is disabled excuse them from having to make a positive decision to believe? I do not know the answer, but I do trust in

God. I trust that he is a just judge, and that he will judge Samuel's case with fairness. I did not worry for Samuel about the logistics of Heaven, as I knew it would be far better for him than what life seemed to present for him here on earth. Life on earth for Samuel would have been tough. I had to accept that fact, and I had to not want that for him.

I could now imagine Samuel finally being healed and finally free of pain. I thought about Heaven and where Samuel might fit into it, but I did not question the details of its existence. It seemed right to hope for something better for Samuel, better than he had experienced with us here on earth because of his physical limitations.

Yet having a belief that he was in a better place did not take away our earthly pain of losing Samuel. We each grieved the fact that he was given CHARGE Syndrome to start with. Why had this been allowed?

***

As Roddy and I lowered Samuel into his grave, my whole body protested. This was my baby; I did not want to place him here where worms and decay would come. I wanted to have him, to love him, to hold him, and to get to know him as a person and a friend. I wanted for him one day to call me 'Mum'. Yet this would never happen now on earth. Roddy and I, together, had to lower him into the hole, and after a short pause we had to turn our backs and leave him there and return to the world beyond the cemetery.

It is a special spot, where Samuel is buried. His cemetery is at the base of the South Downs on the English South Coast. If you visit, you will find a lot of bird life. You can hear the noise of the cows and the sheep in the paddocks alongside the cemetery. Ahead as you look past his grave are the rolling hills of the South Downs. They are a protected green belt, so we do not expect they will ever be built on. To me it is a peaceful place. A good place to rest awhile. Whilst I did still want to keep him close to us by burying Samuel in my back garden, I came to realise that this was the right place for him.

We had been told that Samuel would be buried on the other side of the cemetery where they had newly consecrated a specific area for children to be buried. He would be the first child to be buried there. I felt sad that he would be alone, but it made sense that he would one day be with other children. I did not want that to happen; I did not want him to ever be joined by others as that would mean some other family would have to go through similar grief.

On the day of the funeral we were walked by the funeral director to another part of the cemetery where a small plot had been dug. This was where a plot had been allocated to Samuel, presumably at the last minute as we had not been informed. It was the last place in the old section of the cemetery. When you are part of a formal ceremony with others present you can't exactly call out in protest, 'I thought you said he would be buried over there!' I could not start to negotiate something different. I had to go with what had been arranged by the funeral directors.

Later when we returned to where Samuel was buried I became happy with it. He is buried next to another baby and they are surrounded by grandparents. We later discovered the grandparent of one of my dear friends is buried just along from him, so we feel he is in a proper family and not buried alone in the children's section.

***

The cemetery became a place of refuge for me. I found in entering its gates my heart skipped a beat. There was a lightness about me as I was going to see where Samuel was. After having to deal with so many people around me who refused to mention Samuel's name or to acknowledge his existence, it was good to be 'reminded' that he was real, that he did have a permanent marker, a presence on this earth that could not be denied.

Yet despite liking being at the cemetery myself, I was aware that I wanted the boys to share this same liking with me. I did not want the boys to ever feel that going to the cemetery was a burden. Like some contract with the dead, that if we visited them daily it meant we loved them more. I wanted them to want to go each time we went, and to view it as a 'treat' and not a chore. So we did not make daily visits, but whenever we were passing we would pop in. Often this was when we were heading out of town – maybe off on holiday. We would stop to tell Samuel all about it, and of course tell him we wished he was able to come with us.

One such time, we were off on a big trip. We were going to Australia. Ben asked at the cemetery, 'Does Samuel move to a different part of Heaven when we are in Australia? Would he move to the Australia end of Heaven? Are there different countries in Heaven?'

When the boys came to the cemetery, I encouraged them to have fun. The rules we made were that we had to respect others and their ways of mourning their loved ones, so if other people were present at the cemetery we were quiet. However, if there were no other visitors in the cemetery the boys could run, chase, and play hide-and-seek all over the place. Sometimes they took their scooters to scoot along the paths. They loved finding rabbits hiding in the cemetery and chasing after them at speed. For the boys, the cemetery was a place of fun and not of fear.

***

After Samuel died, going to church was hard. I felt vulnerable and exposed in church. It took tremendous effort to still attend. Our regular church was the place where we had held Samuel's funeral. Many times, I would be standing in church and instead of concentrating on the present moment all I could visualise was Samuel's white coffin sitting on that stage. The image was so clear I wondered whether others could see it too.

Then there was the singing. Oh dear, no. That always, without many exceptions, set me off crying. More keenly than ever before, I would read and listen to the actual words we were singing in the songs. These words confronted me. How could I not think of Samuel at this time? But also, I was thinking further, beyond him. I felt as if, in my silence, when the words were too hard to sing, I would be transported from that earthly venue to a place beyond. I was being given a small, imperfect glimpse of what Heaven could be like, with countless worshippers sharing the one song of praise to God. I imagined Samuel there amongst them. I struggled with why I wanted to have him back with us when surely his life in Heaven was a billion times better, and more than what we could ever offer him here on earth. Why was I sad when my son had run his race and reached the goal?

Worship in church has changed for me since Samuel died. It has been enhanced and deepened. It is odd, as often now I cannot sing aloud at church. The words are too demanding on me, emotionally. In the quiet, as I listen to others singing and tears roll down my cheeks, I have a close spiritual encounter, as if God is talking with me in the midst of my grief as my Comforter and as my Counsellor. These songs draw me to a place where I long to go. A place where all the questions and worries, the fears, the hurts, the pain of this world will be forever replaced.

For me corporate worship is now a far more humbling experience. Since Samuel, I have been known to cry more than I ever would have before. Quite frankly, that is not always easy, especially in new environments where people don't know why I cry. I am a private person. I have not previously often (if ever) cried in public. Singing exposes my rawness. It cuts to the soul. Yet, despite my open exposure and how uncomfortable that feels, I am thankful to Samuel for opening my eyes to really read the words, and for opening my ears to really hear what we are singing and saying. So many times, I want to sing the words but the emotion and the cost of what we are saying hits me and I find myself silent.

Music is a method of healing the broken hearted. Listening to songs of grit and of comfort really help me. The words, the harmonies, all work together to speak to my soul. My best counselling sessions are often just sitting on my own or with Roddy, listening to music. Often in silence at these times I feel closest to Roddy. Words are often inadequate as they cut across each other and we don't meet at the same juncture. Wherever his grief may be, I find the music lets us each silently express it.

***

The other problem I had in church after Samuel died was that I would be listening to the talk and find myself thinking, yes, that sounds good preacher person, but would you still say that if your son had been buried and God had not answered your prayers for him in the way you wanted? I started to hear voices in my head accusing the preacher. I had a strong desire to stand in the middle of church and ask, out loud, whether the person speaking would still testify in the same way if he had been challenged with his own son's death.

Maybe I was unstable. Or maybe I was just more attuned to the need for truth and transparency from those who are tasked with preaching to us.

For me, the fact that one day each of us will face our Maker was very real. I had seen the frailty of life with my own eyes. I found that half-baked Christianity did not work for me. I wanted to hear truth and authenticity, and know that the speaker was genuine, that his or her words would hold true even if he or she was challenged.

I was reminded of a poem shared with me by a friend in my teenage years. I could still recite it as the words still rang true, and its moral had greatly influenced me in life. Edgar Guest was a British-born American who became known as the People's Poet.

SERMONS WE SEE

I'd rather see a sermon than hear one any day;
I'd rather one would walk with me than merely tell the way.
The eye's a better pupil, and more willing than the ear,
Fine counsel is confusing but example's always clear;
And the best of all the preachers are the men who live their creeds,
For to see good put into action is what everybody needs.
I can soon learn to do it if you'll let me see it done;

I can watch your hands in action, but your tongue too fast may run.
And the lecture you deliver may be very wise and true,
but I'd rather get my lessons by observing what you do;
For I might misunderstand you and the high advice you give,
But there's no misunderstanding how you act and how you live.

When I see a deed of kindness, I am eager to be kind.
When a weaker brother stumbles and a strong man stays behind
Just to see if he can help him, then the wish grows strong in me
To become as big and thoughtful as I know that friend to be.
And all travellers can witness that the best of guides today
Is not the one who tells them, but the one who shows the way.

I wanted to see evidence of real faith in action and not just talk. Genuineness of word and action was the only attitude likely to register on my radar.

If church was so hard, why did I bother? I could have just not gone. Saved myself the added stress; stayed away. I could still have practised my form of faith and worship outside of the church community, surely?

I went to church because I knew that if one week I decided not to, I might never enter the doors again. Though it was a tough place to be, it was the one place I could be certain that, at some point, faith and God would be discussed. The very things I was struggling with would be open dialogue in this place. Looking at loss through the eyes of faith was the only thing that was working for me. So it made sense to have the dialogue.

It was not that church contained a whole bunch of exceptional people who were always caring for our needs. In fact, a lot of poorly prepared people awaited inside those doors – with many notable exceptions, of course. But, you see, church is a place full of broken people trying to make sense of the nonsensical world. It is not full of perfect specimens of humanity. It is a place of people who can acknowledge their imperfections.

What would be the point of gathering with a group of people who were all sorted, together, whole? If you can't attend church when you are broken and bruised, then when can you grace its doors? Doesn't it make sense to be drawn into fellowship when we are most vulnerable and in need?

As a reader you may have found sense via other avenues of help. May I ask, is it a sense that makes sense to you when things go wrong? When bad things happen to good people will your sense hold? Will it make sense of the senseless?

CHAPTER 11

Missing Samuel

D uring the summer after Samuel's passing, I decided to use some of my maternity leave. To stay at home and not to return to work until Ben started school in September 2010.

I was raw. I had delivered a baby in the spring, and the very next season he was not with me. I saw babies everywhere, as did the boys. They were great, and said lovely things.

'Oh, just like Samuel.'

'Mummy, maybe that baby would be Samuel's friend.'

Whereas I just thought: why did your baby live and mine have to die? Surely, I would be just as good a mum, if not better. I hated having these thoughts, but I had them.

I tried to cope by ignoring babies and not dealing with my feelings toward them. I thought they just added to my grief. I was very confused about how I should be feeling. I suppose there are no rule books as to how we should feel in these situations, but I was searching my heart for a proper response. Yet I was receiving mixed messages in my mind.

I wanted to have a response that acknowledged my pain but didn't spill over into bitterness, and destruction of other people's lives and my own. It would be all too easy to feel bitter and cynical about what had happened to Samuel, but I did not want to go down that path. I knew in advance that it would only serve to ruin me. Many times, my mind wanted to take me there, to tell me that I did not deserve this, that this was unfair.

I fought that path by trying to focus on what I had. I did not want my hurts to ruin the very good things that were evident in my life.

***

There were countless times when Samuel came to mind in the everyday actions of life. When I least expected it, the very present dilemma of Samuel would come.

The United Kingdom's Waitrose supermarket chain was running a community scheme. After you had spent your money shopping at the store, you were given a green token to place in one of three boxes to support your chosen charity. Each month, different charities were selected.

In the past, I had not thought too deeply about the selection process – just popped it into one of the boxes. After Samuel's death, the token seemed to burn in my hand as I read the descriptions for each charity. I could not decide. They were all relevant to Samuel. There would be the Sick Children's Trust, helping the blind, the heart foundation, and so on. I was in a panic at the supermarket under the pressure of choosing a box for my token.

This only served to make me aware yet again of how many problems Samuel had been given in life. I constantly protested in my head, standing there staring at those bins. Why could he not have been given just one of those things? Surely being blind would be enough, or deaf – why both?

Later, after a very special local charity formed, I would know exactly where to put my Waitrose token. For now, Ben and I would be looking together at the box wondering together where to deposit our token. I would often let Ben decide. He easily chose his target.

***

As part of the routine hospital process after a baby dies, I met with the geneticists up in London. They liked to help families and give feedback about the condition. They also wanted to learn from each family, so that by compiling more and more data on families and links, they might be able to help others. This was our opportunity to ask any questions we may now have about Samuel's condition, and how he and we were treated whilst in hospital.

The medics confirmed that the chance of having a baby with CHARGE Syndrome was extremely rare, that as yet they did not know why CHARGE Syndrome occurred. I was again told that none of the genes from Roddy or me were indicators, as quite frankly they did not know what the indicators were for this condition. I think it is correct to say at that juncture in medical research it was unknown how CHARGE Syndrome developed in a foetus, and it was not hereditary but a spontaneous mutation.

***

In the summer of 2010, there was one baby born who became very special to me. He was born six weeks after Samuel died, and transferred up to London for an urgent heart operation.

This coincided with the invitation to Roddy and me to go back to St Thomas' to do our six-week recap with the staff.

My friend Charlotte contacted me to say that our mutual friend, this baby's mother, Robyn, had been transferred to London. Whilst recovering from her caesarean section and staying by her son's hospital bed, she had experienced intense pain. Her doctor had believed it necessary to check it out. What they uncovered was cancer that had already spread from the breast to the liver. She had been instantly transferred to the private cancer ward. Charlotte wondered if I might visit her, since we were at the same hospital that day.

I didn't know Robyn that well – she was an acquaintance, and we had not had an opportunity to form a deeper friendship. I knew she had lost her first baby to cot death. I thought that in time we might be able to talk, and comfort each other in our shared baby losses. She was heavily pregnant when I came home after losing Samuel, so it did not seem the right time to approach her at the school gates.

Now I had an opportunity, but I did not know what to say or what to do. I had already heard from Charlotte that the outlook for Robyn's type of cancer was not good. However I also had this feeling that somehow, I must go to her, and that we had been given our appointment on this day for that reason. So, I went up to Robyn's hospital room, knocked on her door, walked in – and have never regretted the friendship that was cemented between her and me, both in tears on that day. Sometimes, true friendship is built through tears and not through laughter.

In her remaining lifetime, Robyn was a brave and courageous woman who would care for me as a friend through dark and troubled times. I treasure the many times we spent time together. On that first day, we just wept and laughed and then cried a bit more.

She said to me, 'E-J, can life get any worse than this? I have just been given a newborn baby who has to have major heart surgery, but I can't be by his side as I have just been diagnosed with unbeatable secondary cancer. Can life get any worse?'

I did stop and think about it for a brief moment. 'No, life could not be worse.'

Her dear baby came through his operation and is now a strong and lovely boy. His mother was to face two years of gruelling cancer treatment.

Despite the treatment and the difficulties faced I think Robyn taught me a real lesson. I recall during her treatment she said to me at one stage 'What does God want from me at this time in my life?'. I reflected on it and was amazed here was someone asking what God wants from me as opposed to what do I want from God. She could have petitioned God with a string of requests but here she was asking what she could do for him. Sometimes we meet the wisest people in the unexpected moments.

***

It was good that I was at home that summer, during what was meant to be my maternity leave. Although I headed back to work before the end of my allocated time, I was off work for the early days when we all needed each other the most.

I wanted to be there for the boys, to be the one to answer their questions about Samuel, and just to befriend them through those early stages of grief. We were all in this together. Parents and children, helping each other navigate the uncertain and unpredictable paths of grief. We did not all feel sad at the same times. We did not all want to talk about it at the same time, but we were there for each other, allowing each of us to survive as best we could.

Despite their many tears for Samuel, overall it was a happy summer for the boys, and I was so glad about that. They often played games where they included Samuel. I looked out the window and the boys were in the back garden together. I saw they had a gap between them, their hands down low as though each holding the hand of someone walking between them. I heard them chatting away to Samuel, their imaginary person. They were showing him how to kick a ball, and how to run after them. I was struck by how much they would have loved to have him in their lives.

They had so much love to give. Why were they not given the chance to show Samuel this love? So many other children we saw seemed to hate the very existence of their sibling and would love to be without them. Why were they allowed to have it while my boys were denied? So much did not make sense to me.

Ben was the child who outwardly seemed more concerned about death. He coped better when he was busy and distracted during the day. In the quiet times when he was home from nursery and just with me, he would talk to me more about Samuel. He would tell me all the hopes and dreams he had for him. Ben also told me once that he was frightened of becoming an adult. He asked me how he could stop himself from growing old. He said he had wanted to see Samuel grow old and see what he would have been like. I think in a way he felt some sort of guilt at becoming an adult himself when Samuel would not be able to. It was hard navigating some of these conversations. You never knew when they were going to come and how to find the words. Trial and error.

At night-time, it was Ben who would wake often, after Samuel died. He had not done this prior to Samuel's death. He would wander up and down from the boys' bedroom to the bathroom, thinking he needed the toilet. When I got up and asked him what was the matter, he would hug me and cry, and tell me how much he missed Samuel. He also told me he thought the adults should all be buried together. I think it was the act of burying Samuel that had this unsettling effect on Ben. I wrote in my journal that it was clear to me Ben found the act of leaving Samuel at the cemetery a sad and lonely experience. He had told me, 'The day we buried Samuel was the worsest day of my life.' Maybe, on the day we buried Samuel, Ben felt most keenly the separation from the brother he had loved and wanted. Burial is final, and it took seeing that act to make it a reality for Ben.

The other matter Ben expressed to me in his night-time wanderings was a desire to sort out what was true in the world and what was make-believe. In the middle of the night, we would sit together in the bathroom. Ben would ask me, 'Mummy are dinosaurs real? Are tigers real? Is Noddy real? Is Jesus real?' And always these night-time conversations would end with the question, 'Was Samuel real?'

For all these questions, I answered as truthfully as possible with the knowledge I had. I tried to reassure him of the truth of Samuel's existence. I think that even at this young age, Ben was going through a process in his mind of working out what was real and what was false.

Later in his life, Ben would do a funny dance when he was entertaining us. He would include a hand gesture which according to him had two variations. One way was 'just pretend' and the other hand gesture was 'the real thing'. Today as a family, we often still comment about what is 'the real thing'. I use it as a guide for what is good and true to think about versus what is just passing and of little value. To work out what was true and real, genuine not fake, was what mattered, and Ben helped teach me that aged only four.

I was pleased that Ben's night-time wanderings did not last long. He soon settled and accepted the truth about Samuel's passing. Yet I think for him there was always a yearning for his younger brother to be with him.

Only recently, when we were looking together at a photo of Samuel, Tom told me how when he first saw Samuel it was such an amazing feeling that came over him. Tom could not recall when Ben was born, but to him the feeling he experienced when he saw Samuel for the first time was so clear. He said he was so pleased that the baby was real and so gorgeous, and he loved him so much.

Then Tom turned to me and said, 'Mum, you should have seen how pleased Ben was with Samuel. He loved him so much. He told me all the things he wanted to do with him and to show him. I think Ben was so very, very sad when Samuel had to die.'

I think Tom is right – it was a strong bond Ben had for Samuel. I am thankful for that bond and for how much the life of Samuel taught Ben and Tom. I am thankful to Samuel that, because of his life, we as a family were able to talk so openly with each other about life and death and faith.

During these early times, we often found ourselves talking about what Heaven would be like. Tom and Ben often wondered what friends Samuel had made in Heaven. Of course, as humans we can only imagine Heaven within our limited human knowledge of life. To the boys, friendships and relationships were an essential part of their daily life, so to them they must also be essential in Heaven.

We were asked, 'Who does Samuel play with? Does he play football? Are there massive stadiums in Heaven?' This is what prompted prayers like, 'Dear God, please make more footballers Christians so that the games will be good in Heaven!'

I wrote down one of my conversations with Ben. He said to me, 'If Samuel was here, Mummy, I would give him a kiss and a cuddle. When I get to Heaven, I am going to run to find the part where Jesus is, as he will have Samuel with him, and I will run to him. Mummy, do you think

Samuel is crying for his Mummy in Heaven? As it will be hard for him, Mummy, as he may have to cry for a long time until you get there.'

I thought about this and the fact that Samuel would not be crying for me, as in Heaven, from the sources I have read, there are no more tears. I felt an intense need for Samuel, but he would not need me, as he had all he needed in Heaven. I tried to explain this to Ben, that Samuel would be at peace and that it was now harder for us without him than it was for Samuel without us.

CHAPTER 12

The Gap in our Lives

At the end of that summer, Ben was so pleased to graduate from nursery and finally be at school with Tom. We all smiled for the obligatory first day at school photos.

Yet as I left him in his class for the day, I wandered down the hill alone. My hands felt useless. They were not pushing a pram as many other parents in Ben's year group were. From that day on, I often thought of Samuel as I walked down that hill. Not that he had ever been on the school hill. He should have been there beside me, but he wasn't. In my pain and hurt, I tried hard to counsel my own brain to be thankful for what I had and not to focus on what I did not.

No matter how thankful I was, there would always be a gap in our lives that could only be filled by Samuel. No matter how hard I tried to logically deal with loss, I couldn't accept it as good. Loss is bad. There is a gap, a hole in my heart for Samuel.

I made an unspoken deal with myself as a type of coping strategy. I decided not to get too heavily involved with Ben's school year group this soon after our loss. The younger siblings of the children in his class were often the topic of conversation amongst the parents, and I had to remain silent. We would have many more years with Ben in that class. I would get to know the parents gradually, as I got stronger for the task of numbing myself to pain.

Ben came home on one of his first days of school and told us they had played a 'getting to know you' game. The children were all in a circle, and you had to jump in the circle if your answer was 'yes' to a question. For example, you would jump in if you had a house with a red roof, and then jump back out again. Well of course one of the instructions was to jump into the circle if you had a younger brother or sister. Ben was so pleased to jump into the circle for Samuel. The children in his class said, 'But we didn't know you had a baby brother.' He told them all about Samuel and how he was in Heaven, but he would always be his brother. I was so proud of Ben that day. He stood up for Samuel in his own way. He jumped into the circle and did the vital thing of acknowledging Samuel to those around him.

***

I was astounded by one elderly lady who phoned me to tell me she had initially felt sorry for me in my loss of Samuel, but then she had seen me and Roddy out with the boys down the street. We had all been laughing, and so she realised we were not hurting and we were not sad. She hurried to add that, for two years after her husband died, she had not been able to laugh or face life. Clearly, she said to me, 'You have been less affected than I have.' I am telling the truth; this is what this lady had the audacity to phone and say to me.

I responded to her phone call politely, trying to put the phone down as soon as possible and escape to hack a bush in my backyard. In my head, I felt anger mounting. I am not sure how I was able to hold my tongue. I think it was only because I was too stunned to activate the tongue to respond.

I knew just how much effort it was taking me each day to get up and out of bed, and try to give Tom and Ben a mother who could love and care for them and occasionally laugh with them. A mother who they could be out with in the public arena. Contrary to that lady's opinion, we were in no way unaffected. After losing Samuel, I would cry daily and hurt regularly.

For me, sometimes the outwardly happiest days would be the hardest. I wanted Samuel to be there with us, to share those times with us. It felt wrong smiling without him present, but I did it – not for myself but for Tom and Ben primarily. How could I say to them that I believed Samuel was in Heaven, a wonderful place to be, and then spend all my days long of face because he was not with us? I had to in some way practice what I preached, and in turn help them to a deep and lasting understanding of the hope that Roddy and I held. Never did I deny their pain and hurt or my own at the loss of Samuel, but I was aware that in the midst of grief we had to display to the boys hope for the future. To me it was the only real hope to cling to and to long for.

Acknowledge the loss

One of the most important lessons I learnt during this time of early grief was that when friends, family, or acquaintances suffer a loss it is vital that I acknowledge that loss in some way.

I found myself in situations in our town where I was being deliberately avoided. People would cross the street not to have to pass me. I would have conversations with people I had not seen since I was pregnant, and they asked me about anything and everything, but nothing about my pregnancy or Samuel.

I started to wonder why people did this. Why did they deliberately appear to avoid the biggest thing in my life? Did they think I had a disease that made me now untouchable? It was a very isolating experience.

I learned that lack of acknowledgement by others is a common experience for people who lose a child. The modern western world is more familiar with cure. It is not common for people to have to confront death in this way. It is a common response in the awkwardness of the situation for people to fail to acknowledge the death, and I have learnt that this may be because they think that this will help the grieving person to be able to move on and not dwell on the pain.

For me, however, I only found the lack of acknowledgement by others more hurtful. For me, it was a better response if people made some type of direct and specific acknowledgement of my loss. This may have been by giving me a hug, then acknowledging that they did not know what to say but they wanted to acknowledge our loss. This simple acknowledgment was enough for me to feel supported. Clearly if they were only acquaintances then the hug part could be skipped, but the verbal acknowledgement of loss had great significance for me.

One friend took some time, but she did come up to me in the playground at school and say, 'EJ, I have started to write so many letters to you and each one has been screwed up and shot into the bin. I just don't have the words, hun.'

I hugged her and said, 'I don't have the words either.' Her care meant so much to me.

In many ways I understand why people said, 'I don't know what to say.' I also had no answers as to why Samuel was born with CHARGE

Syndrome, and had it so badly that he had to die. I really wanted them to still acknowledge him and our loss.

I asked my close friends, 'Why do people do this? Why do they fail to talk about Samuel to me?'

They replied, 'It's just that it's so hard for people to know what to say and what to do.'

I found it hard to accept this. When people denied the existence of Samuel, the effect on me was like one who sees a wound open and raw and just comes along and stabs at it again. Many a time I returned to the sanctuary of my home to shed tears about people's denial of our loss.

I also acknowledge that prior to Samuel dying, I was just like them. I did not know what to say, and I went through life managing to avoid these types of scenarios. For those I hurt, I apologise now and ask humbly for their forgiveness. I hope it is never too late to apologise.

I have learned that it is positive to talk of life. Roddy puts it in a good way. He says that by talking about the child who has died you are acknowledging their life and not just talking of their death. It is beneficial for the grieving person to be reminded of the realness of the child's life. Others acknowledge the value in that life when they speak of it. When people talked to me about Samuel or wanted to find out more about him, my heart would leap. He was real. His existence had weight and value.

I have learned that if I hear of someone's loss I should not avoid them but confront it and acknowledge it. I at least then give the grieving person the chance to respond or not. I can take my lead from them. If I make myself visible and available and give them space to talk if they want to, then there will be a chance, there will be an opportunity. I do not want to miss it. I also fully acknowledge that everyone is different and may grieve in a different way, but I also acknowledge that surely there is no harm in showing or saying that I care.

Trust the silence

If I do not know what to say to a grieving person then I need to tell them that. I know that sometimes there are no words, but sometimes words are not needed.

A friend suffered the death of her baby girl at 22 weeks. Her friend, on hearing the news, came straight to their house. He knocked on the door, was welcomed in, and gave each parent a hug. Then he sat in a seat and cried with them. And then he got up and left. As far as I am aware, on that first visit after their loss he did not say a single word. He showed great love for that couple in their loss by openly mourning with them and showing them he cared. He did not feel any need to fill the silent void or to quote great words of wisdom; instead he cared enough to grieve with them. We can grieve communally in silence.

Many times in my very early grief stages when I was very vulnerable, I had people who I am sure were well-meaning try to fill the void of silence by quoting wise words to me about how they thought I should be, and the joy I should have at the wonders of Heaven. My response I never verbalised – I just internally screamed. Their advice came across in a superior manner. This type of talking at me turned me sour to the words that were being spoken. The good intentions of the people did not give my soul the warmth and healing I imagine the givers thought they were giving. I would think, who are they to tell me what to believe? Have they ever had that tested in their life? I looked at their outward personal circumstances. Their children appeared to be healthy. They did not know the pain of my loss, so what gave them the qualification to tell me how I must be? Or how I should act?

At that early stage of loss, the advice that helped me I read in solitude, or with Roddy as we grieved together. I felt words of comfort spoken directly during some of those dark moments.

To my younger self I now say, whatever your approach to comforting your family member or friend, first acknowledge the human condition of loss – the pain, the emptiness, the hurt – and then let that sit for a while, and please do pause prior to offering your words of faith and hope.

The hand of friendship

I have experienced that when we acknowledge someone's loss, the grieving person realises they can talk about their loss and this can be very beneficial. Oh so beneficial. It gives the grieving person the chance to lead the conversation. Maybe they want to talk or maybe they do not, but let them take the lead. This is not about me it is about caring for them and letting them know they are supported and not alone. My goal is to offer the hand of friendship. The grieving person is free to take it or leave it.

There were some people who chose to become our friends at the time we lost Samuel, and did not walk away. They had been merely acquaintances before, but they proactively came to us and acknowledged our loss and offered their hand in friendship. I give those people praise. It was a bold and brave move not to walk away as you easily could have done. We never expected your love and friendship, but you chose to come and support us.

I am not saying I would actively look through the death columns in my local newspaper to seek out and visit strangers. But if someone in my circle of contacts experiences loss, I want to tell myself to take time to acknowledge it in some way and show that I care. It may feel uncomfortable. I may feel unprepared, but I must take courage. I know that just showing up may be the real difference in a grieving person's life at this time. Acknowledgement of loss and the hand of friendship was a lifeline for me. Without their love I would have sunk.

I took Ben to his friend's birthday party soon after Samuel died. I did not know many of the parents well, but they all knew of my pregnancy and our loss as they had children in Ben's nursery class. Some appeared to deliberately ignore me that day, but there were a handful of parents who came up to me and found a moment just to acknowledge our loss and to express their condolences. I am most grateful to them. Those people's kindness helped me so much by showing their interest and care.

The people who acknowledged our loss did not do so in a loud and confrontational manner. They looked for a time where maybe I was on my own, then came alongside me and spoke of their sadness at our loss. I think it is the coming alongside others in their loss, whatever that loss may be, that is important.

***

When Tom and Ben went back to school, I returned to my work as a solicitor in an investment bank in London. I was not expecting people to be demonstrative about my loss. I did not expect everyone to say something about it. But I did expect those who knew about Samuel's death to acknowledge it or make some reference.

How wrong I was. I was often avoided at work. I had thought to myself, these are sensible, educated people. Surely they can handle this? I was left to deal with it almost entirely on my own. I use the word 'almost' in the previous sentence because not all were silent. One person did acknowledge the death of Samuel. He came alongside me and offered the hand of friendship.

This was of course the corporate world, and death of a baby was never going to be on the agenda. I think it would have helped me if I had been asked occasionally how I and the rest of the family were doing. If some mention of Samuel's name had been made. If I had been given the opportunity to talk about him. I am a talker, and speaking about Samuel was a joy for me. Having his name verbalised in my work environment would have helped to 'normalise' his death and to make it more open.

The asker may have had to deal with tears. But maybe there are times that even tears in an investment bank in London are okay. Good practice, in fact.

I have since been told by a colleague that he never knew about Samuel's death, so I am assuming it was not publicised widely. Again, I suppose people thought that by suppressing the news they were helping me.

The wall of silence about Samuel in my workplace did not emotionally help me. I would have coped better had I been given some opportunity for release during my working day. Instead I had to exist in a silent world where anything and everything was discussed apart from my family life, as no one wanted to touch on those wounds.

I do not think that any of these people were bad. In fact, I had some of the most fantastic colleagues possible. In terms of the logistics of arranging time off, and my return to work, they were beyond amazing. They could handle the practical stuff, just not the emotional. I truly believe that modern western society is ill-equipped to handle infant loss.

I would leave work most evenings and cry heavy tears as I walked along Cannon Street towards London Bridge and the train. Crying, and weaving in and out of fellow commuters. My tears were a release of the tension I felt all day at work when Samuel was not mentioned. In the busy London rush hour, no one stopped. I did not expect them to. I was free to grieve in the midst of all the chaos. A tearful walker unnoticed in the mix of urgent human activity.

When I expressed my disappointment, Roddy did not disagree that lack of acknowledgement added to our hurt. However, he cautioned me, telling me he thought I expected too much of people. You see, the calm and measured response does not change – it still guided him daily. Roddy thought it might help me if I lowered my expectations of others and then was pleasantly surprised on the occasions where acknowledgement did come. He must have had it tough at work himself. Imagine returning to work to sit and listen to all of his patient's ailments when he had just witnessed such loss. Yet he did not complain. Very impressive.

***

There are gems of people out there in society. I have had the privilege of meeting some of them through the experience of loss in my life. There were people who chose to be our friends because of our loss. They literally came into our lives. I had known some of these people in passing, but had never spent any meaningful time with them. They took the time and found ways to show great care for us as a family.

In our experience of loss, we found that a new community of people formed around us. We were of course extremely grateful and thankful to those we already knew and who continued to give us support and friendship through our loss. We were also so thankful to these new people who came alongside us, but they were rare, and therefore I see them as precious in our lives. Our community of friends now included some other parents of infants, children or adults who have died. I was so strengthened by their support. To find people we could share anything and everything with. To have a conversation about our loved ones, or to talk about the practicality of choosing a headstone, or the dilemma of whether to cremate or to bury, in an open and natural way. May be this would not be palatable conversation to people who have not been faced with it, but for those who have, it has become our everyday.

Of course, we did not have everything in common with the people we shared grief with. We did not all agree on religious teachings or spiritual aspects. Some of us chose to bury, some to cremate, some to scatter, and some to keep in a jar or a cuddly toy on the sofa. No way is right. No way is wrong. All actions or inaction were our own individual expressions of love and care for our loved ones. But together we had lost, and we grieved, and we could laugh and cry together in the midst of that grief. The moments where we had been with those who, too, had lost precious people were wonderful. What an odd word to use, you might think – how could talking about death be wonderful? When you feel the pain of loss and are able to share with those who have been through a similar experience, it is indeed wonderful and refreshing. It feels like a great release. Corporate care and understanding. We felt less isolated and more 'normal' with this group.

Through these people who came across our path, I had the privilege of hearing many stories of loved ones who had died. I consider that their stories are now a valuable addition to my life, and an acknowledged part of it. Often, I didn't have the joy of meeting in this life the people who had died. I remembered their story as others expressed them to me. I was given a small glimpse of them and their unique personalities. The verbalised gift of their stories added greatly to my own world and life view. I was personally enriched by them and the friendship of those who grieved for them.

***

Early in my return to work, I had an odd encounter with one of my fellow commuters. To get to work in London, I had to travel by train for almost two hours each way on every working day. The fellow commuter realised I had not been commuting for a while and he had missed me, which was kind. I asked him how he had been over the past few months.

He said, 'Oh, it has been terrible. Just awful.'

I said, 'Oh no! Why?'

He said his dog had died and it had been so hard on him and his partner. The dog had been fairly elderly and it was not entirely unexpected as far as I could work out. I of course offered my condolences and said how sad it must be for him.

It would have been okay had he stopped there, but oh no, this poor man chose to go on. He said people did not understand just how hard it was when you lost a dog – it was worse in his opinion than losing a loved one. With the loss of a dog, you found all their things around the house. He and his wife had been bereft the other night when they had found in a cupboard an old dog lead that had once belonged to his dog. So this was why it was harder than losing a person. A person does not have a lead.

Clearly, this was a bizarre situation to find myself in so soon after Samuel died. Had the man thought to ask about me or my family he may have realised just how ridiculous it was.

Perhaps it was not entirely his fault. Maybe, sadly, he had never known the love of a human so much that he would grieve for their loss. Yet he had known the love of his dog, his faithful friend, and it had grieved him deeply.

However, experience with the man and his dead dog did teach me that each of us may only understand situations, for example loss of a loved one, up until the point of our own experience. It takes people of wisdom and love to actually be able to understand the loss of others if they have not experienced it first themselves.

The problem for me was that I was hurt that he could think the loss of an old dog was worse than my loss of a baby. He never meant it this way; he didn't even know my story to make the comparison. I was highly sensitive at the time and my mind had already made the comparison and left me angry. I suspect that pre-Samuel's death, a comment such as this man's would have passed me by, but with my own world view highly focused on my own grief, I measured his comment alongside my grief and found it to be wanting.

I realised after this conversation that I needed to work out a coping strategy to deal with these types of comments that would come out of the blue. I had to have a plan for the unexpected, random comments that may bruise my open wounds.

This commuter helped me, although he did not know it. He helped me to develop what I called the Numpty Theory. It is terrible to admit it, and a part of me is ashamed to do so. I only include it here as I did use it and it helped me. I have shared the theory with a couple of friends who suffered loss. They said they found it helpful as a coping strategy in the initial stages of grief. People can be very raw in these early stages and I found this a way of developing some skin – giving me protection against the unexpected.

Whenever I came across someone who did not acknowledge my loss, or someone who I felt belittled it in some way, instead of getting angry with them directly, or dwelling on it and becoming bitter, I just thought in my head, 'You Numpty! I won't let your unqualified words hurt me. Those words are going to mean nothing to me.' And so I blanked out their comments. It helped me to feel less wounded. As a result, I did not let the hurt fester. I was able to dismiss the comment and move on.

Without some sort of coping strategy, I think I would have drowned because of my sensitive prickly state. I have seen this happen with others where they can enter a very black and lonely hole and believe that no one else can enter it and help them out. I found that for me personally, by being able to dismiss the comments that hurt me I was still able to connect with the rest of the world and not switch off into isolation.

The Numpty Theory is of course not at all kind or loving to others. It is a protection mechanism when a person is weak and vulnerable. Real care for others is to love all people as equal and not declare them numpties. Yet in practical terms, this helped me not to dwell too deeply on the pain caused by their comments or lack thereof.

Later, I had to address this attitude and find a better way of dealing with it.

***

Another way I attempted to deal with my anger was to garden. I took great delight in grabbing the loppers and hacking any random bush in our backyard. My parents would have been appalled. They were amazing gardeners and their garden was always a pleasure to view. Mum has always said it is her way of being creative. She creates beauty in planting and nurturing.

I was not planting or nurturing, I was hacking. Random bursts of intense chopping helped release tensions when they started to form.

I also found refuge in running. I am a keen runner. I have been since school. I would often run through the Botanical Gardens in Wellington before school, and loved the buzz it gave me. Wherever I have lived since, I have owned running shoes and run the streets. I run at no particularly great speed. It is just a way to get outside and soak up the air and enjoy a change of scene and get some head space.

For months, I had not been able to run. I had been pregnant, and because of the extra amniotic fluid I had to stop running earlier than some. I had also been holed up in hospital for months, so the ability to get out and enjoy nature had been cut off.

Now I had times where I was free. Free to run on the South Downs in open countryside overlooking the sea again. Even though I had running buddies I used to run with in Eastbourne, at the early stages of getting back into it I chose to run alone. For one, I was not up to their level straight away – not that they would have minded. But also, sometimes on a run I would stop and stand there alone, looking out across the English Channel. I would just sit, just be, or just cry. Then when that was done, I would head home, refreshed by the freedom of exercise and the freedom to express emotions in open countryside.

I find the need to be alone to cry important. I live a people-filled life, so time alone can be scarce. When I find solitude, that is often when I release the tears. Sometimes it can feel uncontrolled, but sometimes I think that is necessary. Without release, I may explode. Like Samuel's amniotic fluid building up with no natural outlet, it was always destined to be problematic. Once the fluid was drained, like my tears draining away, he was able to carry on existing. When my tears were released I could also carry on existing.

CHAPTER 13

The Wider Family

Many people were affected by Samuel's passing and the frailty of life that his short time on earth had come to represent for us all. None more than us as a family, but as an extended family as well, many of us were changed. My parents had shared so much with us re Samuel's scans and eventual birth, diagnosis and short life. They had been a fantastic help to our family, coming to England from New Zealand to be with us. Together, my Mum and Dad tried to keep home life as normal as possible for Tom, Ben and Roddy (who had to return to work during that time) whilst I stayed near the hospital to be with Samuel.

When Samuel died, Mum and Dad were greatly hit by the question, 'Why in this order? Why not us first? Why take the youngest among us and let the older live?' I think it is a type of guilt we all take on when we love a young person and they die before us. There is no denying it seems the wrong order in life, and it is only natural to question.

Many times since the loss of Samuel I have seen and heard Dad cry for his grandson. My Dad is not a crier. Prior to the loss of Samuel, I had only personally witnessed him crying three times.

It was not easy knowing that our baby had not brought joy to my parents but instead much grief. They have had to work out their own answers to these questions. I wish they had never had to contemplate such things.

The boys, too, had to work out their own answers. They had questioning heads. When I heard their chatter, I was challenged by how they did not blame God for the bad things that happen. They trusted that God took care of Samuel now and didn't blame him for Samuel's death. If only we as adults could be so accepting.

Tom and Ben taught me much about faith. They directed my thoughts back to the simple truths when my mind would want to wander, to become angry, to try and complicate matters. Their simple faith was like a healing balm to my soul.

**

The beliefs of all my family were tested again within a year.

On February the twenty-second, 2011, we were all together in Christchurch, New Zealand, where my extended family live. It was less than a year since we had lost Samuel. Our pain was still raw, so Roddy and I thought it was good to have as many holidays as possible with our family who were also suffering greatly. That is how we came to be in Christchurch on half-term holiday break.

The day started like any other. We were nearing the end of our stay, so we took the boys to a shopping mall to choose something to buy with the holiday money they had been given. Ben did not take long deciding. He had always wanted to play rugby, so he headed for the sports shop. He decided on a round plastic object that you place the ball on to kick your conversions – he called it a 'conversioner'. He was very happy with it. Tom took longer with his purchase. Eventually, he chose the book *The Lion, the Witch and the Wardrobe*.

Because Tom had taken so long, I was late home. The lunch I had planned with my mum and sister for 12.30 pm was pushed back.

Therefore, at 12.51 pm New Zealand time, Roddy and the boys were having lunch at home with Dad. My sister Joanna was driving Mum and I into the centre of town, late for our lunch date.

We were just passing Hagley Park, a large green space in the centre of Christchurch, when an earthquake measuring 6.3 on the Richter Scale struck. I thought Joanna had temporarily lost control of the car – it was all so sudden and not part of my usual experience.

Joanna said, 'No, that was an earthquake, and it was a big one. I think we should head home.'

Ahead of us was the city, we saw so much dust in the air. We now know that many buildings or parts of buildings had collapsed, and killed people walking by or trapped inside. We now know that the place we were due to have lunch was part of the worst devastation. Buildings around it crumbled, and many people lost their lives.

When Joanna turned the car around, we saw walls and trees strewn across the road. Power was out. There was no mobile phone reception. Roads which had been perfect only thirty seconds ago were now awash with water as a result of burst pipes below. Traffic lights had failed.

Christchurch had experienced a disaster. In only thirty seconds, the landscape and cityscape had changed, and it will take our lifetimes and perhaps more to rebuild. We did not know all of this at the time. We just knew we needed to establish that our loved ones were safe, and then see how we could help others.

We had left my parents' beautiful home and garden when we drove out only ten minutes previously. We returned to discover huge holes in the ground and cracks in the walls of my parents' home.

We gathered together outside, and hugged each other, and shared our stories. We were so thankful that we had each other safely accounted for. In all the subsequent difficulties my parents were to face with the insurers and the stress of living daily life in a disaster zone, they were consistent in saying, 'We have each other, and that is the most important thing.' The stress they had to go through didn't help with their grieving, falling on top of all this destruction around them. Their honest response would be that to have your family alive and with you is of far greater value than all the solid bricks and mortar of a home.

I am thankful we were in Christchurch at the time of the earthquake, and that we were able to support each other through the initial stages. Had we not experienced it first-hand, I believe we would not have had as much insight into the situation. Of course, it was not our home, our school, or our community that was affected, but we caught a glimpse of what true devastation looks like.

We were able to fly back to England a few days later when the airport reopened and escape the situation, but I left my family behind with a heavy heart. I knew the Christchurch people had a long road ahead of them, rebuilding their lives out of the rubble.

***

Living through the earthquake and initial aftershocks reminded us again of the fragility of life. There is truth in the saying that we are to make the most of each day we are given on this earth, as we do not know what is around the corner for each of us.

There were many what-ifs, buts and maybes in our earthquake experience. We could have easily been killed, hurt or at the very least caught up in the trauma of the worst damage of that day. If things had gone according to plan and I had been on time to lunch, we would have been right in the heart of the worst damage. All of my family were saved. 185 others were taken that day and many seriously wounded.

I think often of the pain of the people who lost their loved ones on that tragic Christchurch day. It causes me to consider the wider experience for many who lose loved ones in sudden tragedies. Unplanned, unpredicted, unexpected. There must be such sadness in the event itself, and in the re-enactment of the moments before it in your head. Where were you? Where were they? Could your actions have changed anything? Over and over, the scenarios would replay. These thoughts must be great burdens to carry.

After the earthquake, the boys' talk and prayers changed. I noticed that they started to consider more about world events. A Japanese earthquake and tsunami killed eleven thousand only a couple of weeks after the Christchurch earthquake, and we were struck by so many more world events. I wondered whether these tragic world events were ever going to stop.

CHAPTER 14

Ben's Headaches

At Ben's Year One parent-teacher interview, his teacher told us great things about how well Ben was doing in class. It was the end of October 2011.

Then, just as we were getting up to leave the room, she hesitated and gave a half laugh. She said, 'You may think this is a bit odd to mention but I thought I would anyway.'

We waited.

'Ben often asks for the sick bucket to be beside him in class. He hasn't been sick, but he asks for it a lot. Being a teacher of younger children, I know to listen to them when they think they're going to be sick.' She laughed. 'I've had too many accidents by ignoring them in the past. It's probably nothing, but I just thought I should mention it.'

We were puzzled. Ben had never said he felt sick to us at home, or asked for a sick bowl. Maybe he was just too hot in class, or a bit unsettled. Was this the start of attention-seeking behaviour? But then, that seemed so out of character.

We had a lot of questions in our heads, but we had no answers. We thought it certainly odd, but very soon dismissed it.

Two weeks later, Ben started to be sick. It was random. I would get a call from school about it, I would go to collect him, and he would be bright and perky and asking what was for lunch. Then, in the next breath, he would be asking whether he could go and play football in the garden. Not very sick-child behaviour, I thought.

However, school insisted he had to be off for 48 hours in case he was contagious. So we had a lot of juggling with work each time it happened. Then, as quickly as the sickness began, it stopped.

A couple of weeks after the sickness stopped, the headaches began. I thought it was quite a grown-up concept for a child to have a headache and to express it as such. I dished out the pain relief and thought it would go away. Again, they were random. Ben did not have headaches every day.

A month after they started, they became more frequent. It was the Christmas school holidays and Roddy was home with the boys. He dropped Tom at a party and went to the park to play football with Ben. They lasted ten minutes at the park before Ben said he had to stop because he had a headache.

When I heard this later that evening, I became worried there was something not right. Ben would never turn down football with his Dad for a mere headache. We had to get to the bottom of it. I thought maybe his headaches were a result of eyesight problems, so I arranged for an eye test.

That night, Ben woke in the early hours, screaming out with the pain in his head. The next day I took him to the General Practitioner (GP). We told the GP our story. She went through everything with us. He had to walk up and down the corridor to see if his balance was alright. Touch his toes. She tested a urine sample, temperature, blood pressure. None of these standard tests revealed any abnormality.

I said, 'It's only the headaches.' Then I thought of another friend whose child had headaches. She had been to her GP numerous times about it, but it was dismissed each time. It took her child having a seizure before his brain abscess was discovered. That thought niggled at me as the GP smiled and sent us on our way. However, I was also relieved that the GP had assured me all was well and I had nothing to be worried about.

***

I told myself, he will grow out of this. It is all just a phase. There is nothing we should concern ourselves about. Mind talk.

That night was our church pantomime, a big event on the local calendar. The theatre seated three hundred, and for an amateur show it was always considered a good night. In our family it was particularly Ben who loved panto.

I had been in the production the previous year, our first Christmas after Samuel's death. All proceeds raised from that panto had been sent to St Thomas' Hospital NICU ward, in memory of Samuel and in thanks to the staff for their great care of him. We were very grateful to the church team for suggesting this and following through on it.

I had played the part of Peter Pan, the boy who would never grow old. I had realised the irony of that role at the time, but refused to let the emotion control me as I wanted to act well for Samuel.

When Ben saw me after watching that show he got so excited. He said, 'Mummy, did you really fight the pirate?' Then he said, 'You were amazing.' His little face beamed.

This year, I had decided not to act in the panto. I had gone to the first read-through of the script and had just not felt comfortable being involved. This was odd, as I would never usually miss out. Looking back, I believe I was saved from not being involved. I would have missed a lot of what was going on at home, being at rehearsals and performances. I would have blamed myself for not being there, and not being aware of the critical nature of Ben's condition. As it was, I had nothing external to blame.

We were having fourteen people for dinner before the show that night. As Ben loved panto, I told him all afternoon that he would only be allowed to go if he ate all his tea (as his appetite had been down of recent) and if he did not complain of having a headache or appear sick in any way. He managed to convince me he was fine.

So we went. I sat with my friend Charlotte, and had already discussed with her the GP visit. We both looked along to where her boys and mine sat together, and saw Ben's smiling face as he laughed at all the classic panto gags. We both concluded he looked okay. The only indication that things were not right was when Ben turned down the offer of sweets in the interval.

He asked instead for pain relief. He said he had a headache.

***

That night, initially Ben slept, but again he awoke in the middle of the night crying with the pain in his head. The next day, I took him to the local hospital. The same checks were done that the GP had performed just the day before.

All was fine, just as the day before. Again, I insisted it was just the headaches – no other symptoms – and that they were becoming quite severe. So this time they decided to give him an MRI.

Roddy came from work to the hospital at 4pm that afternoon, just in time to join us as Ben went in for his MRI. I sat in the room with Ben as he lay still. The loud banging of the machine began.

The room had a large window along the side and I could see straight into where the radiographers were. As I rubbed Ben's legs to comfort him and to assure him of my presence, I looked through that window and my heart sank. What I saw was people staring at the computer screen, and more and more people entering the room, and going over to look at the screen where the radiologist was pointing.

I learnt one certainty about hospitals in our time with Samuel: the more medics interested in your case, the worse your situation. Why were they all in that room? What were they seeing on that screen? My head pounded.

When the MRI was completed, Ben and I were taken back to the children's ward. The consultant asked Roddy and me to go into the parents' room with her. I started to cry and stood my ground. I did not want to go into that room. The last time I had been in a parents' room, it was to discuss Samuel, and the consultant's face gave me a terrible feeling that something similar was about to take place.

I wanted to escape to a room called a 'child's room', not a parents' room. Surely in a child's room you wouldn't have to deal with hard stuff. I didn't want to be the adult in this scenario. I thought that if I didn't hear what they wanted to say then it hadn't happened.

The fact that I was a parent who had a child I was responsible for lying in the ward meant I had to go into the room with that label. What other door was open to me? Time had called us to be a parent yet again.

I was a mess. My emotions spilled out all of a sudden. It was dawning on me that something serious was happening to Ben. I kept apologising to the consultant, saying I would be better if it were not for Samuel – I'd had so much bad news with him I could not imagine any good news coming in a parents' room in a hospital.

She presumably had no idea what I was mumbling on about. She tried to be kind to us, but it was also her job, despite my tears, to break the news to us that Ben had a brain tumour of considerable size. It was pressing dangerously close to the base of his brain stem. Ben would have to be immediately transferred to King's College Hospital in London to have the tumour removed.

We were then shown the MRI that all those medics had seen earlier in the room and had pored over. I saw on a screen in front of me the big black mass that was Ben's tumour. Undeniably, it was there. The tumour that could change a life.

I saw it but I couldn't take it in. There was a photo of it, but we wouldn't be asking for a copy of it. We wouldn't be taking it home from the hospital and back to our house to be placed in a family photo album with other momentous moments like birth and first day at school. This black blob would just have to sit in the memory of Roddy and me, engraved in our minds.

I hate black blobs on scans.

***

Roddy and I had to tell the boys the news. There was a loud protest from the boys. They wanted to go ahead with our plans to go to Scotland the next day to celebrate Roddy's fortieth birthday and then Christmas. They had been really looking forward to being with their cousins and family.

Instead, we would be spending Christmas in hospital. We had to explain to them that we had no option. Ben needed this operation as soon as possible.

I rang my friend Charlotte. I felt that one Eastbourne person should be aware of what had happened, and that we were not going to Scotland but to London instead. Within minutes Andrew, Charlotte's husband who worked in the hospital, was with us. He was brilliant. I will never forget how he just stood with us, trying to give us strength and support as tears ran down all our faces.

It is the only time I have ever heard Roddy ask the why question, but he said it to Andrew that night. 'Why? Why us? Why Ben?'

***

The why question is something people often talk to me about. They seem to think it must be a big part of my thinking. Why have I been given this deal of cards in my life? Why me? Why my children? But actually it is not something I have given too much thought to. I have always thought: why not us? If bad things can happen to the people in the house next door or the person down the road then what is to stop them from happening to me? Why should we be immune to trouble? Whilst I had placed my trust and faith in God, I also knew that God did not promise us a life of ease when we followed him. I did not think that only good would happen in my life and I would be saved from all the bad. I figured that bad things could still happen to us, but it was in how we dealt with the bad in our lives that our faith and hope could be revealed.

I may not have questioned why God gave us these troubles, but I did question God's judgment in allowing this to happen to us. As parents, Roddy and I tried to be loving and caring and all of our children were wanted. Yet illness was allowed to strike our household. Not once, but twice. Other children were born into homes where there appeared to be no evidence, or at least minimal evidence, of love and those children had to live a life of pain and suffering inflicted by other humans onto them. So I did question God's decisions in our lives when they seem so wrong from an earthly perspective.

Again I am reminded that God's ways are not our ways. There is no way that I would have allowed Ben to have a brain tumour, had I been God. In fact, many things would be different in the world if I were God. But that is just it. I am not God. The fine balance of the universe and its many facets are not mine to control. We were in a different hospital with a different child, but again our world was spinning out.

CHAPTER 15

A Christmas Gift

en was immediately given steroids to relieve the pressure the tumour was creating on his brain. He and I were transferred by ambulance to King's College Hospital, London. Only one carer was allowed in the ambulance with Ben. Roddy and Tom returned home to contact immediate family and pack, so they could get up early to be with us first thing for Ben's operation.

It was a very fast ride up the motorway with the ambulance lights flashing, then through the busy South London streets on an ordinary Friday night. The pace of the ambulance and the emergency status made me start to realise what a precarious state Ben was in.

What had started as a puzzle only a day or two earlier had now changed in an instant to an extremely critical situation. As Ben managed to sleep and I clutched a sick bowl (for myself this time, not Ben), I tried to make some sense of the last twelve hours. All we knew was that Ben had a tumour. We did not know what type or how he got it. We just knew there was an urgent need to have it removed. I perceived that the task of removal was not going to be a simple one.

Ben would later tell his Granny that he realised how lucky he was. He'd had a ride in an ambulance and Tom had not. He told Granny he had decided not to talk a lot about it to Tom, as it might make Tom sad he had not had an ambulance ride. Ben said he hoped one day he would have another one and maybe Tom could come too.

Granny said, 'Maybe it is best not to have too many ambulance rides.'

When I heard of this conversation from mum my reaction was, 'Please, no more ambulance rides.' One was enough.

The ambulance team rushed us up to Lion Ward, the paediatric neurosurgical ward. Our ambulance driver Matt sat down by Ben's bed. He looked up at me with tears streaming down his face as he told us his story. Ten years ago, his son had been rushed to this very ward because he had a brain tumour. The quick actions of the ambulance crew got him there in time for the operation that he believed helped save his son's life. They were able to operate. He indicated that there were some ongoing complications with his son's condition, but this hospital and its fantastic team had supported them all the way. He showed me a photo of his son, on the board out in the corridor. He said it was because of what he had seen that day ten years ago that he had changed his job and become an ambulance worker himself. Yet in the ten years he had worked for the service he had never had the privilege of doing that same journey of taking a child from Eastbourne District General Hospital to King's Neurosurgery, and he was honoured to do it for Ben today. Matt also said, 'Maybe that was why I drove so fast.'

Matt reassured me that we were at the right place with the best team in the world, and they would make Ben better. He shook Ben's hand and gave me a hug as he said, from one parent to another, 'I know your pain and confusion at this point, but you will get through it.'

Again, I was struck by the people that are put on the journey with us in order to somehow lighten the load – to give us courage when we ourselves are all out of our own private store. Already I had met a parent who had gone through similar and had offered the hand of love and care.

Despite still being in some pain, Ben must have heard this conversation. In subsequent weeks and months, he often talked about the ambulance driver who cried. His display of emotion had an effect on Ben.

It reminded me of the time when Jill, Samuel's nurse, cried when Samuel died. As dealing with illness is a part of the medical professional's job, you do not often expect to see them cry. The few times I have witnessed tears from medics, it has affected me as well. Their very humanity shows just how much they care, or maybe just how bad the situation is.

***

That night, Ben and I met Mr C, the person who was to be Ben's neurosurgeon. He was a fantastic man, not only with his skill with his job, but also with his ability to relate to his patients.

Within minutes of meeting us, he had Ben laughing. He tried to explain to Ben what the operation would be like that he was planning on doing at seven the next morning. He told Ben he had a squirrel in his head that was very naughty. He was going to take that squirrel out of Ben's head and throw it in the bucket, and he hoped to get all the squirrel into the bucket.

I did wonder about the terminology at times, as Ben might have imagined a full-sized squirrel, and that could have rightly caused some worry. My concerns were unjustified, as Mr C's approach seemed to work for Ben. He never later complained of squirrel nightmares.

Ben took the matter of the operation on board, but like a true child he was soon spending more energy thinking about what colour hat Mr C was to wear when operating on him than any more details of the actual operation. They decided together that red would be the best. Being a Manchester United fan, Ben's favourite colour was red. Mr C supported Fulham, and so he and Ben managed to talk football stories into the wee small hours.

I kept on thinking Mr C should cut Ben off and go to bed as he had an important operation in the morning, but you could tell this was all part of his fantastic doctor service. His chatting with Ben helped put Ben at ease in a less than easy environment.

When I was alone with Mr C, in a more serious tone he told me more details about Ben's condition and the operation he would face in the morning. He had seen the scan and advised me the tumour was large. Whilst the scan showed the surgeon where the tumour was in the brain, it did not show the detail of whether the tumour had yet attached itself to the brain stem. It was clear it was precariously close to the brain stem. Mr C would only know when he opened up Ben's skull exactly how close it was. His intention was to remove all of the tumour, but he warned me that if the tumour was on the brain stem then he may not be able to take it all out, as he could damage Ben's brain.

I saw the need for haste to stop this tumour from growing more. I could understand why the operation had been scheduled for seven in the morning, and why even though it was Christmas Eve and meant to be his time off, Mr C had taken on this operation.

Roddy has often said since our experience with consultants taking care of both Samuel and Ben that more of these hospital consultants should be receiving the Queen's honours. We have had the privilege of meeting some remarkable people in the hospital system. Many times, we have seen evidence of medics going the extra mile for their patient. The passion and dedication these medics give to their jobs is something we think should be publicly recognised.

Mr C did not finish with our family that night. He went a further step and phoned Roddy back in Eastbourne to tell him what the plan for the next day would be, and to answer any questions he might have.

Back in the ward with Ben, we prepared to settle down for the night, but it was to be a broken night. Through the night, blood samples were taken, but they were not done well. Ben awoke in the middle and moved his hand, causing blood to squirt all over the bed.

The other traumatic experience was a further MRI scan at two in the morning. Ben was clearly exhausted, but he also became most upset at the hospital staff insisting he take off his trousers and only have his underpants on. Tom had always told Ben that you are never to show girls your pants. Here Ben was, in front of a number of female medics, being asked to take off his trousers to reveal his pants. I had to broker a deal with the staff that they all left the room. We got the trousers off, and then the sheet over Ben and his pants: hey presto.

With all that drama even before we got into the MRI room, I had my doubts whether we were going to be getting any clear results. MRIs require a patient to be perfectly still in order for the best imaging to be taken. They are very noisy machines. The sound you hear is like a builder drilling or banging, and the patient is lying flat in a tunnel listening to this noise. Ben had lain still for the Eastbourne MRI, but that was almost twelve hours before and he had not had much, if any, sleep since then. It was now getting closer to three in the morning and he was understandably protesting at all the demands that were being put on him. On top of all this, of course, he had a headache. It took two hours before they were satisfied they had enough images and we were able to return to the ward.

***

Roddy and Tom arrived at 6.30 am. They'd had to leave very early from Eastbourne to get there before Ben went into the operation.

I'd had the privilege of spending time with Ben the night before, so it was appropriate to give Roddy the task of going down to theatre with Ben. Whilst I wanted to have all the time with Ben, I had to share him as of course he was Roddy's child as well. Roddy cuddled him while they administered the anaesthetic.

Again, I was seeing one of my precious children being wheeled off to an operation for which we had to sign the usual forms, agreeing to all the risks. There was a real risk that Ben might not survive this operation or that, as a result of it, his brain may be affected.

***

Roddy returned to the ward an hour later, and then the waiting began. When one person receives a diagnosis, the ripple effect can be enormous. Here were Roddy, Tom and I sitting in a room in London on Christmas Eve whilst Ben was undergoing brain surgery. Our happy, bright, intelligent, well child was having to go through this. I am not sure I will ever know how this could have happened. It was not part of the plan I had in my head for Ben's future.

Ben was the child I thought had been born with exceptional abilities and character. I had treasured these thoughts in my heart. Life had been easy for Ben so far. Apart from the loss of Samuel eighteen months earlier, Ben had really not had many other challenges. Ben was one of the tallest in his school class, and probably the best sports person. Academically, he was excelling. Most importantly, Ben was a really nice guy. He was the person in the class that you wanted to be friends with. Ben was fun, happy and loving. At six years old life looked sweet for Ben. I used to think he could be anything and everything he wanted to be as there would be nothing holding him back.

Now, this brain tumour. What did it mean? How would he be affected? Would his personality be changed for good? Would they get all the tumour out? Most importantly, what type of tumour was it?

We had a lot of time to fill, so we wandered out of the hospital to try to find some breakfast. King's College Hospital really seemed to be in the middle of nowhere in terms of finding shops and gathering some familiar bearings. We found a greasy spoon and ordered breakfast.

What a nice surprise to hear that Roddy's three brothers had flown down from Scotland. They were now just down the road. If Roddy could not come to them for his fortieth birthday, they had come to him. I was very pleased they made this effort at such short notice. It was a great distraction for Tom as well. He was able to go and play with them in a park nearby. Roddy and I returned to the hospital room to wait.

By lunchtime, Mr C returned with the good news that the operation had ended and it was successful. He had managed to remove all of the tumour and it had not been touching the brainstem.

Roddy said, 'You have just given me the best birthday present ever.'

We will never forget Roddy's birthday, because on that day Ben was operated on and came through it all so well. It was a day to celebrate.

Mr C told us the tumour would now be taken to the laboratory, where they would thinly slice it and put it through various tests in order to determine whether it was a benign tumour or whether it was cancer.

I had visions of that tumour. I imagined the slicing of it and its process through the laboratory. I envisaged it like a biscuit making factory where the slices from different people were on a conveyor belt, each processing by. Some would be benign and others would not, and there may be no rhyme or reason why one was and one was not. Those slices were all just random selection.

As it was Christmas time, the laboratory was operating on reduced hours. We would have to wait longer than usual. It would take about a week before they had the results of Ben's tumour. We put that aside, as for now we were just happy to be collecting our Ben.

We both went to the recovery ward to get him. His hair had been shaved at the back of his head, and he had a very large plaster covering where the operation had been. He took some time to come round, but he was able to talk to us. We were relieved, as we knew the operation had been so close to his brain stem and it is such a small area to be operating on. Anything could have happened to cause damage. Truly, the work of these surgeons is amazing.

***

I slept in a camp bed beside Ben that Christmas Eve. We were visited by Father Christmas at four in the morning. Ben was given four presents. At the time Ben was too drugged to notice much. He later said four presents seemed so much and he thought he had been spoilt. He also wondered, how did Father Christmas know he would be there?

I would think about Ben's comments again the following Christmas, when together as a family we would lay our Christmas gift for an unknown child under a tree at a different hospital – the Royal Marsden Sutton. A gift for a child who would be in hospital that Christmas.

Christmas morning, I was alone with Ben in hospital and he was slowly coming round. In the quietness of the high dependency room I decided to try and encourage Ben by telling him about all the people who had sent him best wishes from around the world. He listened to me telling him about the people who had contacted us to send their love, and then he said to me, 'And God and Jesus too, Mummy. They also love me.'

I smiled. 'Yes, Ben, God and Jesus do love you.'

He randomly then said to me, 'I want to stand up for Jesus, Mummy.'

I thought of how my parents had often talked with the boys about a song they both loved and cherished when young: 'Stand up, stand up for Jesus you soldiers of the cross'. I think Ben was thinking of that when he said he wanted to stand up for Jesus. I was amazed at how this young boy, lying in a hospital bed having just had brain surgery 24 hours previously, could not blame God for the imposition and pain on his Christmas Day but instead want to stand up for him. Again, the boy's faith encouraged me.

That Christmas day, Tom was fantastic. He turned up at hospital with some of Ben's presents from home. As he sat by his bed making up his own and then Ben's Match Attax books for their football cards, he said out loud, 'This is the best Christmas ever.'

Roddy and I looked at each other, disbelieving. The surroundings were not looking that great from our perspective.

But now I have to agree with Tom that it was a great Christmas. That Christmas, we were able to be with Ben and care for Ben. We did not have the turkey or the stuffing – in fact, we ate hardly anything as all the shops were shut. But we were together, and we had our two boys with us, and that was priceless.

CHAPTER 16

Waiting

The following week was unbearably hard. Uncertainty can cause so much stress.

The best result would be if the tumour was found to be benign. We would be sent home after the week when the main healing of Ben's wound had happened, and we would continue the process of healing at home. There would be follow-up appointments at the hospital, no doubt, to check on Ben's progress, but that would effectively be it for the treatment. We would be back to normal life fairly soon, and would have just had a wakeup call that we needed to appreciate having Ben in our lives.

I earnestly pleaded with God that it would be that result. It felt like it should be that result. Hadn't we already had enough? If hard times were being dished out, surely our family plate did not need to be topped up right now.

I felt the need to remind God that this was Ben, and he and we had already endured enough. Maybe my prompting would help God make his decision to let Ben's slice be benign. I finally had decided that straight talking was necessary for my spiritual path.

My limit had been reached. Enough was enough. We needed good results in order to check that my pleadings were working.

However, there was another option, which was that Ben's tumour would be cancerous. What that meant and the subsequent follow-up treatment I did not want to contemplate, but it was on my mind.

***

One day during that week, friends came to London to see a production of *The Railway Children*. They kindly contacted us to see if Tom would want to go with them. He was delighted to get away from boring hospital routine. There are only so many times you can play Connect Four in a hospital playroom and get excited about it. I took Tom into central London by train, and then was in town for three hours in order to collect Tom afterwards. Roddy stayed with Ben in hospital.

I filled in time wandering around the shops, not really seeing what I was looking at. My mind was distracted and on overdrive. I got to Victoria Train Station, where I was due to collect Tom in about an hour. I thought I would grab myself a coffee and a muffin.

I sat and drank and ate on my own, just one of the many people filling Victoria Station on that day. A man who appeared to be out shopping with his partner and teenage child had his coffee in his hand and was looking for somewhere they could sit. He found a place but was clearly disgruntled by the process, and said in a loud voice, 'Why is it that some people come here and sit at a table and hog it and don't move on for others?'

He was not pointing the finger at me but at another couple, but his dissatisfaction with such a minor matter really rattled me. I felt anger welling up inside that he could be so pathetic about his petty wants when he had nothing to truly complain about. I thought of Ben sick in hospital with real needs and reasons to complain.

I stood up, looked directly at the man, and told him clearly what I thought of him.

I told a stranger in a coffee shop that he had a pathetic reason to complain. 'You've got your seat, so why make other's lives a misery by complaining. I have a real reason to complain. I have a child maybe dying in hospital. I just wanted some time out relaxing with a coffee, and along comes you and your selfish complaints.'

He was gobsmacked and started blurting out, 'It wasn't you, love.'

I picked up my bags and stormed out of the coffee shop. If anyone had lit a match near me I may have spontaneously combusted. I was at breaking point.

I still can't believe I did it. An open rant was not my usual response to others' petty selfishness. I think it showed in some small way the amount of tension we were all under.

I went away from the coffee shop visibly shaking, and only just had time to recover my composure before seeing Tom and our friends. I was probably better hiding away in hospital and out of the real world for a while.

***

The week was a painful one for Ben. In order to regain movement in his head he was encouraged, and sometimes forced, to do physio.

Roddy was often by his side for this. Tom and I would escape along the corridor to the playroom for some distraction.

We did not go far enough away. We could often hear Ben's screams of pain, even at that distance.

It hurt. Put your hand to the part of your head where your neck joins your skull and imagine having that cut open. Ben's scar went right up the back of his skull. Now imagine, after having that cut, that you have to force yourself to lift your head and turn it. That was physio for Ben.

When our children have to face such pain, as parents we want to take it on ourselves. Because we can't, we feel useless in the face of it.

***

On the ward that week we met some great teenagers who were visiting their friend in hospital. He had been in a racially-motivated fight two months earlier, and had been sent to King's College Hospital for surgery and rehabilitation. Sadly, his brain had not recovered, and it was predicted at the time that it may never recover from the blows he was dealt. I had heard about the attack, as his story had reached national news. His friends were so hurt and sad. They filled in time playing Connect Four with Tom.

The position these young people were in seemed hopeless. Their friend had been in a deep coma for weeks and was not communicating. They visited him daily. They hoped he would somehow register they were there, and that might help him. Life in hospital exposes you to the reality of other people's lives. It sometimes helps us if in our daily lives we are reminded of what goes on in the world of hospital land.

***

So the week passed. On Friday, Roddy and I were to hear the results. We went into the parents' room to meet with Mr C. We left Ben and Tom in the safe care of the hospital staff.

Again, I did not want to go into the room, but part of me wanted the waiting to end – and the head-hurting thinking of different scenarios over and over again.

In the parents' room, we were again told unfortunate news. Ben's tumour was cancerous.

He had a medulloblastoma, and would require eighteen months of treatment at the Royal Marsden in Sutton, under the care of Consultant S. For Ben's type of tumour, there was a 75% chance that he would survive past the five-year mark. Mr C had prepared his own research, and statistics for his patients had been higher, at 80%. He gave us the positive news that as all the tumour had been removed it put Ben in the best position. He would now hand over Ben's care to a consultant who would be taking care of Ben's oncology treatment.

All I could think about was Samuel. I was in another parent room in a different London hospital, but I was again hearing bad, bad news.

My mind was protesting against the doctors and what they were saying. My head said, but this is not meant to happen. In my mind, even as the consultant started to talk to us about treatment plans and options, I was telling God he had gone far enough.

I reminded God that from my earlier prayers that week he knew I was believing him up until this point, but if the outcome was cancer then I didn't know what I would do in terms of my ongoing faith in God. If cancer was diagnosed, I felt God would have overstepped the mark and gone too far. He could control this sort of thing. Didn't he hold the whole world in his hands? Hadn't we and many others prayed on an almost twenty-four hour watch that the result would be benign? How could we get through this and keep our family and our faith intact?

Did the doctors not know what was at stake when they delivered that cancer verdict? My head told me the consequences of this diagnosis would reverberate more deeply than the cancerous mass that had been in Ben's head. This diagnosis had the power to shake the core of my existence.

CHAPTER 17

A Plan

Consultant S came to meet us at King's with a plan for Ben's treatment. Ben would be given a couple of weeks at home to recover from his operation, then he would need to attend the Royal Marsden Hospital in Sutton (South London) each weekday for six weeks to receive radiotherapy to his brain. The radiotherapy would initially focus on the part of the brain where the tumour had occurred as well as the rest of the brain and spinal cord in case the tumour had spread.

The strength and intensity of the radiotherapy administered to Ben would be determined by the doctors at the Marsden, taking into account the results of further tests Ben would need to undergo prior to his treatment. Another important test would be a lumbar puncture, which would check for any spread of cancer cells along the spinal cord.

Ben would also receive weekly doses of one type of chemotherapy whilst undergoing radiotherapy.

After his radiotherapy he would be given a month at home to recover and rebuild his strength. Then he would begin a year-long plan of chemotherapy which would consist of nine six-weekly visits to the Marsden to be given three days intensive chemotherapy into his system. This would be followed by further chemotherapy which could hopefully be administered weekly in Eastbourne.

The oncology team were in the process of trying to establish whether Eastbourne District General Hospital would be able to handle this level of care for Ben. For Consultant S, it would be the first time he had worked with Eastbourne as the backup team, and he wanted to assess their capabilities. If they did not meet his standard, then we would be under the support care of paediatric oncology in Brighton, a forty-five minute drive from where we lived.

All this information. Dates, times, plans. The next eighteen months suddenly determined for us by hospital decree.

It was a lot to take in, whilst my head was pounding: 'cancer, Ben has cancer'.

Yet again, I was calm with the hospital staff. They appeared to be lovely people and it was not their fault this was the result of their investigations. I did not feel like lashing out at them. Whilst I did not want to believe what they said, they were the professionals, so I had to trust that they knew what it was. I was also aware we had to work with these people in order for Ben to make a full recovery.

The journey would be long, that was obvious. Eighteen months was the time line, but if there were any setbacks along the way – for example, infections – then we were told it would only further extend the length of his treatment.

***

I cannot recall how we told Ben and Tom the news, or whether we even did at that time. We could hardly take it in ourselves, let alone have the courage to explain it to Ben and Tom.

Roddy and I stayed in the parents' room for a while after the doctors left us, in order to gain enough physical and emotional strength to return to the ward and to our sons.

I have walked this journey with Roddy, and at times it has taken us to the closest level of personal interaction. At others, it has taken us on polar-opposite routes. What two people can ever react or grieve alike? Yet in marriage we are called to be there for each other in sickness and in health. So many times, we interpret this as sickness of the spouse; we imagine having to be their caregiver in their later years. Would we have ever imagined on our wedding day that we would first be called to be there for each other in the sickness of our own children?

We packed up our bags and lifted Ben into a wheelchair for the trip out of the hospital to our car. He had hardly walked since his operation, and lifting his head was still extremely painful, but Ben bore it all in a stoic manner. We had been advised that he could have paracetamol whenever required, but by this time Ben had been so put off medicine that despite his obvious pain he would never knowingly take a painkiller again. He preferred to go cold turkey, from intravenous morphine to nothing. As a result he suffered more pain than he should have, but if the child won't take it then it is hard to force them. We were aware there were a lot more medicines to come, but we would cross those bridges when we got to them.

We took our time driving home, with Ben in the front seat on the lowest recline, as any sharp movements were hard for him. Two hours later, it was such a relief to be home. I thought what joy this homecoming would have been had the results been different. Over time, we had to accept that the results were what they were, and somehow muster the strength for the long journey with cancer ahead.

The four weeks Ben was home were not free from hospital visits. We drove to the Royal Marsden on many occasions for various tests to check whether the cancer had spread and to test Ben's body functions. His body was about to be hit with radiotherapy and a variety of chemotherapy drugs. The doctors needed to establish how it would cope with all of this.

It felt like we were starting from a good position, as Ben had always been such a healthy and strong boy. Surely his physical fitness would help him to handle the treatment better?

CHAPTER 18

Treatment Begins

Ben went up with Roddy to the Marsden for a kidney scan. A male prisoner was led into the same waiting room. The prisoner was handcuffed to police on either side of him. This prisoner had cancer, and he had his scan just before Ben.

Ben was fascinated. It probably had something to do with his enjoyment of playing with police Lego. He was full of the story on his return home that evening.

It made me think about that prisoner. What had he done in his life to get himself into prison under such maximum security that he required a double escort to a hospital room? I also wondered whether he would complete his treatment and make a recovery. I wished him well as I did all cancer patients, but it still made me wonder. Here was Ben, starting his life, having inflicted no real harm on others as far as I was aware, and here was this prisoner whose actions I could only imagine – and yet both had cancer.

Ben and this prisoner were in a similar position. Cancer is a real leveller of our human condition. No one is immune.

***

One of the first tests completed at the Marsden was a lumbar puncture to check for any tumour spread. If there were signs of this, then the doctors would give Ben a stronger dosage of radiotherapy. We are just talking degrees of bad here, as the other levels were seriously high as well. However, in the world of medical care any good news is gratefully accepted. In our household, by this time good news was never really expected.

When our consultant radiation oncologist told us that the cells had not spread – the spinal fluid was clear– I literally could not thank him enough. Ben was in the room when we were told. He looked up with a faint smile of embarrassment – at my loud and happy reaction, I suppose. I hugged Ben. I would have hugged anyone and everyone in sight, but the consultant looked a bit awkward at my overenthusiasm so I spared him the hug. Maybe I was clutching at straws, but each bit of better news helped me believe that Ben's story would be different to Samuel's. I had to hold on to that hope.

You see, no matter how hard the cancer road ahead of us would be, it was always expected to be better than Samuel's journey. We still had Ben, and we had every good hope that we would have him with us for a very long time to come.

My friend Sarah called to see how everything was going. When she heard what we were facing with Ben's treatment, she was clearly shocked. She said, 'Oh, that sounds terrible. I don't know how you can cope with it all.'

My response was immediate. 'Yes, it may sound bad but it really isn't – not in comparison to what we had to face before.' I think she understood what I was referring to.

To me, nothing was as bad or as final as death, and the pain attached to losing your much-loved and longed-for child. I fully realise that statement could be challenged by those who experience the very real and long term pain of caring for a loved one who has to daily suffer through physical or mental ill health, and maybe death would be a relief. However, I can only speak for what I know and what I have experienced. Due to my life experiences, I can say that looking after Ben through his cancer treatment, whilst tough in many ways, was at no point hopeless. Belief that these dark days would one day end and there was hope of a better time to come brought strength for each new challenge.

***

We went up to the Marsden to have Ben's radiotherapy mask fitted. The mask was made of a strong plastic turquoise mesh-type material. In a session with a play therapist, Ben was able to shape and mould masks for his toys and play with pieces of the material. He liked that the material was squidgy.

We tried to focus on the positive, as though this was all 'fun', but Roddy and I were nervous. How would Ben actually react on the day when he was held down and not allowed to move as a large sheet of this heavy plastic material was pressed down and moulded over his face and chest? We wondered whether Ben would be able to lie still for the time required as the mask makers did their job. They also had to tattoo various permanent markers on Ben's body, to guide the radiotherapists in the weeks to come.

On the day his mask was fitted, Ben did well. It was Roddy and I who found the ordeal quite traumatic. Ben had to be held down by various staff members as the sheet was moulded over his head and shoulders. I suppose it was no tougher than the operation, but Ben was sedated for that and we were kept in a waiting room. We did not have to sit and watch. For the fitting of the mask, we were in the same room, standing useless in the corner, just watching.

I am not sure whether the staff made it up just to make us feel better, but when the mask was completed they said Ben had made a smiley mask. The reason I was not sure whether this was correct was that I wondered whether it was a grimace and not a smile.

Preparation for long term treatment also meant the fitting of a 'portacath' which would be used to administer certain drugs. A permanent portacath would reduce the need for regular needles into the veins. It required an operation to insert the port under the skin, just below the ribs. Ben had to have anaesthetic for this procedure, so nil by mouth had to be enforced. It was a long haul, as Ben had started to like his food again since his brain surgery. Having to wait until mid-afternoon for his operation was hard going. We talked about all the food he could have once the procedure was over. Ben was relishing his food at this time.

However, this enjoyment of food was all to go once radiotherapy started. To see my son's body that I had nurtured and cared for from birth gradually fade away was hard for me to handle. As parents, we want to care for their physical and emotional needs, and one of the ways we do this is by feeding them. To have food become a battle between me and Ben, all because of the nasty effects of treatment, was something we were to discover going forward.

For now, we were happy that the portacath, commonly referred to as 'Ben's port', had gone in. We had to ensure we took good care of it, so that no infections could enter his system through that easy-access route. Infection means delays for oncology treatment, and can lead to serious illness for the patient. Naturally we wanted to avoid that.

***

The day for starting radiotherapy soon dawned. We had read some of the information given to us, and it was not pleasant reading. Radiotherapy to the brain can be brutal. The list of possible long-term damage to Ben seemed endless. Once you added the chemotherapy list, it was not for those with a weak stomach. I had not previously queried medical process; I used the same tactic and approached radiotherapy with the same level of numbed resignation. Of course I did not want my child to suffer permanent brain damage, hearing loss, eyesight problems, growth and hormone complications, stroke, heart attack … I could go on. Pretty much, add anything nasty and it was probably on one of the lists we were given.

But I wanted my child to have every chance of survival. I committed him to the care of the medics with hope that their skill and treatment would save Ben from cancer.

On his first day of radiotherapy, Ben had to have approximately thirty minutes of radiation. This required him to lie still under the pinned-down mask, all alone in the room. He was in an adult room, and the machine was adult-size with a large step up. Ben, ever Mr Independent, wanted to get onto the table all by himself. Over the next few days, the radiotherapy team devised a way to create a step onto the bed so he could do just that.

We also had another drama with those pants – not a great start. This time, I thought we had prepared well. He was wearing soft tracksuit trousers – no metal. I thought you were not allowed to have any metal parts on your body, as these would react with the machines. Well, I learnt that day that, yes, that was the requirement for the MRI, but for the radiotherapy machine the main issue was to have no bulk around the body; all the measurements they used were so precise. So this meant that the tracksuit pants were too bulky and would have to be removed.

We had another pants drama on our hands. The radiologists were female. Ben knew Tom would not think it was right for them to see him in his pants.

A solution was found. Ben agreed to wear a hospital gown. In different circumstances, it could have been comical as of course they only had adult sizes. His little six-year-old body was swamped in it. He had to hold it up like a wedding veil so he did not trip over it. I was pleased that Ben had found his solution to the problem and was working out his own way of adapting to the hospital environment. We managed to get around this on subsequent visits by Ben wearing a pair of small swimming trunks, as we all agreed it was okay to let girls see those.

Because of the intensity of the radioactivity, I was not allowed to stay in the room with Ben. I helped him get settled on the table with his mask fitted, and then I had to walk out whilst still verbally giving him reassurance that all would be alright. His young body was lying there in an adult-size machine and I had to leave him to face this alone.

I realised this was only the start. Roddy and I could not take from Ben the treatment he had to face. As his parents, we would dearly have wanted to swap places, but we couldn't. We had to be strong for Ben, so he felt relaxed and comfortable in that environment. But we had to walk away and out the door; there was no option to stay.

I was allowed to talk to him through a microphone into the room in order to reassure him. Knowing Ben's personality, I wondered whether this might hinder things rather than help. He had shown us already, by how he coped with the operation and other tests, that he was best with minimum fuss and attention. It worked better for him if the medics just got on with the job as fast as possible and essentially ignored him. He was a no-nonsense boy, just like his Granny, who the boys sometimes called a 'no-nonsense Granny'. No fuss, just get on with the task at hand, and the quicker started then the quicker ended.

I left the room to go and watch with the radiotherapists, to see if I was needed in any way. They spoke to Ben over the intercom, and told him about what was happening in the room. Over subsequent treatments, they even built up jokey banter with Ben. He pretended to them that they were 'Done!' almost before they had even begun. He gave a bit of cheek back to them over the sound system as they teased him back and laughed.

I was proud of the way Ben handled that. It had been a big ask for him. Some children his age were not able to handle the radiation procedure and required daily sedation before receiving it. This first time was considered a test, to see if he would comprehend the need to do the procedure, and whether he would cooperate with the team. If not, they would need to resort to sedation. If he wriggled and moved, they would have to use anaesthetic each treatment. This would mean restricting food before treatment and would just add to the stress of the procedure and the stress of keeping Ben's body in good shape for all it had to face. Ben worked out his own coping strategy. Despite the awfulness of the treatment and the environment he managed well.

Whilst in the room or waiting for him to come out, I would often just fill in the time by praying. I knew no other way to fill the void. I would pray that Ben would stay still and endure this. My mind would often wander to picture the good luck card that one of Ben's friends at school had sent him before his treatment began. She had written 'I hop the medson worx'. Spelling mistakes and all, she was spot on. We all were just hoping that this medicine would work for Ben.

On leaving the radiotherapy department one day, we saw a young child being wheeled along the corridor back to recovery on a bed. She had clearly had to have anaesthetic to get her through the radiotherapy process. I felt for her parents, and realised how fortunate we were that Ben did not require this, as he managed to stay still for the treatment.

***

I have learnt that with cancer, as in many things in life, there are no two stories alike. One part of the journey may be easier for some, then the next stage may be harder. You may even have the same form of treatment and yet somehow your body may react differently than the other person's.

The more I learned about cancer and about life, the more I realised that each journey was unique, filled with its own joys and challenges. As onlookers to others' journeys, we cannot say that just because we have had a similar journey we have had the same one. All are individuals. That is how we are made. With our individual portions, we have to exist. For that girl, radiotherapy required daily anaesthetic. We had been saved that for now, but did that make our journey better?

In the hospital, I observed different children and adults going through cancer treatment. Some seemed clearly worse than others. It was as if we had entered a new level of life itself. The real world outside was now irrelevant. We were now in a world where all had cancer. I admit we were starting from a weak point; it was hardly a world of great statistics or happy ever afters. However, some people's stories were better. Some had only a couple of months of treatment with a higher percentage expecting full recovery. Others had longer treatment, but if they completed it all then they were virtually assured of success. Then there were others who had no hope of recovery, no matter how many of those toxins their body accepted.

I started to realise I was feeling envious of those who I thought were in a better position than Ben. I gave this bitterness of mine a name. I called it 'cancer jealousies'. I am ashamed to say that my cancer jealousy was directed at totally the wrong person, as I was soon to learn.

Whilst Ben was having radiotherapy, there was another young boy called Krish who had the slot for treatment either before or just after Ben. For those six weeks, we would see him and his parents in the waiting room every weekday morning. Krish would have his treatment and literally bounce off the table. He would come through to us all, smiling, holding his little bead of courage to add to his string, and asking whether he was able to have a donut for morning tea or not. He was so full of life and energy.

Ben would get off the table subdued. He would look pale and weak. He would often turn down the offer of a bead of courage, as he wanted only to escape the room. When Krish mentioned donuts, Ben's eyes would roll and his tummy lurch.

From the very first session of radiotherapy, Ben had been sick. I was surprised it had reacted so quickly with him. I had thought it would be a gradual build up. But oh no, after his first treatment we went to town to try and find some swim trunks for him to wear on the radiotherapy table. We were just walking into the shop when Ben said, 'I feel sick.' As I had no sick bowl with us, I grabbed him and tried to direct his head at the public rubbish bin for him to use instead. From then on, the sick bowl was our constant companion. Ben hated food, and I hated having to try to force him to eat.

Yet here was Krish, having 'the same' treatment and reacting so well. I initially felt upset as Ben was finding it so hard, but this other boy seemed to be having a walk in the park in comparison. When I discussed this with Mum, who was also with me on a treatment day, in her wisdom she cautioned me. She said, 'I can see the obvious visual difference between Ben and Krish, and yet I think that Krish's family are in a bad way. I can tell from his dad's eyes that he is very, very troubled. I think we should not judge what we do not know.'

How right she was. I discovered later that cancer jealousy was working in the opposite direction as well. Krish's family had heard we had hope that Ben would recover. In their honesty, they later told me they had decided our family were a nice bunch of people, that all would go well for us and Ben, and we therefore had no comprehension of the cancer battle they faced. They had written us off. They did not think it would be helpful having much to do with us, so they had determined not to get too involved with us.

Their decision to protect themselves from us reminds me of the people who had sick babies in St Thomas' at the same time as us. One group of parents in the special care unit had babies with jaundice, or babies on the road to better health having been born premature. They were all working towards taking their babies home one day. Those parents talked in the shared breast pumping room as if the trauma of not having their baby at home yet was the worst thing in life.

For those of us breast pumping from the neighbouring intensive care ward, the experience was totally different. Many of us could not comprehend ever having our child at home as there were so many hurdles to pass before that day. In that room, pumping milk, I often chose to stay quiet and not talk to anyone, let alone to discuss Samuel's story as his was just so different. In the story unfolding for me each day, my hope for Samuel's survival was being chipped away. How can you compare the two experiences? Both are bad and hard; I would not wish either on anyone. But where there is hope there is life, and there is a promise of better days to come. When hope is removed from the situation, there is deep agony of the soul. It can often be a lonely road.

Little Krish's love of life, big spirit, wide smile, and easy nature touched all of us who met him. He was only four and Ben was six, but each had developed a brain tumour. Ben's was operable and meant to be recoverable from. With current known treatment, Krish was not. His parents had been told that Krish had at best eighteen months to live. The treatment he was receiving was simply to delay his inevitable death by five years of age.

One day during treatment, Ben and Krish played together in a children's play area near the hospital. As they played together that day in the park, around all the other apparently healthy children of the neighbourhood, the boys had an instant connection and affection for each other. They later sat beside each other on a couch watching TV, their two little bald heads touching. Ben put his arm around Krish's shoulder and said, 'This is the life.' I shed a silent tear for the bitter blow this statement threw at my heart.

That day, I had heard Krish's story. As Ben was later to describe it whenever we talked about his friend, 'Krish has a worser brain tumour than me.'

You see, we can fall into the trap of judging others from what we see on the outside but fail to really know their story – the truth about who they are and what they are facing. How often we all do this.

Krish's life prior to developing cancer had been one of great joy. He was a much longed-for son, and he brought hope to a family who had already faced much pain. His later passing, only nine months into his treatment and just short of his fifth birthday, caused heartache and deep despair for his family and friends. In seeing a small part of Krish's journey, I saw what it was like to be a parent who has no hope. Our story was meant to be different – we had hope that Ben would survive. Although our time through Ben's cancer treatment was rough, all along we thought that he would come through it and we would be out the other end with Ben still in our lives.

Krish's family had had this hope taken from them at the start. It was a desperate time for them.

***

We talked to Ben about losing his hair. He appeared unperturbed by it. He told me that it would be quite cool to be bald, as then you would really know what rain felt like.

So when his hair started to fall out a couple of weeks into the treatment, we all hoped his attitude would not change with the reality of it. It did not. Ben faced hair loss as if it was only a minor irritation. Some friends advised us to get his hair cut really short before it happened so there would be less to come out. However, as he appeared unconcerned about it, we thought his free time at home was better spent with us and his friends than sitting in a barber's waiting for a cut that would all too soon happen naturally anyway.

When Ben's hair did fall out, it came out in large handfuls. He found it an annoyance on his pillow at night, and often it got in his mouth as he slept. He had a playdate at his friend Rufus's house the Saturday his hair started to come out. By the time he got to his friend's house, his head was patchy, with bald bits. I wondered how he would feel when others saw it, but did not want to make it an issue, so we went up to Rufus's house excited about the fun times ahead. Ben rang the bell.

Rufus scampered down, opened the door as Ben took off his hat, and, as any six-year-old would, said, 'Ben, your hair looks funny.'

Ben said, straight up, 'Yes, it's coming out.'

Later that playdate, Rufus's Mum, Sarah, heard the boys in Rufus's bedroom, again talking about Ben's hair. She heard Ben say to Rufus, 'Look! It comes out easily. Do you want to have a go?'

Ben's attitude helped to normalise it. We were all able to cope with this aspect better because of Ben's response to it. Later that Saturday, Tom very lovingly combed all of Ben's hair out into a bowl for keeps.

Ben's loss of hair and other people's reaction to it was hard on Tom. When we were out in public, he saw people staring at Ben. He wanted to hide Ben away and protect him. I explained to Tom that it was great he felt that way and wanted to protect Ben, but as it did not appear to be a big issue to Ben, we should try to develop the same laid-back attitude – that really it was the least of the issues. Hair loss had not hurt Ben, whereas some of the other things he was facing had and would. However often I said this to Tom, he still felt concerned.

Tom was particularly worried about how people would react at school when they saw Ben. His scar after the operation had been enough of a curiosity in the playground when he was back at school briefly before starting radiotherapy, and that was minor compared with total hair loss.

Ben did go back to school for very short times after radiotherapy, and students' stares were like water off a duck's back.

For Tom, it was harder. The hardest was when a boy in the playground said to Tom, 'Your brother may die.' That hurt. Tom held on to the hope that the boy's words would not be true.

Ben's ease with hair loss was evident in that, despite the various hats we had purchased for him, he was not keen to wear any of them unless it was cold outside. Generally, he preferred to go without a head cover. I would find myself in a supermarket or walking down a street, wondering why people were looking at me. I would look around and, sure enough, Ben had decided to whip off his hat, apparently oblivious to their stares. To me, Ben without his hair looked adorable, like a little old man. He seemed more vulnerable, and I just wanted to scoop him up and protect him. I realised he had to cope as best he could in the real world. I was thankful he coped so well with this side of his treatment. I also had to take it in my stride.

We had one funny incident in a bookshop. Ben loved books, so to fill in the endless time between radiotherapy appointments we would often be hanging out at a local bookshop, looking at the Biff and Chip books – a series that was on his school reading list and which Ben enjoyed. I had wandered off to a different section of the shop as Ben trawled through the books on the shelf.

I became aware of a small girl who kept going round the corner and then back to her mum, as if there was some great curiosity round the corner. Of course there was: it was Ben. I headed over to Ben and we laughed about her looking at him. I told Ben I felt like making a funny face at her, as it was only hair loss.

Ben's bald head became a curiosity to many. Only when it was cold did he have a hat on. I came to love his bald head and often kissed it. The photos of him at the time still display his wide smile. His resilience in the face of much adversity is an inspiration to me.

CHAPTER 19

Support Gathers

W hile Ben was having daily radiotherapy and weekly chemotherapy, we were offered the use of a flat near the hospital, kindly provided by the generosity of The Rhys Daniels Trust. The travel distance to our home in Eastbourne was judged just sufficient to have a flat offered, if available. We would therefore not have to make the daily commute to the hospital. We were very fortunate that a flat was provided during our entire radiotherapy treatment. We were aware of others who were not given a flat as there were only three available. They had to travel daily, and this added extra strain on their family life and their child's health. Had we had to travel daily, it would have been at least a four-hour round trip by road. As Ben suffered from additional tiredness and sickness through the treatment, it was wonderful that we did not have to add that car travel on top of it. I also think it was a benefit for me, as my mind was constantly on Ben. No matter how hard

I tried not to be, I was worried for him. To add four hours driving on busy English roads would have piled more pressure on me.

***

A cancer diagnosis has a knock-on effect to an entire community that surrounds the patient. You cannot navigate the journey alone – support is needed.

When Ben was diagnosed with a brain tumour and required an operation, my parents dropped everything. They had been on holiday when they heard the news, and had come back from their holiday to fly over to us. Despite Dad's worse health in colder conditions, they came out of their New Zealand summer to our British winter to support us all. We were all so grateful for their sacrificial actions.

I had negotiated time off work to be with Ben during the six weeks' radiotherapy. Mum and Dad were there to look after Tom and Roddy at home, as Roddy was back at work. Mum and Dad would also stay on, after I returned to work, to care for Ben during his time at home recovering.

Mum did not want to leave Dad for too long on his own. She also wanted to help support Ben and me at the hospital during radiotherapy. So we developed a routine whereby Mum would travel up to the flat with Ben and me on the Sunday night and stay with us until Wednesday, when Roddy would come up on his day off work to see Ben and me and help out on the long day when Ben had both radiotherapy and chemotherapy as well as blood tests. Roddy would then take Mum back to Eastbourne Wednesday night, and Ben and I would stay on until after the Friday treatment and head home for the weekend.

***

The flat we used was a five minute walk from the hospital. We often had early morning radiotherapy appointments, and after that, every day except for Wednesday, we were free to leave the hospital. It was an intense six weeks of filling in time.

At the start, I tried to encourage Ben to attend the hospital school. I was concerned that he would be missing a year and a half of his schooling, so any schooling would be better than none. However, when we tried the school, on the first day Ben found the noise and the smells in the hospital school hard to handle. He did not complain. I could just tell by his general lack of enthusiasm that it was not great.

Radiotherapy heightened his sense of smell, and the smallest thing could set off his nausea. I'd had bad morning sickness with my pregnancies and imagined it may be similar. So I thought it would be best if Ben just came back to the flat with me. We rested, or worked on the work my friend Emma had kindly supplied us with. She had produced amazing workbooks, all bound in a Manchester United folder – a folder of love and care.

I find it painful to describe this time of our life. It was only six weeks, but they were long. Each day, we ticked off a further treatment, but the list before us still seemed to stretch just as long. On one side, I think of it as extremely precious time for me with Ben, with minimal distractions from the outside world. I think with warmth of the times we would cuddle in together for hours and I would read to him, something I have always enjoyed doing with my boys, or if he had the strength then he would read to me. We each gained pleasure from this shared companionship.

On the other side, the memories are painful for me as Ben was not well. He often had a headache. We were told this was most likely a result of the radiotherapy. He did not want to eat, and if he did he was often sick. He did not like taking his medicines, yet in order for him to be able to keep his food down it was advisable to take the anti-sickness medicine. The effect of all the drugs was making his bowels close up, and he was badly constipated. The only way we could deal with this was by the administration of yet more medicine. At times, even sleep was difficult, as Ben's headaches would wake him. I was negotiating all this unpleasant stuff with a six-year-old.

I was his carer, and he was my son. I had so many conflicting thoughts going through my head. I did not want to undo all the good of the character he had developed over the last six years. I did not want to spoil him. I was aware that in order to be kind I had to be firm, yet I had to agree the medicine was revolting stuff. I thought I might be more understanding if I could imagine what the radiotherapy and chemotherapy must feel like.

I thought about how I had felt when pregnant with the boys, and the yucky taste that seemed to be permanently in my mouth. The thought of food was enough to make my stomach churn. I thought how Ben's treatment must be worse than this, as each smell and taste seemed to be revolting to his palate.

One night in the flat alone with Ben, I was trying to get Ben to brush his teeth, a task that had never been a problem before cancer treatment. However, the taste of toothpaste must have now become unpalatable. He was protesting, then he turned to me and said, 'Mummy, will I have to brush my teeth in Heaven?'

I was not prepared for that question. It was not a topic I was too keen to be discussing with my six-year-old cancer child but discuss it we did. I paused and sat with Ben on the edge of the bath as we considered his question. We thought of a few options but then agreed you would not have to brush your teeth as there was nothing perishable in Heaven, so presumably no tooth decay. We ended up hugging each other and longing together for Heaven.

One of my lowest points occurred in the early stages of radiotherapy. At every part of Ben's day, I felt like I required master skills in manipulation – to convince Ben to lie down for his treatment, and then to take his anti-sickness medicine two times a day. I had just spent two hours trying to negotiate patiently with Ben to take his medicine, but he kept up the excuses and the procrastination. I had tried every negotiating method in the book. I needed to call on all my skills, but I was weary and I was angry.

I felt like a failure. Despite all my efforts, still the medicine remained in its syringe. I lost my patience and screamed and shouted at him. To try to calm down and count to ten, I went into the bathroom and slammed the door.

In floods of tears, I knelt down and pleaded with God to listen, and to make some part of this horrible, long and arduous journey more bearable. There in the shower I verbally reminded God again (in case he had forgotten) that he had allowed Ben to develop cancer. As a result of cancer, Ben needed all these medicines, and yet Ben was not willingly wanting to take them, and it was making my already difficult job that much more difficult.

I informed God that it might just help if he were to make some parts of the treatment easier. He had allowed Ben to have cancer and we had no time to 'deal' with that right now, but could he at least somehow work the miracle and make Ben more accepting of the medicine he was meant to take? Then at least I would feel like I had some help along the way.

The answer was not a quick fix. However, this brokenness and total collapse did help me. Sharing my burdens lessened the load on my shoulders – all the small aspects I had been trying to carry on my own.

Over time, Ben managed to take his medicine a lot more quickly. We also worked out that he liked to have some personal control about it. The medicine was measured in millilitres, but Ben got into his head that the measurements were in grams. So he took control and would suggest we started with half a gram in order to test it. Then he would have a sip of water to take the taste away. Then maybe a few minutes later he would have a whole gram, and a repeat of the water. So over time we managed to get the entire medicine down. It was never easy, but it was certainly one hundred percent better than when we started. I was reminded of how each day we have to have faith, and trust that miracles can be active in the small things as well as the big.

***

Weekends were a welcome change. They were a break from hospital appointments and the close quarters of living in the flat. On the weekends we were able to go home to Eastbourne. However, for me it also felt like a readjustment each weekend to be back with all the family and our friends. It was hard to explain to all how we were doing. There was such a long road ahead of us I did not want to be complaining this early, yet the journey was not proving easy so far.

There were certain breaking points for me. Once, I came home and was horrible to Dad as he gave me a hug. I was so worked up and stressed I could not handle it, and pushed him away and threw things at him or near him. I was rotten. The other time I unloaded on my friend Emma about how horrible the week had been. I was a wreck.

It felt like we were in a pressure bubble up at the flat. In coming home each weekend, there was a slow release of the pressure of the bubble for a period. Yet at no point during Ben's cancer treatment did I ever feel entirely free of that pressure. The bubble would be ready to inflate again the same time next week.

I thought it would not be until the end of Ben's cancer treatment that we would ever be free to safely breathe again. When I voiced this to Roddy, he said, 'Well, by that time we will just be holding our breath in a different way between each check-up. Hoping that the recovery is complete.'

During the treatment stage it was not expected that the tumour would return, but it was when Ben's body was free from the chemicals that we would really know if the chemicals had worked and he was free from cancer.

I have never found uncertainty easy. I realised I had to take one day at a time and no further. That would have to be the story of my life for eighteen months, plus five years, until we could breathe again and feel Ben was cancer-free.

***

It was wonderful to have Tom and Ben with each other at the weekend. Tom was also able to spend one week, his half term break, up at the flat with us. He was a welcome distraction amid all the activity of the hospital.

He was nine years old now, and old enough to question what was happening to Ben. Tom had a conversation with Mum one day that she has often mentioned, and for which she feels concerned that she may have misled him. He was walking with Mum and said 'Granny, do you know what Ben has?'

She responded, 'Yes, I do, he has cancer.'

Tom said, 'My Granny Flora had cancer and she died.'

Mum said, 'Yes, but there are many different types of cancer. The one Ben has is different than Granny Flora's. The doctors do not think Ben will die.'

Tom also found the end of each weekend hard, as he would have to say goodbye to Ben for him to go back to hospital. He realised this was what Ben needed, but Tom told me he was confused for Ben. He just wanted to cuddle Ben and keep him safe. In his own way Tom was coping, but it was far from easy seeing his once healthy, strong, rugby-build brother losing strength and not having the same ability to play endless football in the garden with him. It was also not easy feeling that life was not ordinary, and was somehow beyond Tom's own control.

Tom also found it very hard seeing Ben's body getting smaller. He told me that one of the hardest things about Ben having cancer was seeing Ben get skinny. When you saw Ben in the bath, as Tom did, you could see his once-covered ribs now exposed.

I also found this a very hard thing. Again, it was something that as a mother I felt I should be able to help him with. There were so many aspects of the treatment I could not help with, but at least with feeding him, surely that was my job?

I thought the answer was just to find the right food that could tempt him, draw him in to be able to want to eat again. In any spare time I had, I would trawl the supermarket aisles looking for tasty treats to surprise him with. Yet when I put them in front of Ben, he never responded with any relish or joy.

All food was a challenge. The best example of how hard food had become for Ben was with breakfast cereals. Our boys had always been good eaters – we had been fortunate that way. I had certain ideas about how to achieve a healthy diet, and one was that there were certain meals that were essential, such as breakfast. Also I thought it was best to deal with children's fussiness by not giving them much choice. Simple options, simple life. So in our house there was often no choice at breakfast – it was bran flakes or nothing.

Ben loved his bran flakes. He would relish his breakfast and eat with gusto. My friend Melissa once stayed with us on holiday. She had been out for a walk in the morning and came back and there was Ben having break-fast. He informed her it was his second breakfast as one was not enough! There was a lot of banter that holiday about Ben's second tummy that could hold his second meal. At the time, I used to imagine him as a teenager, eating us out of house and home.

Then came radiotherapy and chemotherapy. I would put Ben's bowl of bran flakes down, and his eyes would roll. I knew he did not want it. He suggested that if we got a different cereal he might like it.

I thought now was the time to break my rules, but only for the cancer season. Thus the introduction to our cupboard of Coco Pops, Weetabix, Multi-grain Shapes and so on.

Then, with a cupboard stacked with different cereals, we fast forward to another breakfast at the London flat.

My patience was as thin as a tissue and Ben had pushed his small serve of cereal around the bowl and managed to eat nothing. I asked him to please eat.

He said, 'It's just that there's nothing here I want to eat.'

His comment was a red rag to a bull.

I am ashamed to say that I totally lost the plot. I screamed, shouted, and opened all the cupboards to show him all the boxes. I said I purchased them all for him and yet he said I did not have what he wanted. I was so distraught.

I stormed out of the room back to that bathroom to rage and storm and count to ten (at least).

I later confessed all to our specialist nurse at the hospital. I felt that as a carer I had failed. I had been left alone in charge of Ben and I had lost it and become angry toward him.

The truth as I see it now was that it did not matter what I put in front of Ben. Since his cancer treatment, all food had become unpalatable. Ben just did not want to upset me by saying that. He was just not interested in food, and probably could not understand my growing obsession with it.

***

Why was I so obsessed? Because I wanted to avoid Ben having to have a feeding tube. For me, a feeding tube was one less thing than Ben should have to deal with. I did not want him to have another thing that would be a curiosity to others.

If I am truthful with myself, it was also probably because I felt that a feeding tube would show me to be a failure as a mother and provider. I realise now this was wrong, but it was an intense time. I did not have much else to focus my energies on so I can understand how I became controlled by wanting to help Ben with this one thing. The one thing of food, which I had totally failed at. The task was an impossible challenge against toxins that were beyond my control or Ben's reasoning.

Each week when he was weighed, I dreaded the result. As the pounds rolled off him, the hospital staff thought it would be inevitable that Ben would need the extra assistance of a feeding tube during his treatment. It was all just a matter of time. We had a lot of time ahead of us, with still over a year of treatment planned.

As with all these things, I worried more than Ben did. He was unconcerned about the imposition of a feeding tube. He said he just did not know what it would feel like, and could not decide if he wanted it or not until it was in, and then he would know what it felt like. I commend Ben for his attitude and approach to new issues along the way. He dealt with them far better than I did.

***

I wondered how Ben was dealing with all this, emotionally. His whole life had been turned upside down.

He was not able to go to school on a regular basis as he was in hospital. Even when we were back between chemotherapy sessions, his time at school was very restricted. Here was someone who loved school, loved his friends, and loved his Saturday football. Yet he was in a period of time where he could have none of them.

To my knowledge, Ben never complained about any of the things that had been taken from his life. He just seemed to accept it as a new way to live for a period of time. He understood that treatment for his cancer would not be a quick fix, and he would just have to be patient and see it all through.

As I was privileged to spend a lot of time with Ben at this time, I was able to have some great talks with him. Some of our talks helped me to see what strong and good character he had developed. Ben was laid-back about his own needs at school, but he was concerned for others. He was worried that he was not at school, as there was one boy in his class who the others did not always allow to play with them. Ben would pray for this boy at night, and ask God to make his other friends include this boy in their play while Ben was away.

I thought about this a year later, when I was part of a special footy fun day on the school field where Ben had played. I saw the boy Ben had mentioned playing the parachute game. He had a huge smile on his face and was loving it. As I watched on, I thanked God that it looked as if Ben's prayers had been answered for this boy. Little miracles along the way.

I often think of Ben's nature as being an example to many, and I talk about it with Tom. Ben did not worry about losing his friends whilst not at school, as if that happened, well then, they were not true friends anyway. He seemed to even understand that. He also knew that in time he would be able to catch up with all his work and his football. We of course did not know how much the cancer treatment would have affected his abilities. But we hoped that a level of normality would one day resume in the McNicol household.

I talk with Tom about how truly great sportsmen and academics are not the people who need to shout from the rooftops about their achievements. They are the quiet ones who achieve the results almost as a side-line thing. Sure, they work hard, but a large element of their greatness comes from the inherent abilities they started with. Ben also had innate abilities, and he did not have to shout about them as they were there before us, plainly presented for all to see. He had nothing to prove, as he had in him that elusive gene which allows you to naturally radiate talent.

However, Ben had another gene, and that one was cancerous.

***

Once when we were at home on the weekend and watching television, there were a lot of adverts for the Race for Life, a cancer research fundraiser. The adverts had hyped up slogans like 'together we can beat cancer'.

Even at the time, sitting there with Ben, thankful for all the medical advancements that had been made so far, I still questioned the assertiveness of these slogans. I knew there were certain cancers that humankind with all its progress so far could not beat. I thought about my friend Robyn, and Ben's friend Krish, and knew their outlook was not good. I knew further research would make things better and I was thankful for that.

I still find it hard when I hear or maybe read a magazine article where people express their views about how they were strong and positive and that is why they were able to 'beat cancer'. Well, if there was ever a stronger person in the world than Robyn, or a more positive and sunny nature than little Krish, I would be surprised. They did not beat cancer, despite the greatest efforts from all.

To me, you do not need to be exceptional to beat cancer. You just have to be extremely fortunate. I do not fear cancer. I am just very respectful of it and its ability to bring down even the strongest and the bravest of people.

I realise people use this strong emotive language to give courage, and the hope that there will be a day when all cancer is eradicated. Like many, I look forward to that day and support the work of these agencies that are working toward it. I realise that giving people going through treatment a boost to be more positive does help some with their emotional state, and this of course gives us all hope for better treatments in the future.

Ben would often talk about cancer after he saw these adverts. He turned to me and said, 'That is what I had, Mummy. I had cancer, but Mr C took it all away and I just have to have this further treatment to make sure it doesn't come back ever again.' That was a good summary of his present state. He was so accepting and trusting.

***

Eventually, Ben's time of radiotherapy was up. The hospital staff had kindly made him a special award for his bravery in action. He was presented with a printed certificate with the Manchester United crest on it. How good to go home and have this short break before Ben had to start his next load of chemotherapy. A brief respite from hospitals, we hoped.

Unfortunately, during the month at home we were not free from hospitals. Ben had two three-day admissions to the Eastbourne District General Hospital because of spiked temperatures. I was now back at work, and so Roddy and I were juggling the many demands on our time once again.

I found that people at work could talk about Ben a bit, as he was alive (unlike Samuel). A few would ask how his treatment was going, which was much appreciated by me.

My boss was especially fantastic at trying to come up with new ideas for how to get Ben interested in food. He even arranged for a relative of his to get a whole box of chocolate fish (a Kiwi treat) to him so he could bring it back from New Zealand for Ben. He was always being creative and trying his best to help. I was very fortunate with his care and desire to help Ben.

I learned that a sick child made more palatable conversation than a dead one. People felt they could do something practical to help, and that was some people's way of showing they cared.

***

Had Samuel lived, the twenty-second of March 2012 would have been his second birthday. After picking up Tom from school, we all went to the graveside to remember Samuel, by sitting there with his body beside us in the ground.

It was such a cold day. When we got to the cemetery and were getting out of the car, we realised that Ben did not have a hat to wear, so Grandpa kindly lent him his woolly hat. Ben grinned for the photos as we each posed by Samuel's graveside.

We were pleased to see that the spring bulbs we had planted together in the summer had come up and were in bloom in time for Samuel's birthday. As I stood there by the grave, Ben came up to me and gave me a hug. Then, as he often did at these times, he looked up to my face to check if I had been crying.

He told me, 'I think that I am going to see Samuel in Heaven one day, Mummy, but it will be a very long time away when I see him.' We hugged, and I was encouraged. I felt like I was being reassured that Ben would live to old bones.

***

My cousin Kirsten sent us a CD by the singer Laura Story. Her song 'Blessings' was written in response to Laura's husband's cancer treatment – the long road that it was and yet how in the pain they could still see blessings. One day I was listening to this in the kitchen at home and tears were present. Ben came into the room, saw me and came to cuddle me. He asked me if I was crying about Samuel.

How could I answer him? How could I tell Ben that, no, this time my tears were for him, and for all the treatment he was having to go through, and how it seemed so unfair? I could not tell him that, as Ben had never once said to me that it was unfair. I did not want to drag him down to my level of misery and anger. I thought my confusion and anguish should not be detailed to Ben.

I was again struck by the wonders of childlike faith and childlike trust. When trouble strikes, we adults often like to see something and someone greater than ourselves that we can blame, and unleash our sorrow and anger on. Yet it has been my experience that children do not tend to react in this same manner. They are far more accepting of what life presents to them.

Ben was very trusting and very accepting. He did not like the treatment, the painful operation followed by many tests, the medicine, and then the difficult radiotherapy and the chemotherapy, and the effects this treatment had on his body. Yet he did not blame God for this.

I do not know what was happening inside Ben's head and how he was being prepared for the future. What I do know is that, despite not liking the treatment he had to face, he still went to it and took it and learnt various coping strategies in dealing with it. In my opinion, this is true bravery and courage. I admired Ben for it, and we could all see the evidence of real depth of character and courage being developed in Ben's young life.

***

Ben's first three-day hospital admission for chemotherapy was scheduled for the eighteenth of April 2012. First, he had to have an MRI scan to check there was no evidence of any further tumours. When Roddy called me to let me know the results, I had to pull over the car to hear the news.

Oh, the joy! What great news. We had something to celebrate – the results were clear! Ben was considered in a great condition to be able to start his chemotherapy. It was such a thrill to hear, and we quickly publicised it to our friends. We were all needing this positive boost, to give us strength to face the nine three-day sessions of chemotherapy ahead over the next year.

Roddy had taken leave from work to be with Ben in the hospital for the three days of his chemotherapy. The vague plan we had was that we would each do alternate three-day sessions with Ben. Roddy was eager to get on with it, and to start ticking off these sessions in the diary.

Ben went in on the Wednesday. He had to have a drip in place for the three days. The drip would either contain fluids or chemotherapy drugs. He bravely began his session. I came down to visit them both on Thursday evening after work. When I walked into the ward and saw Ben lying there, I couldn't help but want to jump up on the bed next to him to give him a cuddle. Oh if only, if only it could be me attached to that drip, I thought. Yet again, we could not take the treatment from him. He had to go through it alone.

That night in hospital, I met the mum of a boy who had also had a medulloblastoma but was two chemo sessions in advance of Ben. It was great to meet another mother caring for a child of a similar age with a similar condition and to discuss treatment and coping strategies. It was also lovely to see her young boy. He looked so much like Ben. He too had no hair, and I suppose baldness can make you look alike as you have less distinguishing features. When I saw him, I felt a real rush of maternal love for him. I was shocked – the feeling was so powerful.

This mum said to me, 'When you come here to the ward you realise how, compared with others, we have it easy. There are so many with a less hopeful prognosis than ours.'

Whilst I felt terrible for the others, I was pleased with the hope she thought we both had. Ben's treatment was to be long and hard, but I believed we would get through it. We just needed to keep up our stamina for a year longer.

Ben's first session was complete on the Friday, and he travelled home with Roddy in time for the weekend. Now would begin a time of trying to help him at home with the effects of the chemotherapy. In the latter weeks before his next treatment, we would also be trying to help his body get stronger, to be in the best position for the next round of chemotherapy treatment.

Mum and Dad needed to return to New Zealand as they were not holders of British passports; they had been with us close to three months and they needed to leave before they overstayed. There were also a number of pressing things they needed to deal with back in New Zealand – including insurance negotiations. This long after the Christchurch earthquake, Mum and Dad's housing situation was far from resolved, and they had a battle to fight. They knew the real battle was being fought in Ben's wee body. But life's other pressing needs were calling them, too.

On the morning Mum and Dad left to fly back to Christchurch, Ben and I walked with them a short distance to a local park overlooking the seaside. After a short time of football with Grandpa in goal, we all sat down, weary, and looked ahead to the vast sea and the hills of the South Downs to our right. We talked of when we next would meet, maybe when Ben had finished his treatment, maybe here or maybe somewhere else. We were all trying to be positive, to look forward to the day when we met again.

Later that day, Ben and I dropped Granny and Grandpa at the train station. As I held Ben's hand and we both waved until their train left and we could see them no more, I wondered where we would be at with Ben and his treatment when we next saw Mum and Dad. I know they left with heavy but expectant hearts. The outlook for Ben was good. Had they known how things were to change, I know that despite the other pressing needs on their time they would never have left Ben that day.

CHAPTER 20

Waiting Again

It was now May 2012 and one week before Ben was due to have his second three-day course of chemotherapy, his headaches returned. It made no sense to us. We were on week five following his first chemotherapy. We had been told by the medics that this was when things should be getting better before he had to have his next chemotherapy.

I found it a difficult weekend. By this stage in the journey, my mood was greatly affected by how Ben was. We had visitors staying, as we had thought Ben would be in a better stage of his chemotherapy cycle, but it was not the case for him. It made for a long and hard weekend.

I had the privilege of putting Ben to bed on the Sunday night. I noticed that he had all his pillows and cushions piled high for him to rest his head. It reminded me of the fairy-tale story of the princess and the pea, and I told him so.

I did not tell him what it also reminded me of. The last time I had seen Ben make this pile of cushions was in December 2011, five months earlier, when his headaches became severe and the brain tumour was found. I had a sinking feeling about those pillow piles this time. It was a deep fear I did not want to have to confront.

Ben loved books. Any and all types were of interest to him. On this Sunday night, he asked me to read a book called *Jesus the Helper*. I read the whole book to Ben as he listened intently. It was a Ladybird book we had found in his Scottish grandpa's house and borrowed for a while.

The book went through many of the stories from the Bible where Jesus helped an individual to recover from illness. At the end Ben smiled at me and said, 'Mummy, that is what Jesus is going to do for me. He is going to heal me.'

I was so encouraged by these words from Ben. As we prayed together that night, I knew we all had to live through the ups and downs of Ben's condition, and have the faith that Ben did – and believe that Jesus would indeed heal Ben.

I believed that, at any time, God could heal anyone. I am a miracle believer. However, I also knew from my experience with Samuel that there are times when God chooses not to heal in this life and not to make our hoped-for miracles happen on this earth. He has the power, but such power is not always used as we would want it to be – that is my understanding.

That night, I left the boys' bedroom confused. I was concerned about the headaches Ben was experiencing, but I was encouraged by Ben's faith that Jesus would heal him. I felt that God was telling me not to doubt, but to know that he would take care of Ben, and for us all to trust Ben to his care. More faith required, even when the future path looked bleak.

***

The next day was Monday and Roddy and I were both at work. I was in London and Roddy in Eastbourne. Both Roddy and I were regularly calling Debbie, our childminder, to check how Ben was. He was not doing well. We were concerned.

Ben awoke with pain in his head on Monday night. On Tuesday morning, Roddy and I agreed that he needed to go to hospital. I had stayed later than my usual train, to check on Ben before I left. As I was dressing for work, Ben sat on our bed and said to me, 'You look very beautiful, my Mummy.' I had on a new dress. It was pink with navy stripes. I had bright pink shoes to match – Ben approved. It takes courage to this day to continue to wear that dress.

I had to go to work. There was no option as I had agreed to collect our friend Melissa at London Heathrow after work. She had flown over to England from Melbourne, Australia to be our Ben helper for two months. She was planning to help out in June and July, then Roddy and I would take some holidays in August, and then Joanna, my sister, was coming from New Zealand to look after Ben in September, and she would coincide with his seventh birthday in the middle of that month. We were blessed with much support.

Tuesday morning, Roddy took Ben to the Eastbourne District General Hospital. Because of the reoccurrence of the headaches they arranged for Ben to have an MRI scan. We waited anxiously for the results. At work, in between reviewing legal contracts, my mind was wandering to the MRI and the results we may hear.

In situations of tension, I try to be sensible and logically work through things. In this scenario, I kept on telling myself that the MRI had to be okay as only five weeks previously Ben had had a clear MRI. It was hard to imagine that anything could have developed in that short time. Colleagues at work kindly tried to assure me that all would be well. I left work early to collect Melissa from the airport.

I had my mobile phone constantly in my hand, waiting for the call from Roddy to hear the results of the MRI. I walked overland to Holborn Tube station, not wanting to be underground and out of mobile reception. I waited down an alleyway, filling in time till the last possible moment to go down to the underground and make the trip where I would be out of mobile phone reception.

In the alleyway, a number of people were innocently having their cigarette break. It is the first and only time that I have ever felt deep anger form within me against people who smoke. I wanted to scream and shout at those people. To verbalise the loud voices in my head. The voices were saying 'What do you think you are doing? Don't you know about cancer? You have a choice in the matter, but there is a young boy whom I love with all my heart and he lies in his bed, a victim to cancer, and what do you do? You smoke in the face of it as if you do not care.'

Another round of waiting had me straight to breaking point.

I had had enough. The smokers copped it.

***

Roddy phoned. It was good news. As far as the Eastbourne District General Hospital was concerned, the MRI had not appeared to be worrying. They did not think Ben's headaches were the result of a reoccurrence of the tumour. I was ecstatic.

Yet still a concern was there. What could his sickness and headaches be?

I collected Melissa, and we coached and trained our way back to Eastbourne. We went straight to the hospital. It was such a hot evening and Ben's isolation room was roasting. On the bed, Ben's small, weakened frame looked exhausted.

A nurse was trying to talk with him. I saw from Roddy's face, his body language, his eyes, that things were bad. The MRI did not appear concerning, but Ben was in a lot of pain and no one knew why.

***

It was not until Wednesday, late afternoon, that Roddy got the call from Consultant S from the Royal Marsden. That day, he had been advised of Ben's headaches, and had not been convinced by the conclusions reached in the report he had received from the Eastbourne District General Hospital. He wanted to see the recent scan, and compare it to the one that had been done five weeks ago, and discuss it with the radiologists at King's College Hospital who had the scans from the start, for Ben's first surgery. After this comparison, he would get back to us.

In the interim, we could tell that Ben was in pain. The medicine the hospital was providing was not touching his pain. He had no interest in anything, and he was suffering, and we did not know what to do but wait.

Waiting is part of the endless cycle of hospital life. We could not change anything during the waiting time. We were totally in the hands of the medics and the constantly ticking clock.

On Wednesday night, when he was back home with Tom and Melissa, and I was in the hospital with Ben, Roddy got a further call from Consultant S. Roddy then phoned me to report that it was the opinion of Consultant S and King's College Hospital radiologists that Ben's tumour had returned but to a different part of his brain.

Ben was going to die.

Roddy told me this news on the phone. He then told me I had to be brave for Ben, and he had to be brave for Tom. He was about to sit down to dinner with Tom and Melissa, and neither of us knew how either of us was going to get through our respective tasks.

CHAPTER 21

Saying Goodbye to Ben

I sit in the parents' room on the blue plastic fake leather couch. Tell me, why is hospital furniture always blue? Behind me is the kettle and the jars of instant coffee, the Nescafe blend, with tea bags and a jar of crusted sugar beside. This room has a wooden cup holder stand, with arms out for the mugs to hang. Lots of different mugs. None match. A randomly sourced motley crew.

So, I am here alone, with only the mugs to converse with. Alone with the horror of this crushing news burning in my brain. I have been encouraged by Roddy that I need to be brave, but what if I fail?

I do the only thing I have ever known to do in times of total human inability. I ask for God's help. I ask God to help me do what is right for Ben, but I have no idea how I will fulfil my side of any bargain I am making.

I don't offer God anything in return. I am an empty and shattered vessel, needing to be filled with strength beyond my own human capabilities.

I ask for all he has got as I have nothing. In fact, it may be better to say that I have less than nothing. I am all out of options for this task.

***

On the day when Samuel died, I had wanted to run away and not enter his hospital room because I felt that by entering the room I was condoning the horrible act. This time I was desperate to get back to Ben's room as soon as possible.

To be with Benny. To hold him, to hug him, to love him. I had a strong desire to be with him, to be with him forever, and to never let him go. I wanted to go with him and never lose him.

I left the blue couch and the florescent light of the parents' room and walked back into Ben's dully-lit room. I saw him lying on the bed. I tried so hard to be brave, but I couldn't. I am sorry Ben; I just couldn't do it.

I went over to Ben. I hopped up on the bed next to him and hugged him and cried. In the midst of my tears, I wanted to tell him how much I loved him.

I wanted to tell him something else. I wanted to say sorry for all those times I had tried to get him to eat in order to keep him strong through his treatment, and to avoid having a feeding tube. I knew it had been such a chore for him and such a friction between us. I had tried my hardest to be the mother who kept him strong despite the treatment he had been receiving. Now he was going to die and none of that effort meant anything. Useless effort, hopeless trying. I wanted to apologise to him for pushing too much. It all seemed so unnecessary now. Futile.

I told him all these things, but I did not tell him he was going to die; that bit I omitted.

Ben looked at me and in his tired and weak state he tried to give me a hug and said, 'Don't worry, my Mummy. It is not easy being a Mummy.'

Through my tears I smiled at my precious boy, and agreed it is not easy being a Mummy. In my troubled state, I thanked him from the deepest part of my soul for his forgiveness of me and my efforts. I realised again that it was not easy being Ben.

That moment with Ben was the gift I was given that night, in addition to the wonderful gift I had been given six years earlier when he was first placed in my arms.

***

For the first time in a long time, Ben was able to fall asleep and get some rest and relief. I did not want to disturb his sleep, so after a final kiss on his wee bald head, I climbed down from his bed and got myself set up in the camp bed there in the hospital room on the floor next to him.

What a night. What a beautiful night. That whole night I lay awake and I cried – softly, so as not to disturb Ben. Lying there, I had so many pictures in my mind of the Benny that I had come to love and to care for. It was as if my mind was a camera lens, and I saw the photos, all in my head, rolling before me from when Ben was a baby to that day. In my mind I laughed and cried as I had the different pictures in my head of our Ben who had the makings of a superstar.

I was honoured to spend that night with him. I just wish it had been a night that never ended. I longed for the sun to never rise.

That night, Roddy told Tom that Ben was going to die. That must have been one of the hardest things Roddy has ever had to do. Melissa was in the house and she told me she had to leave the house, as Tom's cries were too hard for her to handle. How would Tom ever come through this? Ben was his best friend.

***

By lunchtime on Thursday, the hospital eventually had all the arrangements complete to transfer Ben up to the Royal Marsden Hospital for them to assess the best next steps.

Ben was getting his second trip in an ambulance, but I wish he had never had either. I couldn't help but think about the previous ambulance trip with Ben, and the five-month journey since then. I was so thankful we had been given that time. Time that was hard, but also time to stop and focus on Ben and his care and to appreciate the boy he was. To hang out with him with what had seemed like an endless time of treatment. The endlessness now apparently had an end, but it was not the medically planned one. Ben's body had written its own diary with its own end.

The ambulance journey was hard for Ben. He was in great pain. The only pain relief they had on offer was a new type of medicine he had not tried before. I thought, oh no, how are we going to get him to take this? The nurse suggested I try to administer it for him, and so in the speeding, bumpy ambulance I tried to syringe the medicine into his mouth. He did not swallow much and gave me a withering look. I don't know if he was with us, or in some type of coma, as his lips were visibly white. The pain in his head and body must have been intense. He could not speak and did not cry out. He never complained, I don't think he had the energy to complain, but I knew by his look that things were bad.

I was so relieved to get to the Marsden. I gave the nurse who had transferred him from Eastbourne a hug as she and I had tears together.

We were delivered to the day ward and I tried to explain the situation to the nurse, who greeted us with no knowledge of who we were or why we were there. My blurted story got us immediately transferred to a private room.

***

Ben's specialist nurse arrived. She said to me, 'Do you know why you are here?'

I said, 'Yes, we do. We were fortunate to have been given an extra five months with him.'

She responded, 'Oh, I think we can give him some more time.'

At that moment, Ben had a seizure. His first ever. The nurse pushed the emergency button and staff from all directions descended into the room. The hospital emergency crash trolley arrived and they started to work on reviving Ben.

In the midst of the commotion, I could hear Consultant S's voice shouting down the corridor as he ran to be with Ben. He had to have the quickest talk to me as Ben's guardian, to see whether I would agree that they would not revive Ben if he were to require life support.

My only thought was for Tom. In my head those voices were saying, 'But please, he needs to see Tom. It would not be right for Ben to die before he saw Tom.'

I pleaded for Tom. I knew he would need to see Ben and say what he wanted to say while Ben was still alive. Roddy and I had both been with Ben in Eastbourne that morning, but Tom hadn't, he had been at school. He had not seen Ben since being told he would die.

Consultant S asked where Tom and Roddy were. They were following the ambulance in a car. He called Roddy immediately.

Melissa, Tom and Roddy were travelling together. They had been delayed because of a puncture. As Melissa said in her letter that she later wrote to Tom, 'Life intrudes in the most mundane ways at the least convenient times.'

She also told me how she knew things were bad when Consultant S phoned, as Roddy drove with added urgency after the call. They all had to get to the hospital for Tom to see Ben. It was so important. All his loved ones wanted to be with Ben, but it was only me. Me and a stifling room full of medics.

***

Ben held on. He would always hold on for Tom if he could. He would never have left Tom if he had an option. I believe he was given extra time for the purpose of being with his older brother one more time.

When they got to the hospital, Roddy and Tom were speedily ushered in to see us, by which time Ben was not conscious. He had oxygen assistance and was being held on my lap.

I handed him to Tom, who nursed him so lovingly. Melissa wrote in her letter to Tom, 'The next time I saw you, you were sitting in a hospital recliner chair holding Ben and gently touching his earlobes. He was unconscious but he knew it was you. A nurse was sitting with you both and you were telling her all about Ben.'

***

Ben managed to come through that stage and was able in the next few hours to return to breathing on his own without any intervention. Whilst Tom held Ben, the palliative care team talked with Roddy and me as to what would be the best next steps for Ben. They arranged for the immediate future for us to be transferred to a room within the hospital on the in-patients ward.

We were fortunate enough to have the use of two adjoining rooms. A small one for Melissa to sleep in, and one for Ben and us to share. The palliative care team were fantastic. There at the Royal Marsden, the cancer hospital in southwest London, Ben's palliative consultant who was assigned to us was a lovely lady who was originally from Christchurch in New Zealand. Again, I felt that the right people were being placed in our path on our journey, to help us navigate the rough road ahead.

We all had Ben's interest as our top priority and were working together to determine the best place for him to be. No one was able to tell us how long it would take before Ben died. It could take hours or weeks for death to come. No medic could predict it.

I had just endured the ambulance journey with Ben and seen his obvious discomfort at travelling. My gut reaction was to stay right there in the ward. I could not imagine why we would put him under the strain of returning home or to a children's hospice, as both would require a transfer of over an hour. Our home in Eastbourne was now two hours away from us. We were all now in London, not wanting to put Ben through more agony.

It was clear that Ben needed to have his pain under control by increased medication, and he needed rest. Whilst I would have loved to have taken him home, I did not think he would survive the journey. As parents, Roddy and I had seen such a rapid decline in Ben's health in the last couple of days. We could not contemplate that his current state would last very long. We must have been given some extra insight as to the urgency of the situation.

As Ben's pain was now better managed, with an infusion we could give to him ourselves, we started to see Ben eventually get some relief. The intensity of Ben's pain must have been enormous – his head would have been throbbing.

The swelling around Ben's brain was causing pressure which was the pain that Ben was experiencing. We were relieved that he now had a good and appropriate dose of pain relief. What we had to compromise, of course, was that when Ben was heavily drugged he was hardly ever able to communicate with us.

**

We thought that Ben would not ever speak with us again. We were wrong.

On the Friday morning, Ben had a conversation with us all. Melissa encouraged us to record it on our phone, and we did. Listening to this recording never ceases to cause us sadness, but I am glad we have recorded what he said. Otherwise it would all seem like a dream. However, it did really happen. We have our proof.

Ben talked to us about things that had happened the previous day. He had been aware of them, but unable to join in. Notably he asked us why Tom had been given all those football cards and not him. His mind was still so in-tune mentally, it was truly amazing. The reason we had ended up giving those cards to Tom was that it appeared to us they had failed to alert Ben. We had intended using them as a type of bait to see if the sight of them would stir Ben. He had not reacted to them the day before, but now he was able to tell us all about the cards that subconsciously he had been aware of.

We got them out and Ben and Tom were able to sort the cards together into teams, there on the hospital bed. Ben's knowledge of those football cards was still intact. He knew which ones were new, and which ones were swaps for his collection.

What a precious conversation that was as we let Ben take the lead.

Ben loved Mr Men books and so he told us which Mr Men characters he would call each of us if he was writing a book. He made us laugh and cry with his comments and thoughts about how he viewed each of us and which character we would be.

We told Ben about all the people who were sending him their love, how his uncles and aunty from Scotland were on their way down to see him soon, and how Granny and Grandpa and Aunty Jo were coming from New Zealand, and we hoped that they would be on a flight soon.

This puzzled Ben. He said, 'But why are they coming? Granny and Grandpa have only just got back to New Zealand and Aunty Jo said that she would come for my birthday.' Then he said, 'Oh well, I expect I will let her know what I want!'

This confirmed to us that he couldn't have realised at that point what was happening. He thought he would still be there with us for his birthday in three months' time. He was still a child using the brain he had to work out what birthday presents he would be asking for.

Whilst we did not want to be taxing Ben's energy during this time, Roddy did decide to ask Ben two very important questions. At the time I was shocked to hear Roddy speak them, and yet I was so glad he had the courage to do it.

Roddy said to Ben, 'Do you love Jesus?'

Ben said, 'Yes.'

Then Roddy said, 'Do you know that Jesus loves you?'

Ben responded, 'Yes.'

This is faith, when we cannot see, when we cannot understand yet we still trust.

***

Had Ben been brainwashed into believing this faith? It is correct that by being a part of our family, Ben had been told the Bible stories. He knew we believed them, and he wanted to as well. He wanted to fit in, that was true, but he had shown in his character, even at this young age, that he was not a pushover.

I recall once when Ben was having those chats with me in the flat alone during his radiotherapy treatment, he said, 'I wish I was like the rest of my family. I wish I liked soup and fizzy drink.' It made me laugh, as I had never realised he had observed this difference and had wanted to fit in with the rest of us. But the truth was, Ben did not like soup or fizzy drink and could not fake it just to fit in.

I think as a six-year-old he had also not faked his love for Jesus. To Ben, Jesus was real. He was the one he talked to. Who knows whether he talked with Jesus when he did not communicate with us? Who knows what happened in the troubled mind of a six-year-old facing the end of life?

Near the end of Ben's conscious talking, he said something that none of us who were present in the room will ever forget. We had not mentioned Samuel in the conversation, but it was Ben who did. As always, he was still including Samuel in our family unit.

Ben looked up at us with a faint smile and said, 'I just can't wait to cuddle Samuel.'

I responded, 'Maybe Samuel is not that far away.'

I will always believe that this was God present in the room there in Southwest London that day. I wonder whether Ben was actually already being given a glimpse of Heaven in that room, as otherwise, why would he mention Samuel? Maybe we as his family were also being encouraged to hold on to faith, and to know that when our time came, we too would be reunited.

***

That was our last conversation with Ben. It was precious and memorable.

He then fell back to sleep, and from then on Ben was not conscious to our knowledge.

We knew the end was not far off. We spent the day with him. During that day, Tom spent a short time at the hospital school where he meticulously completed a drawing of Buckingham Palace. Tom has never been hugely into art and so this piece stands out for me. He clearly wanted to do it so well, and obviously it helped Tom to be able to concentrate on some outside task. Methodical and careful, requiring brainpower and skill. When the rest of his world was spiralling at a rapid pace, the task of completing his picture kept him focused on something other than the events occurring along the corridor in the room where Ben was.

We told Tom he could come and go from that room as much as he wanted. It was a total open-door policy. Roddy's brothers and Melissa were present at different times to take Tom to play pool or just hang out together. Tom was able to call the shots on their time and attention, as Roddy and I needed to be with Ben.

***

In the evening, when Tom was ready to go to sleep in our shared camp bed in the room where Ben was, we joined together around Ben's bed and we had our family prayer time.

Ben was not able to add his own words, but each of his family prayed for him, that God would take away his pain. In turn we each committed each other to God's care. There was a reverence that night around Ben's bed, where it felt to me as if time itself stopped still. Our words, however hopeless and faint, were each spoken into eternity. It felt as if God was so close that he was actually in the room with us, calming each one of us, and preparing Ben to go with him. I can't describe it any better than that there was such peace during such a time of horror.

Tom was able to rest, as Roddy and I each continued our watch around Ben's bed. I was physically on the bed, curled in next to Ben. Roddy sat on a chair beside him. So we waited with him, and softly told him over and over how much we loved him and always would.

As Ben's breathing slowed, I watched the clock as it ticked by, and realised for the first time what the date was. It was Friday night, the twenty-fifth of May 2012. As we saw the time ticking toward midnight, I wondered whether Ben's last gift to us would be to show us his eternal connection to Samuel, and in turn die on the twenty-sixth of the month, mirroring the date of his baby brother's anniversary the month before.

Ben did it. He held on until the early hours of the twenty-sixth of May 2012, exactly two years and one month after we had said goodbye to Samuel.

We no longer had our dear Ben. Our second son had passed on.

- - -

CHAPTER 22

After Ben

Roddy and I together prepared our dear son's body, in order for Tom to be able to see Ben smartly dressed in his clean pyjamas when Tom awoke. To lose one brother in this life is a hard burden to carry, but to lose another is for many of us impossible to comprehend. Tom's grief is personal to him, and in my writing I will not intrude upon it.

However, I will share one glimpse into the nature and person of Tom. When he was told in the morning that Ben had died in the night, he jumped up next to Ben and gave him a cuddle, then stopped midway and said, 'But will I hurt his port if I cuddle him like that?'

Even beyond the end of his brother's life, he was wanting to protect his brother from harm. My mind was taken back to the time we had been in the hearse with Samuel, driving to the cemetery, and Ben had said, 'Where is the seatbelt for Samuel?'

The care each of my boys had for each other was a beautiful thing. When they were taken from each other it was heart-breaking to witness. Their depth of love and concern for each other as siblings only served to deepen their pain as they were separated from each other by death.

We told Tom that he would no longer be able to hurt Ben. One thing was certain, Ben's pain had now gone, the world could not harm him anymore. Tom gave Ben a big cuddle. He was his best friend. Tom was only nine years old.

Tom later left Roddy and I with Ben and went through to the next room to find Melissa. He asked her if she knew that Ben had died, and checked that she was alright. Melissa greatly appreciated this and his non selfish care of others. It was unexpected, but again showed Tom's loving nature.

***

Roddy's siblings came to see Ben's body that morning. We cried together.

I felt for my family – my Mum, Dad and my sister, Joanna – who were still in the air travelling, en route to Singapore at the time Ben died. I wanted them to hear the news from us, but I did not want to email them even though they had asked me to update them if there was any change. When they had sacrificed so much to help us and care for Ben, it felt wrong to tell them his precious life was all over by email. Once we knew their flight was in the air again from Singapore, on the last leg of their journey to London, we could then tell others in the United Kingdom, as there would be no danger of Mum and Dad inadvertently hearing from another source. This was after all my child, and it was a small ask to make, I thought.

We decided to stay in London that night. We booked into a hotel near Heathrow airport, so that we could go and collect Mum, Dad and Jo when they landed at 6.30 am the next morning.

We had to leave the hospital, and leave Ben to be transferred to the mortuary. As Ben lay in his hospital bed, with his clean pyjamas and his wee bald head resting on the special cushion, with the teddy bears, that he loved and that his Granny had made for him when he was born, I looked for the last time at my son and my friend. He looked absolutely beautiful, he looked at peace.

But this scene before me was all wrong, so very wrong. This once active, lively boy now lay still, with a faint smile on his lips and a serenity that defied the situation. How could we ever leave him?

***

When someone dies, the world around does not stop. The shops still sell their produce. The walkers still stride down the footpaths. The children still play in the park. After death, everything was different in our world, but nothing had changed in the external world. Life for others ticks on.

We drove away from the hospital and delivered Melissa to the train station so she could return to Eastbourne to give her and us some space. We went to a local store, got some sandwiches and went to the park. What a mistake that was.

It was a sunny Saturday at the start of a UK bank holiday weekend, and the park was heaving with life. Parties of friends and families had formed, and they were laughing and playing and enjoying the warmth of the day. Boisterously celebrating life. Yet our hearts and world were cold and numb.

Ben had been to this park. In the many hours we had to fill in after radiotherapy, we had occasionally sat here. If he had felt alright, we had played. If not, he had sat on the bench with me and watched the other children playing.

I saw a bush where Ben had once hidden in a game of hide and seek. Two boys close to his age came bursting through it, laughing and chasing each other. Yet our son, our boy, was lying still in a hospital mortuary up the road, not able to chase anyone anymore.

How can I describe to you the pain? I can only say that it hurt beyond a definition of pain that I can describe. Everywhere I looked was hurt and sadness. Even in the joy of those boys' games, I had sadness and hurt.

Aching is a good word to describe this type of pain. It is constant, it is unrelenting, and it aches. The bitter emptiness of shock and loss once again. The world we were facing as a family was dark. We had no option to hide, nowhere to go.

***

That afternoon, once we had checked into the hotel and each cried at the things Ben would have liked there, and Tom having been struck by the fact that Ben would not be sharing his hotel bed, we decided to make a few phone calls.

It never seemed an option to us to just shut off. The world around us needed answers. I think, if left on my own, I would have escaped like a hermit, away somewhere, and turned off the phone. But I felt a responsibility for the rest of our family and friends, so did not succumb to my natural instincts. Maybe it was best that way. If I had hidden, when would I ever have come out from solitude? Like a family friend always said, if you fall off a horse you must get back on straight away or else you will never gather the nerve to do it. I wonder, if I had escaped would I ever have gathered the nerve to get back on the horse of life again?

Life just continued. It may have been preferable if a pause in the universe had occurred, but if life were to pause at each death then life would be paused eternally.

For me, the hardest phone call to make was to my friend Robyn, but I was determined she was not to hear the news from anyone else but me. The last we had spoken, Ben had been doing well. His rapid decline had not yet come to her attention.

Even in her own fragile state of health, I had to share our news. Only two weeks previously, Robyn and I had sat together in her summer house talking about the hopelessness of her own situation with cancer. We had physically held onto each other, knowing the pain of our own future separation. I had left her house feeling terribly guilty. How come Ben's cancer journey was looking so much better than hers? I had felt awful that we were so lucky and Robyn and her family were not. Yet I had been encouraged by what she had said to me that day.

She had said, 'No, E-J, do not feel bad, as this is the right order. However bad it may be for me and my family, I have at least lived a life. I am my age and Ben is only six years old. This is the right order.' I now had to break the news to her that the order had not gone according to plan and Ben had been taken first.

There were many other friends we had to contact. We chose to do some personally, as they had been there beside us supporting us on the sidelines all the way. It felt wrong to let them hear this news some other way.

When I shared the news, I tried to encourage each of them who had a faith like ours to continue to hold onto their faith, and to trust that Ben was now safe with Jesus. I did not want anyone to fall away from faith due to God's will not being our will.

**

The next morning, we went to Heathrow airport. We waited nervously to see my family come through the double doors. I have no idea how he did it but Roddy had helpfully arranged with an airport worker that we were able to use a quiet room near the arrivals gate, for us to break the news to my family. It helped that they gave us that place away from the stares of the public to share our very private grief. Yet as soon as Mum, Dad and Jo came anxiously through the arrival gates and saw all three of us there together at the airport, they knew what had happened. They instantly knew that if Ben had still been with us, one of us would have stayed with him.

The grief of our extended family is and always will be something hard to bear. I can write of what I know, and that is that my family's lives are changed forever. The loss of Samuel started that process for each of them, but the loss of Ben sealed it. Their journey through grief has been hard to watch, as I realise it is because of me they have had to face this. Had I never been in their lives, then this grief would never be theirs. I have been the cause of their suffering.

I also give thanks for my family grieving with us and sharing the burdens that we bear. To me, my family are an example of what it is to carry each other's burdens, to walk with each other in our pain. Each of them has truly grieved with us, and they do not forget and have not abandoned us but continue to share our sorrow.

It reminds me that in times when others are grieving, sometimes I do need to step out of my own comfort zone and make an extra effort to have this regular contact. I found walking the road with others to be helpful. If I in turn have regular contact with grieving people, I am not going to be able to take away the fact of their grief, but I may be able to help them with the pain of isolation that many do feel when tragedy strikes.

CHAPTER 23

Remembering Ben

We returned to Eastbourne. We were an unusual household. There was Roddy, Tom and me, Mum and Dad, Jo and Melissa, and Murray, Roddy's older brother. Despite this odd household tribe, the dynamics seemed to work. We were grieving together and supporting each other in our loss.

Murray was fantastic; he simply played endless football with Tom outside in our garden, while Roddy and I were free to prepare for the funeral. Melissa cleaned – she would admit it herself, this became a little obsessive at times. I'm not so sure what the others did, but no doubt they were always looking for a job, something to fill their minds, to fill the time, the endless time that lay ahead.

***

Before Murray returned to Scotland to collect his family for the funeral, he returned his hire car to Brighton. He took his nephew Tom with him. While they were waiting for the train back to Eastbourne, they saw a band setting up their sound gear at Brighton train station. It was the accompanying group for Stuart Townend, a contemporary Christian singer and songwriter.

Out of all the people who were in the busy railway station randomly while the band was setting up, Stuart came and sat with Tom and Murray to chat with them. Somehow, the conversation got around to why they were there, waiting at the station. Murray explained what had happened, and as a result Stuart sent his love to the family. (We had never personally met him before.) He said if there was anything he could do to help, then please get in touch. He gave his personal email address to Murray.

There was something Stuart could do.

As Roddy and I were preparing for Ben's funeral, there was one song I felt I would like us to sing. It was called 'There is a Hope' and it was written and sung by Stuart Townend.

When I mentioned it to our music director, who would be leading the music at the funeral, I was surprised to hear that he was not familiar with the song. He said he could learn it, but a lot of people attending the funeral may also not be aware of it. It might not have such a good impact as a more familiar song. We understood his point and agreed to include a more familiar song.

I did not feel at peace about not having that Stuart Townend song. That night as I tried to sleep I kept on thinking, well, the person who does know that song and does know how to sing it is Stuart Townend, and he has told Murray that if there was anything he could do to help he would, so why not ask him? I mentioned my thoughts to Roddy, and he agreed it was worth a shot.

An email later and Stuart had agreed to sing this song as a solo at Ben's funeral. He was returning to Brighton from a tour in Scotland on the Monday evening and Ben's funeral was scheduled for the Tuesday. We could just catch him before he headed off on another trip the next day.

I had to smile at what Ben might think of this. In my car I had two CDs I had played a lot since the passing of Samuel as I found the music to be an encouragement to my soul. One was Graham Kendrick and one was Stuart Townend. If I played them when Ben was in the car, he often would say, 'Is this Graham or Stuart, Mummy?'

***

I had to pick the clothes Ben was to wear forever. No daily change of clean pants, though I knew he needed them. For his coffin, I was allowed only one pair. One pair for the first day, but what about the other countless days he had to spend in them? I gave him pants and long trousers (despite the season, I thought he may be cold). I also chose a long-sleeved shirt. I thought this would suit Roddy's Scottish ways. Smart. Then there were the socks, Ben liked socks. But I gave him no shoes, because I wanted his shoes for me. They were reminders of Ben. I did not want to put them in a coffin where I could not get to them. I have since regretted not giving Ben his shoes. I feel that the outfit was incomplete. What use is a full set of clothes without the shoes? My efforts were a half-pie job, I tell myself.

I was embarrassed when I handed the clothes to the funeral director in our lounge room. It was those annoying pants, I felt embarrassed about the pants. I felt I had to explain to the director what the need was. Weirdly comical, I suppose. But achingly hurtful.

***

Ben's funeral was another hard but wonderful day. I recall having some of the same feelings I'd had with Samuel's. This was the one day I could celebrate my child's life. For him there would be no coming of age, no graduation day, no wedding day. This was the one day we had been given to share all the joy Ben's life had brought us.

At the start of the service, photos were played of Ben's life with music accompaniment. It was very similar to what I had envisaged that Wednesday night I had spent in hospital with Ben before he died. Seeing the photos roll by caused audible sounds of sadness and grief from the congregation. Roddy had lovingly compiled this wonderful photo and music tribute to Ben. He had chosen a couple of songs to be played in the background. One was 'Blessings' by Laura Story. The other was 'Find Your Wings' by Brent Miller, which tells of all the hopes and dreams we have for a youth – yet in our case they were not to be fulfilled.

The photos Roddy included spanned from the first day of Ben's life to just days before the end of it. The common theme throughout those photos was Ben's ever-present, radiant smile. It was a true testimony to a child who had lived life and lived it to the full. Roddy had tried to include photos with as many people as were present with us on that day, and even with those who had been of an earlier time with us but had since died.

There were gasps in the congregation as they were shown photos of Ben with Samuel. For those who had never seen Samuel before, it may have been a reminder, and to each of them it told a story of just how much sadness we had experienced. Seeing Ben's proud smile as he touched and held his baby brother would have to break any hardened heart.

***

Once again, we entered the church following a coffin. I held Tom's hand firmly. This time, Roddy alone was not able to hold the coffin, but he was ably assisted at each corner of the coffin by his three brothers Murray, Donald and John. I was glad that this time Roddy was not alone, but again there should never have been another time. Surely one was enough?

Ben's service was a reflection on his life and the hope we had for his future. Roddy and I each did a separate eulogy about Ben's life. We were sad, but somehow amidst it we were even able to get some laughs as we retold some of the funny stories about Ben. In my speech, when I mentioned some key people in Ben's life, I looked up to seek them out in the audience. I tried to show his brother and his young friends, by a look, just how much he had loved them, and how much we understood they were missing him even now.

Prominent in that service, I saw Ben's coffin. Placed as the centrepiece, so near to where he and his young pals had hung on the communion rail as they listened to the children's stories during numerous children's talks at church each Sunday. Yet Ben would never hang on that rail again. He now needed no barrier between him and God, as I believed he was with God and was in communion with him.

How odd it felt, that the two youngest in our family knew so much more than their older brother and mum and dad about what the future life holds beyond this earth. If they could return to us, how much they could teach us. Yet seeing that coffin there, I knew that Ben would never return to us. His body filling the physical space on that altar confirmed that for me. Whether I had been in denial before I don't know, but seeing his coffin brought the reality home.

Stuart Townend sang at Ben's funeral 'There is a Hope'. Forever those words are with us, and I will always remember how on taking to the stage Stuart nodded towards Ben's casket, took off his cap and placed it on the piano. Stuart is known for wearing his cap even when inside and playing the piano, but this simple act spoke volumes to us of the dignity and respect he showed to Ben that day. Thank you, Stuart: it was not unnoticed. What a gift you gave to each of us on the day that we celebrated Ben.

Again, the right people were being placed in our path.

***

This time as we left the church in the 'special car', as Ben and Tom had named it at Samuel's funeral, we were not able to travel with Ben's body as he was too big. His was not a baby coffin, so we travelled alone. How silent it now was.

As we entered the cemetery that Ben knew so well, I felt in a sense that we were bringing him home. He had explored this place through the many times he had come to visit Samuel. He had played chase on all the paths, and spotted rabbits playing in amongst the graves. I knew with certainty that Ben would want to be buried here.

Yet as I saw his lonely plot, dug on the hill as the first child to be buried in this consecrated land dedicated for children, I cried out in protest again at why he had to be on his own. Yet I also wanted him to be on his own for a very long time, as no parent should ever have to bury their child next to him. I did not want to inflict this pain on anyone.

As we buried Ben there that day, and as the last person threw their handful of dirt on his coffin, I looked up and over the tops of the other graves to where Samuel is buried. I whispered to Roddy that I wanted to go and visit him too. I knew it was Ben's day, but it seemed wrong to be at the cemetery and not visit Samuel's grave. We moved towards Samuel, and the close family and friends who had accompanied us decided to follow. One by one, they followed.

How come these two children are so intertwined that I can still never grieve for one without the other? They are my sons and I love them equally, and the only reason I think I had the strength to leave the cemetery that day was because of their older brother, who I also love dearly, and who now had a lifetime ahead of him to live with the pain of their loss.

Since that day I have had the feeling that if Ben ever returned to me and had a chance to speak, his first thought would be to say, 'Mum, look after Tom.' I held onto that as a guide, going forward from that day.

CHAPTER 24

Our Community

t was not just us as a family who grieved for Ben. So many people loved and cared for Ben, and his passing had a huge impact on the community where we lived.

As mums, we often think our children are lovely, kind and good, and cannot see the bad in them. I am no different with Ben. From the time he was a very young age, I saw him as a gem. He was one of those fortunate people it was a joy to know. I could go on and on for a long time about the many different qualities of Ben, but you might not believe me as I am his mum.

It might be best to let others do the talking, and to let you read some of the many letters and cards we received when Ben died. How he had touched and affected so many is amazing to consider. He was only six and had only been living in Eastbourne for four years, but his loving nature shone through to those he met.

His teacher and Ben's school class created this tribute:

A Poem for Ben from Miss Bateman and Year One

B is for Ben. Our friend now and always.

E is for energy. You had an energy that would lie waiting like a Lion until something would make you burst into action like a torpedo.... There was usually a football involved!

N is for 'never, never, never giving up!' That was our motto and you demonstrated it quietly and confidently, helping your friends to do the same.

M is for having a marvellous, mathematical mind. You were always one step ahead of us in maths – especially me!

C is for calm kindness. You thought of others and put them before yourself. This was not for a reward, just because you chose to.

N is for no fear. You weren't afraid to 'have a go' and your friends would often follow in your fearless footsteps.

I is for inventions. In star select you could be found 'inventing' a magical machine or splendid spaceship, deep in discussion with your fellow 'professors'!

C is for cool. You are Mr Cool Ben, you wouldn't give much away until a wry smile would creep onto your face and we'd soon be giggling with you!

O is for outstanding! You worked hard to achieve what you wanted, earning a rainbow card for getting all your spellings right.

L is for love. Although we miss you in our hearts, there's not much space for sadness when it's taken up by all the love we have for you, our Brilliant Ben.

Some of the children in Ben's class (aged five or six) wrote down their own thoughts…

'We should write our thoughts in a star shape as Ben was a star'

'I shall miss his jokes and laughter'

'His cheeky smile always lifts our spirits'

'I gave Ben a big cuddle on our first day at school, I think I might have kissed him once'

'He was always kind to his friends'

'He was a comedian'

'I think that Ben will be an Angel in Heaven'

'Ben was nice to us in school so we can think about him with Jesus having fun on the bouncy clouds'

'Time goes really quickly in Heaven because there's so many enjoyable things to do. Ben is playing with Samuel and one day, Mum, Dad and Tom will be with them too'

Ben's godmother, Iona, wrote:

'How sorry we are you have lost Ben, your darling Ben who was loved by so many of us. He was an absolute star who shone out so brightly and one of my strongest memories I will cherish is how he danced on the spot whilst talking to us. He was so brimming with energy and fun and he was so caring too and kind…. We will always love Ben and remember the precious, lovely boy he was.'

Others wrote:

'There is comfort that Ben will bring as much happiness into his new world as he did in ours'

'Your beautiful sweet natured boy of whom you'll always be so proud.'

'Ben was such a very special boy, so kind and sensitive to everyone around him with a lovely sense of fun, we will always remember him so fondly in our hearts.'

'Ben was such a special boy with his little smile that touched everyone who had the privilege of knowing him however briefly.'

Many people wrote to us and thanked us for 'giving them Ben'. When I think of all the love that there is and was for Ben, I am so glad that we shared him with others.

Had I known that he was only to have a lifetime of six years on this earth, I imagine I would have taken a break from work and stayed at home with him. I would have tried all manner of economics in order not to go to work for those six years. I am glad that I did not know what the future had for him for many reasons, but one reason is that we were able to open for him a world beyond our front door, where he thrived and developed to the loving individual we all adored. Ben started nursery on the day of his second birthday. The teacher he had that year wrote to us after Ben died and expressed what pleasure it was to have Ben in the class. *'He was absolutely delightful and really did make me smile every day he was with me.'*

As his family we are so proud of Ben and who he was in the brief life that he was given on earth. I do wonder whether he was given a lovely nature just so that we always knew how fortunate we were to have him in our lives. From a very early stage of knowing Ben, Roddy and I would often comment to each other just how special he was and how fortunate we were to have him.

Does Ben's great personality make the pain of our loss any greater or less? My mum often wonders whether we would hurt any less had he been a more difficult person to love. I am sure it would hurt just as much, but you would also have the difficult burden of carrying regrets in your thoughts of the dead person. You might recall about how they frustrated you and how you lost your patience with them. I am not saying that Ben was perfect – who is? I am also not saying that I never lost my patience with him. I can recall the year between one year old and two years seemed a constant battle between Ben and me, in the challenge of restricting him from mischief. The 'no' word was a constant on my lips.

But despite all that, he came through at a young age to be very special. A true friend. Ben was given gifts of wisdom and courage well beyond what would ordinarily be expected of someone that young. I often hear people talking about how young children are quite selfish, that they have not yet developed the ability to think about others. This was not the case with Ben. I can retell numerous times when he looked out for others. He saw the need, and acted, and changed the situation. It used to impact me at the time, as I thought often about this gift he was given. Even at four years old, he displayed this gift of caring for others. His nursery teacher in his school report for spring term 2010 wrote:

> 'Ben is a happy, sociable member of the nursery, showing increasing independence. He is concerned about his classmates; in Dance when Mrs Robinson asked everyone to make a circle, one boy did not want to hold a girl's hand, so Ben removed himself from where he was and went in between the girl and the boy without being asked. He has a strong sense of belonging to his class and to his family.'

At Ben's nursery, the highest award was to gain a Headmaster's Award. One term, Ben received one of these awards, for 'being kind and helpful and helping the others in his class'. At the time he received it, the nature of the award stood out to me. All others on the list were for measurable academic achievements, yet Ben's was a personality trait they had spotted in him and rewarded. I was so proud of him as to me the achievement in character and personality is of highest value. We knew from an early stage that we were given a treasure.

Ben was bright at his academic work. He had surprised me in this as I thought he would be focused on one thing: sport. I was wrong. He loved to learn and was whizzing through his school books at a rate that kept his teachers busy choosing new ones to send home. After Ben died, many children told us how Ben had helped them in their schoolwork, especially maths. Ben had not told me about these times. He did it to help others. He was a bright, unassuming individual who did much good in the community he was placed in.

When he was no longer in that class at school, they felt his loss greatly. A memory book with photos and thoughts about Ben went with his class every year as they moved forward through the school. In memory of Ben, a blossom tree was also planted on the school field, with a wooden seat running all around the base of it. Together with other school families, we spent an afternoon planting spring bulbs at its base. This lone seat around a beautiful, flourishing tree on the school field is a place where the children can go and sit and have fun, and maybe some of them also take time to remember Ben.

Yet their lives will go on toward other schools, other communities, other adventures. Ben's tree will remain, and each year as spring comes round again, the blossom will burst forth into new life. Other children will sit at its base and play.

In the first year of losing Ben, our dear friend Dee surprised us by placing fairy lights around the tree, so when we walked past it in the evening the lights shone out for Christmas. What kindness. Thank you, Dee. It can be the 'little gestures' that make such a difference. How can you fail to smile when you see a beautiful tree lit up with fairy lights?

***

Our church community also grieved with us. With Samuel we had not experienced the same level of support we did with Ben. I assume this was because many people never met Samuel. They cared for us but may have felt less connected to Samuel, and they did not want to intrude. On the night that Ben went to hospital for his brain tumour to be removed, Roddy contacted someone within our church and the word got out.

We are so grateful to the praying church and wider Christian community that formed that night and remained tight and resolute to pray for him and us throughout Ben's treatment. The group formed unofficially, and continued to meet regularly throughout Ben's treatment, on a Thursday night in our church in Eastbourne. It was not usual for this to happen if a church member was unwell. Even the vicar of our church wrote to us and said that rarely in his time as a vicar had he seen so many from a community come together in communal prayer for one individual.

The Thursday group was such an encouragement to us all. I was pleased that it was not an exclusive group formed for our church members only. They were regularly joined by our other friends in the wider community, some from other churches or others who just wanted to be there to feel it was something they could do in a time when they felt helpless. They wanted to gather with like-minded individuals to bring their petitions for Ben to God.

I never personally attended any of these prayer and praise sessions, as I was caring for Ben, but we had feedback from many.

I know that it meant a lot to Ben. Sometimes on a Thursday, Ben would say to me, 'Are they praying for me tonight, Mummy?'

And I would respond, 'Yes.'

He would think about it and then give me a smile and say, 'That is kind.' I think he wondered why he was being prayed for, but I think he also realised that they must have cared for him, and that did help him to feel loved. Ben was not keen on being the centre of attention, and so we did not push the fact that it was just for him, but I think underneath he was secretly pleased that they cared. That wry smile that his teacher knew so well.

We had developed an email update, prompted by this Thursday group requesting a weekly update about Ben's condition. We sent it to many of our friends and family. Roddy took on the job of sending them. As a couple we did not take time to analyse the situation together. We just did the tasks allotted and worked smoothly as a team. But as I read the group emails each week, it was often an insight to me as to how Roddy may have personally viewed the week so far, and his outlook on the weeks and months to come.

Roddy and I were enormously grateful to these individuals who took on the role of praying for Ben and us. One friend who attended these meetings commented, 'I think that boy has 24-hour prayer.' We had friends throughout the world who were praying, as were their churches and support networks. We were blessed and encouraged that those others, whether nearby or far away, cared enough to sacrifice time for Ben.

I heard feedback about these Thursday sessions, and I understand that there was much pleading for Ben's healing and a miracle to occur, even when things humanly speaking were not looking good. I am thankful to these people for all their efforts, and I believe like each of them that at any time God could have altered the situation. He could have healed Ben, but he chose not to. This is what our family and those who stood beside us in prayer have had to come to accept.

Some from that group wrote to us after Ben's death and said the following:

> 'The church is weeping for you – and trusting in the resurrection'

> 'Standing with you at the cross in prayer'

Thinking of these comments, it tells me that we have nowhere else to go. When life fails to make sense, you need to find an anchor, a place to put your hope.

After Ben died, I tried to encourage each of those we knew in the group that their prayers were not in vain. Ben had died at peace. He had died with a sure and certain faith in Christ, which had only become stronger through the illness he had suffered. Ben never once, to my knowledge, questioned God for giving him cancer, and never once blamed him for his pain. I blamed God, but Ben did not. The fact that his faith had not diminished but strengthened instead – surely that alone is something for us to be thankful for? How can someone in adversity end up being so grateful and trusting of God?

I often wonder whether God was at work preparing Ben prior to his death. I think of how God may have been speaking directly to Ben, and giving him that courage to face each day with the illness he had, and to show us the way to being content in each and every situation. My mum often says that if she can be as brave as Ben if illness comes to her door, then in her opinion she will have faced illness well. How can someone so young teach a person of ten times his age?

I do not think the prayers of so many fell on deaf ears. I simply think that God's will was not to give the answer that we as humans desperately wanted. As Christians we are called to trust God and his purposes, his action and inaction in our lives. This can be tough, but we must walk on in faith even when healing does not come to those we have earnestly prayed for.

I realise that as humans we cannot and will not ever be able to beat death. We of course, in time, will be able to develop new treatments and even cures for all manner of illnesses, but one day each of us will die. This is the only certainty of life, that we will each die.

I wanted to encourage others to be ready for it as Ben seemed to be. In the hopelessness of that hospital bed as I held on to my dearly, dearly loved son, and held him to his final breath, I realised anew that the only true hope is in having a faith in something beyond this world and all its empty promises, as no one can defy death. Only Jesus has conquered the grave.

***

Our community of friends would continue to support us, even in the times we lived far away. If we were not in Eastbourne, then our friend Janet took it on as her task to head to the boys' graves and clean them up, and send us photos on key dates. Birthdays. Death days. She gave us an update on what the cemetery was like on the day she visited, transporting us mentally to the spot. What a friend. What kindness. What a joy it was to receive those regular updates.

Others in the community have visited the boys' graves and found some form of communion and peace there. For some, they visit when death of their loved one has first struck. They have found it to be a place to escape from the world and all its chaos to seek a place of refuge. These stories they have shared with us. For one dear friend who has also lost two children but has no final place for their physical resting, she has also found comfort in borrowing or sharing our boys. Their graveside is a place for her to go, to sit and to think of her loss. We hope she can find some peace. Dear friend.

In Janet's photos, we often notice a new toy or plant beside one or both boys' graves. We often have no idea who has been to visit and placed it here, but it cheers us. We know the boys are loved deeply, even in death, and that makes us smile.

After Ben died, our friend Sarah started a project at the school where Ben attended the nursery. She planted a memory garden. There in the courtyard, with class windows looking on and children with heads down studying, are wooden seats with memory plaques referencing students who have died, or parents of students from the school. There were strangely a lot of deaths within our tight-knit community at a certain period of time that prompted Sarah and the school to undertake this project. Ben shares a seat with two parents whose grieving families have become special friends of ours. Years later I had the privilege of taking my parents to this place for their first visit. It is a beautiful spot, and we needed no words to express our emotion at being there. Sitting on Ben's shared seat, hearing the hum of activity in the school grounds. It is a place of quiet reflection in the midst of the mass of activity of a thriving school. Ben thrived there, and his memory remains engraved upon a plaque, and on many people's hearts as they continue in this school community.

As we cross the road from Ben's nursery and see his tree planted in the primary school field, I am filled with hope. I think of the love that the community gave and continues to give to us. As that tree grows and spreads out it blossoms, year in and year out, I am hopeful that much good can come even out of the ashes of our burnt hopes and dreams.

CHAPTER 25

The Ben McNicol Trust

The idea of the Ben McNicol Trust was born when Ben's good friends, the Pipers, were holding their annual charity café a couple of months after Ben died. Their youngest son Rufus had been one of Ben's closest friends. They all wanted this year's café to receive donations for some charity to help children like Ben.

Rufus' mum Sarah said to me, 'E-J, what can we do that would be specific for Ben? We want it to be for him in some way.'

Roddy and I wondered about setting up a fund for sick children, or some sporting grant to benefit disadvantaged children in our area who showed a real talent for football. We had a lot of ideas and not much clarity, but the Pipers trusted us and proceeded to run the café for the benefit of 'The Ben McNicol Trust'.

We were amazed, as were they, when the afternoon café in their back garden raised over one thousand pounds. This was more than they had ever raised for charity in previous years. We realised that within the community there was a lot of support for doing something specific to Ben's memory. As the community had deeply grieved with us, they also wanted to honour Ben's memory in some practical way.

We opened a new bank account for the Trust, banked the cheque, and thought about what the best use of this money and goodwill would be. I looked into the logistics of setting up a UK registered charity and began the process of applying for gift aid status with HMRC. We looked out a standard Trust Deed and appointed the Trustees.

It was Roddy who came up with the idea of Ben's House. As Roddy said, the greatest help to us in our journey with Ben's cancer, apart from the excellent care at the hospital, was the provision of a flat so that Ben could stay nearby and not have to do the four-hour round trip each time we had to be at hospital. We had used the flat through radiotherapy, but on subsequent trips and tests the flats had all been taken. We had to pay for accommodation, which was not ideal given the lack of privacy in the hotel environment. The alternative was to wake Ben early to drive to the hospital from home.

There was a need for more flats, so that more children and families could benefit from this provision. Our initial enquiries to the hospital showed they agreed this would be a wonderful asset.

We found the flat useful, and the journey would have been many times harder had we had to travel back to Eastbourne each day after radiotherapy. As I was the one who stayed with Ben at the flat there were also many difficult memories for me about our time there. They were precious times with Ben, but they were also challenging as a parent and carer.

I thought of other parents and children who would have to go through the same as us in Ben's House, and I realised how hard would be the stories of those who stayed in the accommodation. Some of course are success stories: the children live. However, the ongoing issues that can be experienced by children who have gone through cancer treatment are not minimal. All lives are affected and all lives are changed in some way.

We thought a lot about what Ben would have wanted us to do. He was such a caring and loving boy. We thought he would want to help the other children who were in the Royal Marsden Hospital. Often, when he was home from treatment, Ben would pray for the children in hospital, that they would be brave, and that they would get better, and that the doctors and nurses would look after them well. It seemed right to do something for those children who were to follow Ben, and not to forget them, as he showed by his example that he did not forget them. The Trust was formed for this primary purpose.

***

The task ahead was daunting. There was a lot of money to be raised. A two-bedroom flat was the goal. At the time we began, a price of at least two hundred thousand pounds was required. It was no small ask. In the early stages of the Trust, I had some sleepless nights, worrying whether we were doing the right thing with the money people had already entrusted to our care. I felt the burden of the responsibility we had taken on.

We were also amazed at how many people wanted to do things for the Trust. I think it was a practical way that people, who had felt so helpless to know what to do or what to say after we lost Ben, could show their love and care. People wanted to see something good come from the legacy of Ben's dear life.

We were, and maybe always will be, still grieving. The first event for the Trust happened only two months after Ben's passing, and it felt like a rollercoaster ride from then on.

Roddy and I handled most of the administration of the Trust ourselves. Neither of us were experts in charity law or website design, but we had to learn, and keep our day jobs going as well. Now that the Trust is established and flourishing, I would not want to stop it, but at the time it was first established I did wonder whether we had over-committed ourselves, and simply added to the pressure of an already pressurised existence. Despite the fact that we received great encouragement through people's generosity there were times I just wanted to stop all the activity and close the doors and grieve, but there always seemed to be another Trust event to attend.

Somehow, Roddy and I were given extra strength and support during that first year of the Trust. At a time when we were both so raw with our grief, we each made speeches and held back the tears in front of new and diverse-sized groups. We pursued funding from various sources. We took the risk and exposed ourselves and our grief, when we were still at a very vulnerable stage.

I am by nature not someone who finds asking for help or money from others very easy. In 1999 when I ran the London Marathon, I paid a large proportion of the required sponsorship money myself as I found it so hard to ask others for sponsorship. Now here was I, one of the lead Trustees of a charity, needing to ask for donations and to challenge others to do the same. Talk about outside my comfort zone!

In all this work, I was encouraged and inspired by Ben and his bravery. I knew his house would help others. So, I had to stamp on my own pride and work towards the goal we had set. After one talk, a lady told me afterward how she thought that I was so brave. I wish I had responded, 'Not nearly as brave as Ben.' Ben was our inspiration for the Trust work.

We wanted to complete the tasks in the manner Ben would have, had he been able to. In all of our speeches, Roddy and I tried to mention some thing of Ben's faith, to plant a seed of the hope Ben had. We wanted to use these opportunities to share, ourselves, some hope during much sadness.

We also received setbacks. Some were major, like missing out on being nominated as the charity of choice for a work corporate event which would have raised a substantial amount for the Trust. The amount could have got us over the threshold. We missed out because it was perceived to be supporting a colleague, me. There was no way I ever wanted Ben's House for us. I had one child still living, and did not want him to need specialist cancer care so that we could stay in Ben's House. The operators of the event did not fully understand this. It hurt when our charity was not given the same platform as other large charities, but we kept pressing on.

It is hard being a small charity, as you are less well-known. Also when raising money for a property there are some organisations who will not give to capital projects so we missed out.

Roddy had two wise comments which helped me handle the rejections better. We have both kept those thoughts as a guide. Firstly, he advised that we resolve, if it is appropriate in the circumstances, to tell people about the Trust once. Then, if they showed no interest we would not push it but stand back and move on. Let them do the follow up, when and if they felt led. We did not want in any way for Ben's name to be linked to a feeling of loathing or dread, like some salesperson or insurance broker who has not understood the word 'no'. Roddy also advised that we must never allow ourselves to feel any bitterness towards those who chose not to support the Trust. Roddy said that was the last thing Ben would want to leave with us as his legacy on earth. He was not a person to hold grudges or speak ill of people. We were determined not to let him down by allowing bitterness to take hold.

**

The positives about Ben's Trust were and still are many. They well out-weighed any setbacks we have had. Through the work of the Trust, Ben's courage and life story reached many people. Those who had not even met him were inspired to raise money for the cause. We saw and continue to see such generosity from many on a large scale, and we are so thankful for that. I can never stop thanking those who have and still do support the work of the Trust. We have seen creative thinking in the ways people have raised funds both young and old. We have been so grateful to you all. It has been a total joy to behold and experience.[2]

It has been our experience that doing some of the small things – for example, a sweet stall raising less than one hundred pounds – can give you the opportunity for other events. We have met people through these smaller events who have become interested in the Trust, and have also been keen to take on larger fundraising activities. From small seeds great trees can grow.

The work of the Ben McNicol Trust has also helped me in other ways. Some of the people who had hurt me before by not acknowledging aloud to me either Samuel's or Ben's deaths, showed that they did care by getting involved in activities of the Trust and raising funds. They still did not ver-balise that they were sad Ben died, but they did something practical, and this helped restore my positivity for people.

The Trust has also provided a way whereby people who perhaps don't know how to speak of Ben or Samuel have found a voice. Instead of asking us how we are doing, people ask how the Trust is doing. Through this inter-est they are showing that they care.

---

[2]   check out the website at www.benmcnicoltrust.com

So much good has come from the Trust work. It has helped many of us to work towards a common goal. It has drawn a wonderful crowd of supporters together.

***

As we continued to raise money, property prices were continuing to rise in London. It soon became evident that the initial goal of two hundred thousand pounds would no longer purchase us a suitable property near the Royal Marsden. The Trustees took the bold step of pulling out at two hundred and fifty thousand pounds and purchasing a one-bedroom flat, with the intention in the future, if funding allowed, to upgrade the accommodation to a two-bedroom flat. We needed to get on the property ladder first.

It was with great anticipation and excitement that we purchased Ben's House in December 2016. Ben had left only a few coins in his money box, but the full provision of funds had come within only four years of his death.

A friend wrote an article about the Trust in a local newsletter in Christchurch, New Zealand. She wrote:

'Ben had an unshakeable belief and a quiet realisation that Jesus would look after him and be with him in Heaven, just as he'd been with him here. Ben serves as an inspiration to us all. Moreover, the actions of the extended family, in establishing the Ben McNicol Trust, show that the outworking of grief can be a beautiful thing for the lives of others.'

Ben's House is rarely empty. Children and teenagers and their families are using it and being comforted by it. We were not living in England when Ben's house was purchased. Roddy made a special trip from Australia to England to the house before it opened to fit it out with all the comforts flat may need. He worked hard for a week, painting and furnishing the flat. As a result, the flat is beautifully kitted out with two single beds in the bedroom and a sofa bed in the lounge, to allow for additional family members to stay. Roddy has tried to create a true home-from-home feeling in the flat, aiming to provide each child and their family a warm embrace as they enter its door.

Two years on, in September 2018, I first had the opportunity to visit Ben's House. It has been so well cared for by the Royal Marsden Hospital, who manage the families' stays. The tiles in the bathroom were gleaming. I have no idea how a cleaner can do that, but they did. It made me smile. What a wonderful gift for families in such need. I could not really believe it was real, but it is, and it serves the community well. What a wonderful legacy from a boy who lived and loved others.

From the day Ben's House opened, and for as long as it exists, may it continue to be a blessing and a comfort to many cancer children and their families. Let it be a safe place. A house of refuge. May it also be just like what Ben's Granny has done by embroidering a special sampler which hangs in Ben's House, with all of Ben's favourite things represented on it — the continual outpouring of a labour of love.

CHAPTER 26

Missing Ben and Samuel

hen Ben died, I not only lost a son, I lost one of my closest friends. I had grown to love having Ben in my life. His family would all agree that life is just not as good without him.

Ben brought much joy and laughter to our family. We have photos to remind us of him, but we long for him to still be a part of our daily lives. I found Tom looking at a photo on the wall of him and Ben, and I let him talk. He said to me, 'Mum, I just wish I could get back into that photo and just be there at that moment with Ben again.'

How true. That is what we all desire, for the Ben we knew and loved to be back with us here on earth, not just smiling in one dimension, flat and fading on a wall.

I grieve for Ben and Samuel. The feeling of grief I carry is a physical longing. I often feel an ache in my stomach. This ache comes from the very base of my stomach. At other times, the grief hits me and I cannot breathe, as if there is a blockage in my throat, and I find myself gasping for breath.

There are periods of time where the tears just flow. I cannot stop them. Do tears have a limit? Now it seems that I have a constant supply. What will it take to prevent a flood one day? It's as if someone has opened the taps and then lost the controls. It is impossible to turn them off again.

Tears are a release. An outpouring of my watery love for them both.

Crying for me is a cleansing, a releasing of tension that builds up. The process can be physically draining. It cleanses me, but does it heal me? I don't think I want to be healed of sadness and grief. I want to always be sad that my children died. I don't think that is a bad thing. It is okay to cry. It is okay to be sad. The loss of a loved one in any circumstances is a sad and broken time.

There are occasions when all three physical reactions happen at once. I may find myself buckled over with the pain in the stomach, trying hard to breathe, and tears are flowing. This clearly is part of the physical side of grief.

For me, this is often a private grief. I have a lot of private tears. Sometimes they come on in public. In these instances, I panic. I have to get out, away to cry in private. For me these tears are a solitary experience, best not shared with the world at large. I suspect the world doesn't want them.

Grief also affects my mind. At times I cannot stop thinking about what happened on the day that Samuel's tube was taken out. I berate myself and think, Why was I so calm? Why did I allow it to happen? I should have protested it more. I should have shouted from the rooftops, 'No, no, no.' Why did I accept it at the time as the right thing for Samuel?

Then for Ben I think about when the cancer started growing in his head. What day was that? Was it a day that I was at work, or was I at home or on holiday? How could such a momentous event occur behind my back

I was his carer; how could I be oblivious to the fact that something had triggered in Ben's body, allowing the cancer cells to start growing rapidly, forming one after the other. Should we have spotted the signs earlier? Then I think, but a child being sick does not make you immediately think: cancer. Realistically, how could we have known? My mind is still in disbelief with the reality of what happened. It will take serious lengths of time to accept it.

Grief has also changed part of my personality. I am less confident than I once was. This may be because my world has experienced such uncertainties. Or maybe it is just that, without my boys, I don't have the family comforts to hide behind. I find this odd, as I was never previously a person who seemed to need others in my life to justify my own existence. I wonder whether I had adjusted to having the others in my life. Particularly without Ben here with me as I had known him well and what it was like to have him in my life, I now feel incomplete.

***

My confidence is shaken in small talk. With friends I have known for longer and for whom I don't have to do the small talk, I seem to cope better. Meeting new people and getting to know them through small talk can be challenging. Often the small talk about my life quickly reaches levels that most new people don't want to enter. It often starts with a person innocently saying, 'So how many children do you have?'

If I answer truthfully, they look at me horrified and blunder out a rapid response, and try to change the subject or get away from me as fast as possible.

If I say, 'We have Tom,' and then leave them to conclude whatever they want from that, I immediately find it feels for me an empty conversation.

The assumption that Tom is an only child does not tell the true story of our family. The three pregnancies, births, and lives of the sons who are always connected to us.

I realise it is very hard for the people who stumble into asking the question about my children. I told Roddy about one experience where I met someone for the first time, and I felt I mishandled it. Roddy was not berating me, but he is a true realist. He said to me, 'You have to understand that these people have probably never, ever had that conversation with anyone before in their life. It is the first time they may have heard of one child's death, let alone two. They are not quite expecting your response. So don't expect that they should know what to say.'

I would have to say that Roddy has different expectations than me about people's ability to react well. He was probably right in that situation. I had expected more, and I misread the situation, and was disappointed at someone's lack of ability to respond well to me.

This, like countless other similar experiences I have had, just underlines to me the fact that my ability to make confident conversation has been reduced since the death of the boys. It will take practice and time to rebuild it.

***

When I think of what we as individuals and as a family suffer because of our loss, I can fully understand people who, when faced with these circumstances, develop deep depression. I see it as an option every day for myself – I will not deny it. I have to make a concerted effort not to let the depression take over the reality of daily life. I try not to focus on what has been taken from us, but to think of what we have been given. Even those boys who were later taken were also first given to us as a living gift to love and care for. That is something I can be thankful for.

The fact that I have not, as yet, suffered from a clinical form of depression does not in any way make me any better than someone who has. The reality of my mental health just means that I am different, and in some way have been saved that further level of hurt and angst on top of the pain we already experience in our daily life. I am not in any way saying I will not need that help in the future.

I would also add that just because I have not entered some form of medical grade depression does not mean that I hurt any less than those who have.

I think of the efforts I made after Samuel died that caused that elderly lady to think we did not hurt, and am now so glad that I did. Had I been unable to cope with daily life after Samuel's death, what would that have been like for Ben in what we now know were the last two years of his short life? Thank goodness he was not consumed with worry for me. He had enough to be sorting out for himself.

People often describe grief as a process. As if someone has to travel a similar journey from the very depths of despair out to a new and different world where happiness can be experienced again. A couple of months after Ben died, I was encouraged by a colleague at work, who I had opened up to, to 'move on' and to 'try to be happy'. The friend's email suggested I just needed to 'get harder and stronger' and then happiness would follow. Whilst I am thankful that she tried to help me, I do not think that becoming tougher is the answer. I think that sometimes my soft and vulnerable state is just a true reflection of what human grief can be.

Of course, there are numerous times I have to be brave and face life front on. I do try hard. But I do not want my experience of grief to make me hard. I want to be a part of life and to still feel emotion, as to me this is the very essence of being human.

***

It would be great to feel happiness again, one day. I often wonder whether, without Samuel and Ben in my life, I can ever be truly happy again. In this world, to be happy and to experience happiness seems for many people to be the ultimate goal. Yet what is happiness? Wikipedia states: 'happiness is a mental or emotional state of well-being characterised by positive or pleasant emotions ranging from contentment to intense joy'.

I have always had a very positive outlook on life. It was one of the qualities that Roddy commented on about me in the speech he gave at our wedding. Yet my positive outlook has been shaken, worn down by the illness and death that has struck my family. I am cautious and wary of the future, because I know that sorrow in life is not always dealt in equal measure. Who is to say I will not and cannot experience any more? My next tragic event may be just around the corner.

Okay, so now I am sounding negative, the very opposite of achieving a happy and fulfilling future. I don't think I have developed a negative view on life. It is just that I realise life is not all as we may want it to be, no matter how hard we try to make it that way. We can't try to be happy as happiness is not a contrived affair.

There was nothing I could have done to change the tragedies that happened to my children's lives, no matter how many positive thoughts or attitudes I exuded. Negative events are a fact of life. I acknowledge that, but I still struggle to think that I could be happy with my life going forward. To be happy, for me, is to be in a state of existence as if those events had not happened. The deaths of my children are not just events, they are import ant people taken from the total equation of my life and my life story. To live as if they had not happened would be a false state of existence.

Since losing Samuel and Ben, the feeling of intense joy has been taken from me. You know, that feeling of freedom and lightness and laughter, with nothing inhibiting it. That is the feeling that has gone. Since losing the boys I have a permanent inhibitor in my life.

If I analyse this, I can see that my ability to 'be happy' was already dealt a harsh blow with the loss of Samuel. After Samuel, if we had any apparently 'happy' events to celebrate as a family, I would take part and smile to the world, but there would always be someone missing in my mind. It was hard to kill that instinct to be a killjoy and shout out to the others in the room, 'But why are you all apparently happy when Samuel is not here?' It did not make sense to me that we were celebrating a birthday without him with us.

We only had a short time between our tragedies, but prior to Ben being diagnosed I was starting to feel some measure of 'happiness' again. Once we knew about Ben's cancer, I was shaken into realising we had to be happy as we had him with us. We had to appreciate and make the most of the time we had with him. I did not waste energy or reserves in considering that the life we had with him may be limited, until it was.

Now Ben has been taken, how can I be happy?

I do acknowledge that in the future, life may hold many good things, either directly in my life or through the joy of seeing good events happen or other family or friends. I can feel some joy for them. Yet in events that would have been shared with Ben and Samuel, there will always be a bittersweet taste in my mouth. Even in life's great celebrations. For me, the experience of intense joy has been stolen.

**

What of contentment, though? I think I can aim at that. Contentment is different from the passing experience of happiness. It is a more fulfilling experience to be truly content, not just the fleeting hype of happiness.

Since an early age, I have been aiming for contentment in life. Since my teenage years, I have had a favourite sentence in the Bible: 'I can do everything through him who gives me strength.' This has been a guide to me through many stages of my life. Not in my own strength but with the power of a spiritual force within, guiding me on.

Just before the sentence quoted, Paul, the writer of the book, talks about learning to be content in whatever circumstances we have in life. He says, 'I am not saying this because I am in need, for I have learned to be content whatever the circumstances. I know what it is to be in need, and I know what it is to have plenty. I have learned the secret of being content in any and every situation, whether well fed or hungry, whether living in plenty or in want.' And what is this secret? What had Paul learned as a prisoner in a Roman jail? He had learnt to do all things in Jesus's strength alone, not on his own. I have found that in my own strength I fail to achieve contentment each time, as there are things in the world that I cannot control. Having a deep relationship and reliance on Jesus, through the good and the bad in life, I have found to be essential and necessary. I don't feel alone in this. I am strengthened and supported.

This is true contentment. Not a smug existence but an understanding of a longer-term hope and a deep-rooted peace.

***

My view on the world around me has changed through the experience of having Ben and Samuel in my life. When I see sick children out in public, I have a desire to race to their side and lend my support to them or their family, but I know that this would be wrong. I have to respect that family and their privacy. Seeing sick children is a reminder of my boys and their struggles. I want to say to these families: you are not alone, we do care. I always find myself wanting to offer a hand to help. Yet how do I do this without appearing nosey and unhelpful?

If I stare at a bald-headed child, I am thinking how wonderful they look. To me, all bald-headed children do. Ben did that for me. When children lose their hair, I think it makes them look similar to each other. To me they look beautiful. A bald head reminds me of Ben.

Yet if I stare and smile at them, the parents may think I am sending out the opposite message – not of love but of curiosity, at the very time they want their child to 'feel normal'. I get that. Didn't I just write about how when we were out in public people would sometimes stare at Ben's bald head and that upset Tom? I don't want to be guilty of the same. So I force myself to be blank and not arouse suspicion, or to look away out of respect for the child and family who I assume want to feel normal.

If a child has a feeding tube or some obvious physical disability, again, I feel a connection with them because of Samuel. But I am faced with the challenge of how I can use this one opportunity to show empathy for them. I cannot imagine a way this can be done without causing embarrassment and drawing attention to the child, when all the carer wants is for everyone to ignore them so that they 'feel normal'. However, it is the very fact of their abnormality that has drawn me like a magnet to them.

These people do not know my story, and even if they did, maybe they would not want to hear about it. No matter how unwell their child is at the moment, they are still with them, and while there is life there may always be hope. To some, our story is just the opposite of that. In human terms, it is a hopeless story. Having help from us or hearing about us may be the last thing parents struggling with their sick child want to be confronted with.

So I turn away from these children, knowing that I cannot enter their world as my intrusion may be unwanted. I cry again for the imperfectness of this world, and for their pain, and my total helplessness in the face of it.

***

When Samuel died, a piece of me was taken with him, and with the passing of Ben a further chunk was chipped away. I am a different person than I was before our loss. Experience of such loss does change you and your perspective on life. How could it not?

We live each day with the reality of their passing. The world around us has constant reminders of our boys. Whether we are near to where they lived or many thousands of miles away, their presence is still real. We see the reminders, but others who are new in our lives do not know. They just see from the outside. To them, we are a family of three. They were not privileged to know the five.

I am a mum; how could I forget my children? Would you forget to think of yours if they were away some place on their gap year? No, you wouldn't. You may wonder each day what they are up to, who they are meeting, and are they happy? It is part of the job of being a loving parent to think not only of our own needs but also of those of our children. It is no different to my experience of my children who have died. I still wonder each day what my children's reality is. Are they just decaying in the cemetery, or has their spirit passed on and they are now experiencing a new creation?

I wonder, and the only difference from my wonderings to yours about your travelling child is that no matter how long I wait at the post box I am not going to get that postcard to inform me of their whereabouts. No need to check my messages by phone, email or social media as they won't be calling. I have to work out myself, with the tools I have been given, what their reality might be.

CHAPTER 27

Asking Big Questions

Is Heaven Real?

After Ben died, and over time as I thought about our loss, I was struck by two major questions for God. These thoughts had not struck me to the same degree when losing Samuel. These two thoughts are probably best explained in this excerpt from an email I sent to my dear friends Netty and Judith, both mothers who had lost babies themselves and who I met after losing Samuel.[3]

'The loss of Ben has sent me down a different course than Samuel. With Samuel I think that I felt a bit more certain re Heaven. I did not question the logistics of it. However,

---

You can read their stories on www.undertherainbow.org.uk

since Ben's passing I feel even more determined to 'know' that Heaven is true, that it does exist, that we can all 'fit in'. I feel concerned that I have given Ben such hope in a place that I have no certainty (apart from through my faith) exists – how can I put it? Ben was so real. He was our son, our friend, he was solid and as a result I cannot imagine him in a waffly place in my mind. It needs to be firm and certain.

'The other thing that I am having to grapple with involves the mountain of pain that Roddy, Tom and other close relatives and friends have been given in the loss of Ben. It is so hard to see what good can come from that pain. How easy it would be to become bitter, angry and jealous, which are all the fruits that we are told in the Bible not to display. How can we produce good fruit from this bundle of pain? And yet it seems to be happening (the good fruit that is). So many have expressed how they have been 'touched' by Ben's passing and our faith. But I struggle with whether for that alone was the only reason for Ben's existence. Was it only meant in order to bring others to Christ? What about our happiness and our family struggles?'

In order to deal with my first question, I looked through the Bible to see what God reveals in it about what Heaven is physically like. When considering the size of Heaven with the Bible's description, I am concerned with the logistics. Can the walls actually fit us all in? The Bible tells us the dimensions of the heavenly city, and by my human calculations it is not big enough. So if it is true, then that must mean we each have a smaller body in

Heaven so all can fit. Or is the Bible giving us a figurative description here and not a literal one? My research from this source gives me no answers.

I also wonder how Heaven caters for children. Samuel and Ben died when they were only young. Surely they cannot and will not spend all day praising God? That does not sound fun for young people. Yet the Bible indicates that they will. Therefore in Heaven do you think we will all be of an age that can handle that, and that wants and desires that? Or do you think Heavenly praise will be so joyous in God's presence that my earthly wonderings are non-comparable? I ponder whether our natural personalities are changed so that we all fit this image of a continually-praising being. Or in Heaven when I get there will I see Ben doing the things he loves and Samuel chasing after him? Then I am back again to the fact that Heaven may be too small to play chase…

So much, so much we do not know, but I trust and hope that God has got the logistics right. I suppose he did create the world, and that has worked for a long time. It is only human intervention that has ever unstuck the equilibrium. In Heaven, I presume that humanity won't be able to muck it up.

I also think about the fact that Heaven cannot just be a repeat of our lives here on earth. What I mean is: how can we be a family in Heaven? That is what I desire to achieve: a 'normal' family life in Heaven. These are the things I have been cheated of, because of illness and death, here on earth. But what would Heaven then be like for those who did not have a loving family here on earth? I believe that I have to accept that Heaven will not translate into my boys running into my arms and staying with me for all eternity, and yet that is my earthly desire for what Heaven should be. However much I desire that to be the case, it can't be correct, as how unfair to others would that be?

Heaven must be radically different to our earthly existence. Not many people think this way, and I have no biblical statements to back me up. These are just my wonderings. But these wonderings are so deeply necessary for me. I can't be pacified by cheap words and empty thinking. I want facts, but they are hard to seek out whilst limited by my own earthly existence.

People try to encourage me by talking a lot about my family's presumed glorious reunion when we all get to Heaven. They think this will satisfy me. Surely that is the hope I must hold on to. I know they are meaning well and want to bring me joy, but silently it is my belief that it cannot be a reunion as we would imagine it here on earth. If it was, then for some it would mean just a transfer of a tough life up to Heaven. By my calculations that can't be right. And Heaven must be right. Must be perfect. I am pitching a lot on that.

My hope is that I will have the joy of seeing my boys in Heaven, but I realise that in order to experience completeness in Heaven I do not need anyone other than Jesus to be there. He is the completion of Heaven, and it is his presence that will be of paramount importance. I believe that in Heaven, Roddy and I won't be any closer to our boys than we will be to a total stranger. This is hard to accept, as I deeply long for their embrace and to be special to them, but I think it is also a wonderful thing to accept, as it shows how we will all be complete in Heaven. It will not be dependent on the presence of others there; it will be God who is its true completion and perfection. God in his infinite wisdom and power will somehow miraculously make each one of us complete in Heaven. My longings will fade away as I finally see what I was designed for.

My random thoughts on Heaven do not lessen my desire to encourage others I meet to consider their eternal destiny, and to have faith in a world to come after we die. But Heaven is not about us. So different to earth.

where we have often made ourselves the centre of the universe we inhabit. Heaven, I believe, is all about God and our completeness in him. It is the wonderful new place he has created for us to enjoy and be perfectly fulfilled in. Notably it will also be about a perfect union of his people with him, and maybe my confusion and thoughts are all because I don't yet know what it is to live in a perfect world. My imperfect view restricts me.

What we are told for certain about Heaven in the Bible is worth reading and focusing on. It is enough to satisfy me that my key concerns for my children are met there, and that Heaven will be good, exceedingly good. Perfect in fact. Reading these sections from the Bible gives me a taste for what is to come, and it makes me hunger for more.

'Now the dwelling of God is with men, and he will live with them. They will be his people, and God himself will be with them and be their God. He will wipe every tear from their eyes. There will be no more mourning or crying or pain, for the old order of things has passed away.'

While on earth, I still long to know more about Heaven, as I believe it is my children's forever home. However, for now it is a matter of having to wait and see, and having the faith that all will be revealed to me one day. I am also aware that on the day it is revealed to me, it will no longer matter. All my questions will be answered, as I will see it for myself as a reality. I will know peace.

The key things that matter are covered in that section of the Bible just quoted. No more pain, therefore disabilities (CHARGE Syndrome) and illnesses (cancer) will be no longer. No more dying, therefore the relationships we make there will be forever, and they will not be hurtful as all our tears will be wiped away.

For the moment, I have concluded my wonderings about Heaven with belief that God tells us as much as he thinks we in our earthly state need to know about Heaven, and no more. It is my opinion that God does not want us to be concerned about the details of our heavenly existence. He does not want us to be so filled with heavenly detail that we miss the daily details of life on earth that we can have an effect on.

Heaven will be what Heaven will be. No amount of my wondering can alter that. We have been shown a glimpse of Heaven in the Bible so that we may spark a desire and want to go there, but he has not taken off the whole wrapper. We can still be filled with anticipation – like a child in the sweet shop longingly looking at the wrapped lolly, knowing that the best is yet to come when the wrapper is removed.

Does Suffering Have Meaning?

The second question I entrusted to others in my earliest struggles after Ben died, is what good can come of so much pain in our lives? Surely as a family we had had enough with the loss of Samuel? Did we require further refining?

We each felt pain in increasing measure. The initial stage of being thankful that Ben's illness was now gone wore off to reveal a question: but why was he given that illness to start with? How could this death ever have happened? These were the burning questions in our minds.

Surely God could have stopped at just giving Ben cancer, as that was a hard enough challenge. Why did he have to take it to the point of death? What good could ever come from the death of someone as kind, loving and faithful as Ben? He still had so much good he could do in this world, and what a great witness he would have been, had he been allowed to live. What a great ambassador for the power of answered prayer he would have made. Surely that would have been a better result?

But instead we were given yet more pain, hurt and broken dreams. How were we ever to survive without Ben's love in our lives? Did God not care that he had taken the joy from our daily lives and replaced it with sorrow? How hard it was for the ones in our family who were left behind. How would we cope? Did anyone care about us when, long ago, the life-limiting condition was allowed entry into Ben's body?

I felt deep burning anger at God for not answering the prayers for Ben as we had requested. I knew I had to somehow get to a point that I could accept his decision, yet it was far from easy, and it was deeply painful to accept.

The pain from God's decision was exacerbated by comments from other people. I felt deep hurt when people tried to justify Ben's death. I acknowledge that this is because others in our life were struggling with Ben's death themselves. However, instead of letting us all just communally agree it was a bad and painful thing to lose a child to cancer, there were people who seemed to feel they needed to go further – to sort it in their head, to find an answer to what I believe in earthly terms is not explainable. People needed to justify it. For example I was told, 'Ben had a good life. His six years had been better than another's sixty years.' Did that justify him having to die? I don't think so.

I was also told, 'You don't know what Ben might have been saved from in the future, had he lived,' My response is that we do know God had not saved him from some future matter, as God had only allocated those years for Ben. My faith causes me to believe that God knows each day he has allotted for each one of us. The six years and 225 days were planned for Ben, and no more. I don't think God saw something bad in the future and then changed his mind about Ben's future and suddenly thought let's make Ben die now to avoid the future catastrophe. That future catastrophe was not planned for Ben.

But cancer was.

The ongoing hurt of losing Ben, the lack of acknowledgement of our loss by some people, and then the justification for his death by others caused me to develop anger, hate and bitterness towards God (who I believed could have changed things). I didn't want to feel this way, but I felt as if God had let it happen and could have saved me from this. When death takes your child from you, you are broken. The truth is, I was probably then, and still am now, highly sensitive. I suppose it is some sort of defence system I have in me to preserve the memory of Ben and Samuel. To believe that their lives were just as important as any other one on earth, and the early end of each life did not need to be justified.

I could see that bitterness could take root in my life, if I allowed it and did not address it.

I am far from perfect. This statement does not spring from any 'guilt complex'. The closer we come to God, the further away we realise we as humans are from his perfect character and his perfect presence. I have come very, very close to God. Put simply, I have had to. It has come to a point in my life that I either carried on with God or I broke the relationship. Why would I break it? Because he had not done what I wanted, so why stick with him?

The God I talk to is not far away in some holy city, enshrined and untouchable. He is right there beside me in the room with me, palpable and real. My conversations are deliberate and direct. When I am angry, I say so. Yet my anger and probable revulsion does not deter God. Living at the extremities, I have found God to stay the course with me. He is still there, ready to listen to my rants – the vents, hurts, pains – however discomforting they may be.

A friend once told me she thought it was my faith that had got me through the loss. It is true that faith in a God who knows pain and ha experienced rejections and suffering is my anchor. But it is also true that my faith could easily have broken me at this time.

I have faith in a God of miracles. He could have changed things, but he did not. I believe he can move mountains; I believe he can cure the otherwise incurable; I believe that healing Ben would have been simple for God. Even the doctors thought it was going to happen. They were not expecting miracles, they just expected that the prescribed medicine would work. We were not calling for the impossible.

Yet God did not save Ben for more days in this world, despite our pleas. I do not understand why he made the decisions he did for my family, and this is still a very deep and unanswered hurt. But it is a hurt that I have to navigate how to live with.

I do believe that God has not abandoned me. I speak to a God who has known suffering. He has taken on human form, flesh and blood, and he has suffered in that body. He is not immune to pain itself. He is not remote, he is present. There is a book in the bible called Psalms. Some parts use poetic language as a way of talking to God or about God where it refers to God's concern for all our worldly pain. In the fifty-sixth Psalm it states:

'You keep track of all my sorrows·
You have collected all my tears in your bottle.
You have recorded each one in your book.' (NLT)

I have experienced the spirit of despair and felt the pit of grief deep within my being. But when I am there, whilst it feels as if I cannot breathe, I have a sense that I am not alone, despite my physical aloneness. I think that there is a God standing beside me collecting all my tears. In my broken state, I feel the need to go back to him daily and ask for him to deal with all my sadness, anger and bitterness. I ask for his strength to live with the decisions God has made, and also in time to learn how to forgive others.

It was time for me to move beyond my judgmental approach to some of the comments I received. I needed to understand how to forgive.

Can I forgive?

Forgiveness does not come naturally to me. I acknowledge that none of the people I am seeking to forgive ever actively intended to hurt me. They would each be sorrowful that they have.

Despite the fact that many did not intend to hurt me, the reality is that I have been hurt. That hurt needed to be dealt with.

I find that I want the person who hurt me to acknowledge that they have done so, and then ask forgiveness from me. Yet it does not happen that way. The people who hurt me do not know they have done it. I imagine that they have long since forgotten what they did or said. At the time I should have probably addressed it, but I was too raw to do that and missed the better opportunity.

I realised sometime after the loss of Samuel that I had to take active steps to learn to forgive the people who had hurt me, in order for me to let go of the bitterness and be free again. It was not easy. My flesh-and-blood response is to want to feed the anger. But I knew it would only ruin me if I let it take hold and smoulder.

It has not been easy to throw off the desire to hold on to hurt. The struggle to hold it is in constant battle with my alternative desire to forgive.

I honestly believe that I need to be proactive and choose to forgive. I do not want it to be superficial forgiveness. I want it to be forgiveness that lasts. If possible, it is my desire to not only forgive but also to forget. To me forgiveness does not feel complete without forgetfulness.

As forgiveness has been hard for me to do on my own, I decided at an early stage to hand it over to God. It felt too big a battle to try to fight on my own. So at many stages of the grief journey, I have simply named the person I need to forgive for their comment, action or inaction. I have asked God to work the miracle in me, and cause me to forgive them and then to forget the hurt. I have told him that on my own I don't want to forgive them, so he needs to work out how it can happen. I don't know what may work for others, but I do think that forgiveness is necessary to free us from further hurt. This has been my way of coping, and it has not been a perfect path, more of a deliberate plod. Recognising that I am hurting, naming it, then waiting for a change to occur. If I didn't face up to the problem, then it would likely fester and affect relationships on an ongoing basis.

In my journey toward true forgiveness, there is also an element of caution in place. I am now at times in a weak and vulnerable position. I do not seek to be hurt again. I believe there are measures of self-preservation I need to put in place, to minimise the likely occurrence of future hurt. One tactic is not to actively pursue the company of someone who has hurt me deeply, as I know it is not likely to be helpful to me. My sister Joanna, who has also had to walk her own journey with hurt and pain from others in the loss of her nephews, would say sometimes for these people there is extra grace required, but we won't always need to put ourselves in their path again, especially if we are feeling raw.

If I am in the presence of someone who I have been hurt by, I am amazed at how being free to forgive them has happened. I also see an element of humour in the process. There have been a couple of incidents in my life where I have needed a helping hand with something, and who has been sent to help me? Why, the very person who had been insensitive to me or had chosen to ignore my story. A person I had named as someone I wanted to forgive. These are the last people I would ever have wanted to feel indebted to. Yet they have been placed in the position of my helper, which forces me to acknowledge that they never meant harm, and I can move on without bitterness toward them.

When we put our faith and trust in God, and hand to him our weak and wilful nature, he is in the business of working those miracles in our lives, and helping us to be people with forgiving and forgetting hearts.

***

Maybe for others, the path towards finding forgiveness of hurts is different. Maybe it has not been your struggle. But if it has, I encourage you to find ways to address the issue. Don't let it fester; it will only consume you.

It is still early days in my journey toward full forgiveness of others, best described as a work in progress. I don't think I could have done this in my own strength. It has taken supernatural assistance. I expect I will need God's strength my entire lifetime to complete his work of love and forgiveness in me.

Just because bad stuff happened to me does not make me exempt from needing to display Christlike attitudes such as 'love, joy, peace, patience, kindness, goodness, faithfulness, gentleness and self-control.' I read that list and the descriptions weary me. I realise how far I am from reflecting them in my life.

I get angry with God. I have sworn at God. I have shouted and raged. I also get angry at others. There are various trigger points for me. The worst trigger event is when my own family, Roddy or Tom, are sad, and I don't cope well with it, as I think it would be different if Samuel and Ben were with us. I want to lash out and scream at God, 'How can we be good and kind when you have given each of us such a pile of hurt?' I want to protect them from further pain, but I can't. It can be a daily, dependent struggle for each of us to rise out of the anger that so easily entraps us, and to walk on with joy.

***

I often wonder whether we would be helped if, for just a short time, Ben were to come back to earth and walk into our home to see us all again. What would that be like for us? Would he admonish us for ever doubting God's planned time for him? Would he tell us to stop being angry and bitter and instead live with a peace that one day we will be in Heaven? To use the time that we have still on earth wisely? Would seeing either Samuel or Ben, and them giving us the message that they are okay, be enough to help us through each day and to live each day with greater purpose and urgency?

The father of Krish, the boy who had radiation at the same time as Ben, said to me at Krish's memorial service, 'E-J, if I could only just see Krish again, to see him, if only for a minute, and Krish would say to me, "Don't worry, Dad, it is all okay. I am safe," then I could be at peace.' I totally agreed with him. Wouldn't that be the answer to our tormented souls? Just to be able to know for certain that our children are safe. Yet, not having this moment of time with our children and still believing is the very essence of faith – believing when we cannot see. I am leaning on God's promises that Heaven is real, and that God will help us to be the people he has designed in us, irrespective of the pain of loss in our lives.

The only reason I can get up each day and exist is in Christ's strength alone. In my own strength, bitterness or jealousy can creep in. However, in God's strength I hold on to the promises he has made for us. Promises where he says he has plans to prosper us and not to harm us and promises for a hope and a future. I cling on to these promises for Tom, as I am continually hit by what he has to face.

Tom is very private, so I do not know the depth of some of his struggles since losing Ben. Roddy and I know as much as anyone in his life what it must be like, but even with this knowledge it is still only a surface view of his pain. I do know for certain that Tom and Ben were as close as two siblings could be. Now that Tom is left without Ben's support and love in his life, he has additional struggles because of it. It is not easy for him, seeing other families, and it is not easy for him only having us at home and not a brother to be with.

Despite his present reality, Tom's experience of a world where he had a sibling is still with him. He has not forgotten how good it was to have his brother with him, and he cannot pretend that his brothers did not exist. I think if asked, Tom would say his greatest hurt at not having his brothers is the feeling of loneliness that he has each day. He deeply misses their companionship.

It is not just having Ben's physical things or photos around that make Ben a part of Tom's ongoing life. It is seeing other siblings and the relationships they have with each other. It reminds him of his loss. Tom is pleased when siblings get on well, and if he sees young children holding hands or helping each other, he smiles at me – no words are needed. I realise he is thinking it is a reflection of his relationship with his brothers. However, if he sees siblings fighting or not helping each other or ignoring each other, he can become very upset.

Once, we were sitting at home and he told me about seeing two brothers fighting at school and saying how they did not like each other. Tom looked up at me and gave me the most earnest look I think I have ever seen. I realised some important message was about to be passed on. Tom said, 'Mum, they just do not know how lucky they are.' The intensity of how Tom told me this will always stick with me. He did not need to tell me any more. I knew the life lesson that he had learnt the hard way. Here were these boys who did not appreciate what they had, yet Tom, who had been such a good big brother, had known the love of his siblings but had had that taken away.

Many times, I am reminded of how Tom has learnt so much at such a young age. As I have mentioned, my boys are very keen on Manchester United Football Club. A year after Ben died, Sir Alex Ferguson, the longest standing manager of this club, retired. Television crews descended on Manchester and in particular Old Trafford, the home of the club.

Tom watched the television coverage intently as they interviewed players and fans and tried to explain the atmosphere and mood on that day. One fan said of the retirement of Sir Alex, 'It is just like a death.'

Tom turned to me and said, 'That is the most stupid thing I have ever heard. It is no way like a death, Mum.' How right Tom was, but how sad I was that Tom knew that truth.

CHAPTER 28

Hope

When you lose someone close to you, you do not just start a new life with them not in it. The memory of them is part of your daily life. Each day I wake, I still think about them.

On anniversaries and special days, like Christmas and the boys' birthdays, people often recognise that these days will be hard. And they are although so far I have found that those significant days have been no harder than any ordinary day. Each day, we do not have the boys in our lives. Each day, we are carrying on without them. Often on those special days, some people take the time to contact us. Some take extra care in acknowledging our loss and sharing with us in our sadness.

On other days it can be unpredictable when the thought of our loss might strike us.

I am in a shop. I am looking for a card for a friend, but I also know it is close to Ben's birthday. I allow myself to go to the area where the children's cards are. I know I should not do it, but I do. I choose the one I would have bought for him, with an eight on it and a football. I hold the card, but I know I cannot buy the card as I do not have an eight-year-old to give it to, and if I did it would not be Ben and I would not be getting that card. So I find myself in tears in a stationery shop looking at children's cards, and the tears won't stop.

I am driving to work listening to the radio. Listeners call in to a talkback show to tell the audience what it is that the listener just can't live without. First up are the usual contenders: chocolate, good coffee, and so on. Then a caller phones and says, 'My children. I just could not live without my children.'

I pause, mid traffic flow, waiting for the radio host's response.

'No,' he says, 'I have to agree. I also could not live without my children.'

I pull over to the roadside, screaming in my head, 'They talk as if it is an option. As if we can choose to live with or without our children. What if the option is taken from us? Are we also to die? I had no option!'

It is not always the big things – selling the house where my child lived with us, or contacting the nursery to let them know the space will no longer be filled by my child because he is dead. No, it can hurt just as much in the small things – the stationery shop or the radio chat show that starts the anger and the tears.

This is the cold, stark reality of learning to live without what I am told by the radio you just cannot live without. Your children. Life without them is hard. It hurts, each day it hurts. I do not know whether this hurt will be with us forever, for a lifetime – as I have not yet lived a lifetime.

I am conscious that as the survivors, even if survival is short (let's be honest, we all will die one day) we also have an opportunity. The opportunity is to live and to experience life with all its fullness and colour. Blotting out the life of the survivor is not something I think that our loved ones would want to leave as their legacy or mark on our lives. They loved us; therefore they must also love this stage of our lives.

My boys are still a part of this latter stage of my family's lives, just in a different form. I carry the memory of the boys with me each day. Some days those memories are large, vivid and ever-present. Some days they are muted. But always they are present.

***

One of the toughest days for Tom on the school calendar is the day when photos are taken. When all the children leave his class for photos with their siblings, he feels his loss of Ben and Samuel deeply. Roddy and I are concerned for him each year, but what can we do? We can't stop the hurt. We look instead to coping strategies. One year, I put a small photo of Tom and Ben in his pocket and told him to look at it and maybe that would help.

If Ben could be there with Tom again, I believe he would, as he would always want to support Tom. But he can't. Also, if we believe what we say we believe, surely, we would not be wanting to bring Ben back from where he is.

A few people have told me they are amazed at the way Roddy and I have parented Tom since losing Ben and Samuel. He is certainly not wrapped in cotton wool, and this amazes them. He is wrapped in love, lots of it. But Tom is given no protective coat by his parents. We have let him experience life to the full. As I edit this book, Tom is away from us on camp where there will be mud, madness and boyhood challenges. My logical brain tell me this is good for Tom. His life should not be inhibited because he is our last reserve. We have no spare, but we try to live without letting him know the burden of that reality.

I try not to spoil Tom. Even though he has hurt, we still discipline him. I try to be logical about this. Even though my heart wants Tom to never experience a bad thing ever again, a part of my logical brain tells me: don't do it, don't spoil him. Make him sweat. Make him realise that hard work gets rewards. Don't smooth the path each day for him.

This same logical brain was in my head when I was with Ben during cancer treatment. He stood in front of the Lego box in a shop, looking longingly at it. I looked at his wee bald head and I felt the tug at my heart which was telling me to buy the Lego box for him, but the nag in my head was saying: No, don't spoil him. Don't undo the good that you worked hard for in the earlier years.

So I listened to the second voice. I turned to Ben and I told him he had to wait for his birthday for that Lego box. Ben did not survive to his birthday.

***

As I am fortunate to be the mother of Tom, this means I have occasionally been at a school playground. I have seen the children of Ben's class, or when at a different school then children who would be Ben and Samuel's ages, had they each lived. I look on at these other children and feel a deep loss. I miss not having my boys with us. I wanted to be their mum and to share in the experience of their joys and sorrows through a long and fruitful life. Having their lives cut short ended this. It killed our dreams for them.

With Samuel, I never had those shared experiences of daily life. From the start of Samuel's life to this day, I do not know whether he ever knew

I was there. I do not know whether he ever saw me or heard me, or even could smell me. Was I in any way special to him? I do not know the answer.

Many people at the time Samuel was alive tried to give me comfort by saying they were sure a child always knows a mother's touch, and despite his disabilities my presence would have been strong enough to break into his world. I hope they were right. I certainly wanted to show him my love, within the restrictions of the hospital environment, the various tubes and hospital apparatus. I am comforted that now he does not need those contraptions, but as parents we are somehow always wanting to be needed. Part of my hurt is not being needed by Samuel and Ben anymore. I can no longer care for them, as they don't need me. I am an empty nester far too early.

With Ben, I had daily contact. I shared his good days and his bad ones. As a family, we knew Ben so well. We know what we are missing in our life without him. Ben, as I and others have said, was just so lovely. He was uncomplicated and a lot of fun to be around. In his six years of life, he made the most of all his opportunities. During his illness he seemed to develop an even stronger, beautiful character. He was undemanding and even more caring and loving to us. Because of death, we now do not have that loving person in our lives.

Yet we have daily reminders of Ben. I might see a child playing in a local park in a 'Ben-like manner' which means laid-back and carefree, happily chatting to themselves or others, content in who they are and what they are doing. I observe those children from afar, and ache for Ben deeply. Or as a family we might go to a swimming pool, and soon we will be looking at each other. No words are needed between us as we know we are all thinking of how Ben would have loved the pool.

At Tom's new school, in a totally new location, new country, we now see the boys that would have been in Ben's year group (he was also enrolled in this school). The boys are playing rugby on the field. We cannot help but stop and watch and think of how much Ben would have been right in the middle of it all. Tom's school motto is 'The Making of Men'. I wonder what type of man they would have made from Ben, had the school been given the opportunity.

I hear children in the playground talking about their hopes and their dreams, and I am reminded that Ben had hopes and dreams as well. I asked him one time during his cancer treatment what he wanted to be when he grew up. I was surprised with the answer. I had expected him to say a footballer, but no, Ben said, 'A traveller. I want to be a traveller, Mummy, and go to lots of different places in the world.' At the time I had a sudden image in my head of Ben as some kind of thrill seeker, footloose and fancy free, checking out the world's best surf beaches. I jokingly told Tom that if that happened then I was sorry, but he would just have to put whatever he had planned that year on hold, as he would have to take the year off to go and keep an eye on his brother. There was an element of seriousness in my joking, as I saw the need for Tom's cautious protection for Ben. I would imagine that in reality, had it occurred, there would have been no stopping Ben's wild and playful nature.

We had hopes and dreams for Ben as well. They don't go just because he has been taken from us.

***

Back in Eastbourne, I have a very special friendship group, formed informally but by a common link. Two of the ladies in this group sadly lost their husbands in the same year we lost Ben, and they both have children Ben's age. Occasionally, we are able to get together and support each other in our respective griefs. We discuss anything and everything.

In all our experiences of death, there is a common denominator. It is impossible to have back what we have lost. Death is final. There is no turning back the clock. No way to unsay something to someone who has died. Your words and your opportunities have gone with them.

I realise it might sound obvious but, reader, please, I urge you, don't miss the joy you have while you have it. I don't believe we did. I just wish that we could have been granted more time with our children, to have more of those experiences here on earth. The overwhelming feeling that we each experience is a deep longing for them. Put simply, we each miss them.

***

After the Wednesday night when we heard there was no hope from the medical side of Ben's condition, and it was predicted that he would die, my friend Melissa said to me, 'E-J, if your God will do a miracle and save Ben then I will come over to his side.'

I couldn't believe it. I had prayed consistently for many years for Melissa to find the hope I had found, and here was the golden opportunity handed to me on a plate. And yet I paused and thought I couldn't fake it. I knew the miracle may not happen, no matter how hard and long I prayed to 'my' God.

I responded, 'Melissa, my God may not do a miracle, but I will still have to go on with faith and trust in him.' We held each other and cried together in that hospital kitchen. The pain was great for both of us. It was not more for me who had a faith than for Melissa who did not share that faith. We stood and wept together in human sorrow.

My faith has not softened my pain of loss; the hurt is no less, in the midst of the event. However, in having a faith we can see a future and have a hope, even out of the midst of hurtful and damaging events. That is the difference.

I often think of some of Ben's final words to us. He said, 'I just can't wait to cuddle Samuel,' despite the pain he must have been experiencing at the time. His face was alight and so full of expectation. I wondered at the time, as I still do, whether Ben could actually see Samuel in that hospital room. I hope he did not have to wait too long for that cuddle.

Has Ben been able to tell Samuel about us, his family? Has he told him how much we longed for him, and how many tears we shed? Has he spoken the loving words to Samuel that I so desperately wanted to give him whilst on earth? Importantly, is Samuel now well? Is he healed from all his many earthly disabilities? Has Ben also been restored to full health? Has God worked the miracles that modern medicine could not do?

**

When I get the opportunity to go to Willingdon Cemetery, I sit on the wooden seat we have placed there in loving memory of both our boys. On the plaque it states this simple message: 'McNicol – In Loving Memory of two special boys. Ben (aged 6) and Samuel (aged 5 weeks).'

One of our boys never visited the cemetery alive. The other boy did. He loved it and he played there, and he talked about Heaven there, and he knew through his own knowledge of a human death what it is at only four years old to contemplate eternity. A world beyond this life. Beyond the body, the material possessions, and the personal successes that each of us may have been given.

At the seat, I can look across the rows to Samuel's headstone. I am reminded by the words inscribed, taken from the book of Isaiah in the Bible, of the hope that we as a family have for Samuel now. Because of word restrictions on a headstone we could not put all the words we wanted, so we chose one sentence (in bold below). I don't have the restriction of words in this book, so I can quote the entire section, and I think it helps to focus on the hope of the future despite our weariness or our disabilities on this earth:

> 'Do you not know? Have you not heard? The Lord is the everlasting God, the Creator of the ends of the earth. He will not grow weary, and his understanding no one can fathom. He gives strength to the weary and increases the power of the weak. Even youths grow tired and weary, and young men stumble and fall; **but those who hope in the Lord will renew their strength.** They will soar on wings like eagles; they will run and not grow weary; they will walk and not be faint.'

At the seat, I can look down to my feet where my second son, Ben, is buried. I think of him as the boy who had so much life in him, so much energy and vigour, he brightened the day for those who knew him. I think about Ben, and I now can agree with my friend who said he had a good life. He did. He had a great life.

I also agree with my other friend, who tried to encourage me to think of all that Ben has been saved from. The world is a place for many of terror devastation and of war – Ben is not a part of that world anymore. He has been saved from the imperfections of human experience.

I smile to myself as I recall Ben telling me what he would do when he got to Heaven, how he would run to the place where Jesus was, as in Ben's mind Jesus would be holding Samuel and so he could then see Samuel. smile because I now realise I failed to tell Ben that all of Heaven is where Jesus is. In my research, I read that he is its lamp, and there is no darkness as his light shines through all of Heaven. Ben will love that, always light time – no more sleep, Mum. How can I be selfish and want Ben to return from that perfect place?

I also believe that Ben did not need to run to Jesus. I think Jesus was with him all along. Once Ben reached Heaven, Jesus was in all of that City. Ben's running days will be over, he has reached his finish line. So I look to Ben's headstone and I agree with the psalmist who is quoted:

> 'Surely goodness and love will follow me all the days of my life,
> and I will dwell in the house of the Lord forever.'

I think of all the good work the Ben McNicol Trust is doing, providing comfort and care for cancer patients and their families. And I think of all the good work Ben was able to do in his short life, and I am thankful. I am thankful to God for all his goodness in giving to Roddy and me three boys, each unique and each wonderful and precious. They are true blessings in our life.

One day, I do hope to see them again. I do not know how they will react. We are told in the Bible that in Heaven there is no crying, so I do not think they have been missing me. Had they been, it would not be Heaven. It can't be a heavenly experience to miss the ones who are not there. But still, will they be glad to see me?

I suppose I am facing the ultimate maternal test, to believe what the Bible says, that it is far better for them to be with Jesus and not here on earth. They do not need me anymore, as their current existence is true completeness. Heaven must be the final, complete story of God in all his glory. No imperfections, and no more human sadness and longing.

Wherever I live or am, I often like to step outside for a moment in the evening, and take a look at the clear night sky. A moment to myself. I see the vast array of stars, and catch a small view of the greater universe beyond those stars. As I gaze at the sky, I think of my two boys and wonder where within that universe their souls are.

As I look at the night sky I am naturally taken to a place where I contemplate the great and powerful God who I believe made all of what I see before me, and I am humbled before him. I am reminded against that backdrop of awesomeness of just how small and insignificant I am. Yet I am also encouraged, as I am reminded that despite God's greatness and his power he still cares for me. He loves me more than I can ever imagine real love to be. He understands my anger, my struggles, my hurt, and wants to be close if I will but let him.

I realise also that he loves each of my family. Those who are with him now, and those who are yet to follow. He will not let our tears flow for no reason. God cares for us all. He made us all as individuals and we were designed to be his companions.

I acknowledge at these times that God has placed a sense of eternity in my heart. He has set in me a desire to know him and to one day be with him. This desire was first placed in my heart many years ago, in my bedroom in Fiji as a six-year-old child. His flame placed in my heart has never been extinguished. Through life's many ups and downs he has drawn me further into him.

Through the lives and deaths of my children, he has also encouraged me to think more about Heaven, of what it might be like. I am so excited. Dare I say it, I might even be happy! when I contemplate what life in Heaven will be. I thank God for this. I also thank Ben and Samuel for causing me to open my eyes and ears to gain a deeper appreciation of what Heaven is like, and for adding to my longing for a better home, a permanent home with Jesus and with them.

On April 25th 2010 I experienced the greatest moment of my life. I spent a short time with Roddy, Tom, Ben and Samuel. No doctors, no nurses. No one else was in the room, it was just us.

My family. Complete.

At the time we knew we would have to say goodbye to Samuel soon, but not on that day. I was happy to live just for then.

At the time we of course did not know that one day, exactly two years and one month later, we would also have to say goodbye to Ben. Had God come down and asked me, 'Will you do it? Will you give me back your children?' I know that my selfish answer would have been *no*, but I was not given that choice.

When God came down to earth in the body of his son Jesus, he gave us all a choice. He gave us an open invitation to follow him. He did not promise us an easy road. He did not say our lives would be simple, sorted and perfect. He did not say we would not be born with CHARGE Syndrome or develop cancer at some point in our lives. He just called us to follow him.

To his calling I have remained faithful, and when I go to this place called Heaven, please tell my family and friends that they won't need to pack my toothbrush. I won't need it there. Ben and Samuel taught me that. Thanks boys. Love you always.

...nna, Kalesi and EJ (aged six) in our garden in Suva, Fiji.

...Gran. Never underestimate the power of a praying grandparent.

Roddy and EJ's wedding day, Christchurch, New Zealand.

Melissa, Tom EJ and Ben on a visit to Melissa in Melbourne Australia 2007.

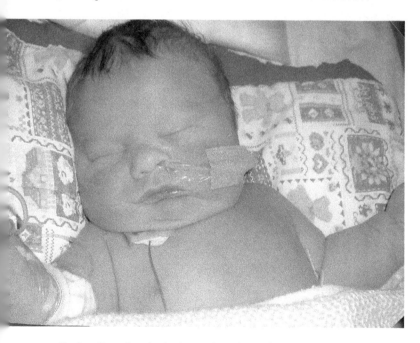

Precious Samuel on the day he was born 22nd of March 2010.

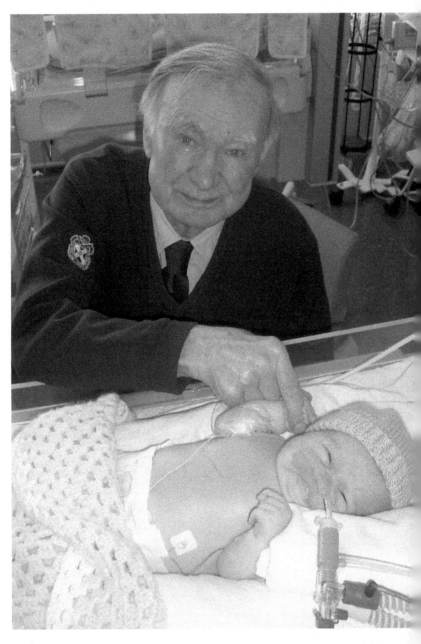

Grandpa McNicol with his youngest grandchild - Samuel Roderick McNicol.

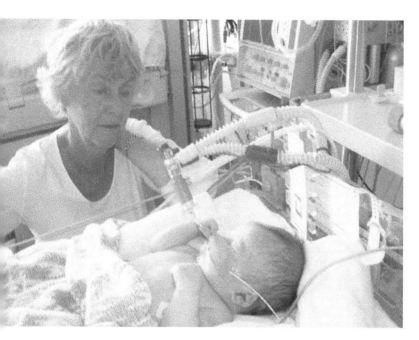

nny and Samuel at the Neonatal Intensive Care Unit St Thomas' Hospital London, 2010.

*Granny and Grandpa John with Tom and Ben beside the
fountain outside St Thomas' Hospital, 2010.*

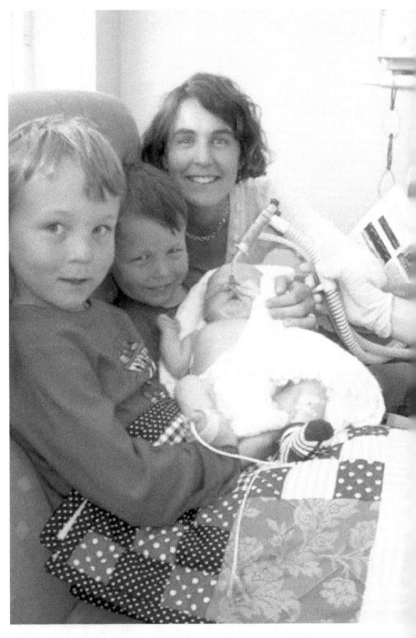

Tom, Ben, Samuel and EJ on the 25th of April 2010 at St Thomas' Hospital, London

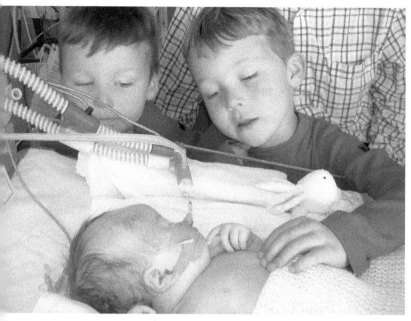

*Ben, Samuel and Tom at the Neonatal Intensive Care Unit
St Thomas' Hospital, London in April 2010.*

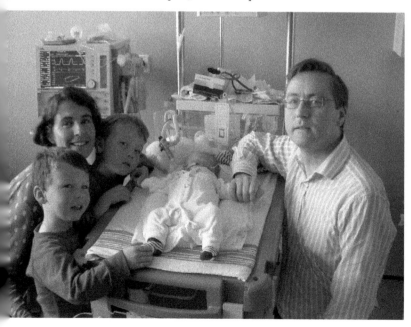

The complete family. Roddy, Samuel, Tom, EJ and Ben on the day Samuel died.

Ben and Tom – best friends 2011.

...orning after the February 2011 Christchurch earthquake. Tom, Oliver, Ben, Granny, Millie ...d Grandpa John. We were fortunate to be able to take shelter at Joanna and Randal's home.

Tom and Ben beside an earthquake crack in Mum and Dad's driveway February 2011.

Ben at St Andrew's Nursery, Eastbourne England.

Ben at nursery 2010.

Ben and his good friend Rufus Piper 2011.

Ben year one school photo. Taken only a couple of months before he was diagnosed with brain cancer.

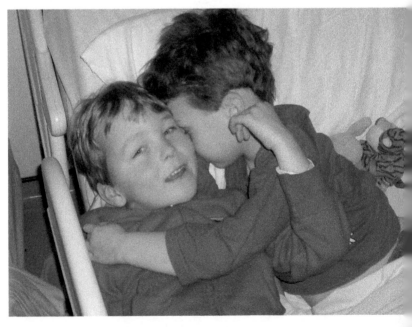

Christmas Day 2011. Tom giving Ben a cuddle at King's College Hospital, London, Engl

Roddy with Tom and Ben April 2012.

Grandpa John reading with Ben in May 2012.

Final family photo at home in Eastbourne, England in May 2012.

We will always love you Ben.

*Charlotte and EJ running the Beachy Head Marathon for
the Ben McNicol Trust in October 2012.*

Ben's House.

Planting Ben's tree on the school field Chrissy, EJ and Dee.